Islamic Political Culture, Democracy, and Human Rights

Islamic Political Culture, Democracy, and Human Rights

A Comparative Study

Daniel E. Price

PRAEGER

Westport, Connecticut
London

Library of Congress Cataloging-in-Publication Data

Price, Daniel E., 1962–
    Islamic political culture, democracy, and human rights : a
comparative study / Daniel E. Price.
        p. cm.
    Includes bibliographical references (p.   ) and index.
    ISBN 0–275–96187–7 (alk. paper)
    1. Political culture—Islamic countries—Case studies.   2. Islam
and politics—Case studies.   3. Democracy—Islamic countries—Case
studies.   4. Human rights—Islamic countries—Case studies.
5. Power (Social sciences)—Islamic countries—Case studies.
I. Title.
JA75.7   1999
306.2'0917'671—dc21   98–44397

British Library Cataloguing in Publication Data is available.

Library of Congress Catalog Card Number: 98–44397
ISBN: 0–275–96187–7

First published in 1999

Praeger Publishers, 88 Post Road West, Westport, CT 06881
An imprint of Greenwood Publishing Group, Inc.
www.praeger.com

Printed in the United States of America

The paper used in this book complies with the
Permanent Paper Standard issued by the National
Information Standards Organization (Z39.48–1984).

10 9 8 7 6 5 4 3 2 1

This book is dedicated to my mother, Charlotte Price.
Without her help and support, this
book would not have been possible.

Contents

Illustrations

Preface

It has been argued that Islam facilitates authoritarianism, contradicts the values of Western societies, and significantly affects important political outcomes in Muslim nations. Consequently, scholars, commentators, and government officials frequently point to "Islamic fundamentalism" as the next ideological threat to liberal democracies. This view, however, is based primarily on the analysis of texts, Islamic political theory, and ad hoc studies of individual countries, which do not consider other factors. It is my contention that the texts and traditions of Islam, like those of other religions, can be used to support a variety of political systems and policies. Country specific and descriptive studies do not help us to find patterns that will help us explain the varying relationships between Islam and politics across the countries of the Muslim world. Hence, a new approach to the study of the connection between Islam and politics is called for.

I suggest, through rigorous evaluation of the relationship between Islam, democracy, and human rights at the cross-national level, that too much emphasis is being placed on the power of Islam as a political force. I first use comparative case studies, which focus on factors relating to the interplay between Islamic groups and regimes, economic influences, ethnic cleavages, and societal development, to explain the variance in the influence of Islam on politics across eight nations. I argue that much of the power attributed to Islam as the driving force behind policies and political systems in Muslim nations can be better explained by the previously mentioned factors. I also find, contrary to common belief, that the increasing strength of Islamic political groups has often been associated with modest pluralization of political systems.

I have constructed an index of Islamic political culture, based on the extent to which Islamic law is utilized and whether and, if so, how, Western ideas, institutions, and technologies are implemented, to test the nature of the relationship between Islam and democracy and Islam and human rights. This indicator is used in statistical analysis, which includes a sample of twenty-three predominantly Muslim countries and a control group of twenty-three non-Muslim developing nations. In addition to comparing Islamic nations to non-Islamic developing nations, statistical analysis allows me to control for the influence of other variables that have been found to affect levels of democracy and the protection of individual rights. The result should be a more realistic and accurate picture of the influence of Islam on politics and policies.

A number of people have helped me along the road to completing this book. Of greatest importance has been my mother, Charlotte Price, who always provided me with whatever support I needed. My sisters, Miriam and Rochelle, have also played strong roles in helping me along the way. All three, along with my brothers-in-law, Paul Friedman and Steve Slater, have always been my toughest critics. I am truly blessed to have such a loving and caring family.

A number of faculty at various institutions have played major roles in assisting my development as a scholar. Dr. Clement Henry at the University of Texas helped me to understand the high standards of good scholarship. He also provided me with the idea of comparing the relationship between religion and politics across nations. Scott Kessler and Lisa Kessler were lifesavers during my two years in Austin and provided me with invaluable feedback and advice.

I am deeply indebted to the Fulbright Program for providing me with a grant to spend a year in Morocco completing research and training. My year in Morocco was crucial in the development of my research and my understanding of the Muslim world. I am grateful to a number of individuals in Morocco who deepened my appreciation for their country and culture. The staff of the Moroccan-American Center for Cultural Exchanges was of tremendous assistance in helping me to become established and assisting with various problems. The American Language Center in Fez played a pivotal role in making my stay in Morocco both meaningful and productive. Daoud Casewit, the Arabic language instruction faculty, and the staff all bent over backward to be of assistance. Dr. Abd-al Hay Labbi served as my academic mentor and guide to Moroccan politics during my year in his country. His assistance, insights, and hospitality will never be forgotten. Several Moroccan friends were also instrumental in providing both companionship and a doorway into Moroccan society. I am particularly grateful to Amina Charrat, whose friendship and candor will always be something that I hold dear. I am also glad to have had the pleasure of sharing my Moroccan experience with Jerry and Lataesha Kurlanski, who also provided tremendous insight. Finally, I also owe my gratitude to the hundreds of Moroccans who talked to me about their country and society.

I want to thank the political science department at Binghamton University for providing me with four years of support while I pursued my doctorate. The department staff, particularly Ann Casella and MaryAnn Verhoeven, were invaluable in providing assistance and support, as were many of my fellow graduate students. Among them are Kathy Barbiari, Martin Hwang, Simon Gomez, Peter Partell, Michelle Kukoleca, Andy Enterline, Drew Castle, Andy Souchet, Paul Senese, Joe Willy, Bob Ostergaard, Yuhang Shi, Roz Broussard, Shawn Blinn, and Mike Andrew. I was particularly fortunate in having the friendship and assistance of Kristin Broderick, John Camabrecco, Chris Borick, Frank Cohen, Rob Compton, Mike Dillon, Mike Mousseau, Craig Webster, Shawna Sweeney, and Demet Yalcin.

The influence of a number of Binghamton faculty has played a key role in this project. I am fortunate to have had the opportunity to work with Don Peretz before he retired. He has been a true mentor, serving as a role model of scholarly production, and his value in helping me along the way cannot be measured. Richard Hofferbert has been an inspirational force and helped me learn to look at things in new ways. He, his wife, Rose, and their collection of animals have also provided me with a home away from home. David Cingranelli has been of great help and stimulated my interest in the issue of human rights and civil liberties. The ideas and assistance of Ali Mazrui, Glenn Palmer, John Bartle, and Michael McDonald were also essential in my development as a researcher. I also owe great thanks to Kevin Lacey, who introduced me to the wonders of Morocco.

Islamic Political Culture, Democracy, and Human Rights

Introduction

DOES CULTURE AFFECT POLITICS AND POLICIES?

One of the most elusive and enduring questions in political science is if and how shared attitudes and values affect political systems. The first half of the question can easily be answered affirmatively after a researcher closely observes the politics and policies that are associated with a particular culture. Smoking, eating, and public displays of affection are against the law in Morocco during the month of Ramadan. Of course, 12 kilometers across the sea in Spain, they are not. Consequently, the tasks at hand are to determine how political culture shapes forms of government and policies as well as go beyond anecdotal evidence to the discovery of patterns that transcend time and national boundaries. I will achieve these tasks, which is the chief objective of this book, by focusing on the question as to whether Islam, when serving as a cultural and ideological basis for government, is associated with democratization or authoritarianism and arbitrary government.

WHY ISLAM?

I have chosen to use Islam to evaluate the influence of political culture on democracy and individual rights because its influence is felt, to a varying degree, in a large number of nations. Also, "Islamic fundamentalism" is a topic that has captured the attention of the public, policymakers, journalists, commentators, and Middle East specialists. In short, it is the most visible and perplexing example of a resurgent traditional political culture.

Islam is also an easily identifiable culture because its fundamental doctrines and precepts are written or have been passed down orally in the *Quran, Sunna,* and *Sharia,* which increases the likelihood that a measure of Islamic political culture will be reliable. Finally, religion and politics are doctrinally and historically intertwined in Islam. Therefore, we have every reason to believe that Islamic culture should influence political systems and public policy.

SIGNIFICANCE

Liberal Development Theory

One of the core assumptions of the Liberal development theory has been that the withering away of traditional political culture is a necessary step in the process of development. Supposedly, traditional political cultures do not foster rationalization, modernization, bureaucratization, or participant societies. This assumption, however, has been criticized by Conservative theorists, who argue that the ties of tradition are necessary to unite nations during difficult periods of rapid growth (Huntington 1967). Consequently, the maintenance of tradition is actually an integral element in moderniza- tion. For example, it may be that Morocco has developed with a compar- atively small amount of turmoil because of the steadying continuity of Islam and the monarchy. In this book I follow the reasoning that tradition and modernity are not mutually exclusive and that development is not a linear process across all spheres of society.

The most obvious evidence for this assertion, again, comes from the ob- servation of cultures as cities such as Fez, Morocco, are living laboratories of the integration of the old and the new. At the same time, one can find many modern elements in thousand-year-old Islamic texts and doctrines. Perhaps Islam, as Gellner (1981) suggested, is more modern than Christi- anity or Judaism. Since Almond and Verba's *The Civic Culture* (1963), scholars have been trying to pinpoint a universal culture that is conducive to political participation. However, it is important to note that Almond and Verba (1963) wrote that tradition maintains affective bonds among members of democratic societies, which fosters trust and unity in compet- itive political systems. Since traditional cultures vary, so should the ideo- logical foundations of democratic societies. Consequently, an "Islamic democracy" would take a form that differs from those of Western liberal democracies.

Islam, Modernity, and Democracy

The debate over Islam's compatibility with modernity and democracy, thus far, has primarily been waged at the theoretical and anecdotal levels.

However, strong evidence based on a large sample of Muslim countries has yet to be produced by either side in this debate. This is because most research has focused on predicting the consequences of Islamic political resurgence rather than systematically evaluating what has transpired during the last twenty-five years. The case studies and statistical analysis in this project will show that Islam and traditional political culture, in general, can serve as a foundation of modern democratic societies. At the same time, I will evaluate the claim that political culture must be included in the study of political development because local cultures affect politics and policies in modern states.

Political Culture and Rational Choice

The study of political culture has enjoyed a recent resurgence and challenged the dominant rational choice paradigm (Diamond 1993). Cultural theorists claim that the assumption that individuals are self-interested utility maximizers may be correct, but this cannot sufficiently explain political decisions. It might be that a Saudi Muslim and a secular American would not make the same choice regarding the allocation of state expenditures if they were operating within the same systemic structures and given the same resources. In this book, I will investigate the assertion that the inclusion of political culture in comparative political study is necessary in understanding why some political choices are unacceptable and what factors shape actors' preferences and help determine their political strategies.

Methodology

This book will offer methodological innovation for the study of Islam through the development of a numerical index of Islamic political culture based on:

- The number of legal spheres where *Sharia*, Islamic law, is utilized and the extent to which it is applied
- If and how institutions, ideas, and technologies that originated outside Muslim world are accepted

Consequently, I will be able to utilize multiple regression, a statistical technique that will permit me to analyze my research questions across forty-six countries to determine if the level of influence of Islamic political culture on political systems has a subsequent affect on democracy and individual rights. This methodology will also demonstrate how statistical analysis can be utilized in the study of Islam without slighting the crucial aspects of Islamic political culture that make it unique and will allow me to control for the influence of other factors that influence levels of democracy and the protection of human rights.

"Islamic Fundamentalism"

This last topic is of particular importance because of the significant amount of attention that has been given to "Islamic Fundamentalism" by academics, journalists, government officials, and, of course, Muslims across the world. Some see Islam as the next great threat to the West and liberation because it is inherently antidemocratic and its values clash with those of secular-based societies. Others see Islam as the salvation for nations that have been the victims of Western culture and economic subjugation. However, as mentioned, systematic studies that investigate whether it is Islam, other factors, or a combination of both, that is primarily responsible for forms of government and policies in Muslim countries are, to this point, rare. In short, analysts have ignored or deemed irrelevant a most basic question. In terms of determining the most important political outcomes—does Islam really matter?

If it is concluded that the answer is no and that regimes are simply deeming a variety of political systems and policies "Islamic," then all the heated debate over whether citizens of countries with predominantly Muslim populations looking to religion for solutions to their political problems is desirable or undesirable and whether Islamic doctrines are compatible with Liberalism have been wasted energy. One must not forget that Kuwait did not hesitate to leave its salvation in the hands of the United States, Iran was a dictatorship under the Shah, and that secular-oriented Tunisia spends a greater percentage of its annual budget on religious affairs than does religious-oriented Sudan (as do many European nations). It might be that religious-based policy in Islamic states does not go beyond the regulation of accepted social conformities and the repression of dissent. Of course, secular authoritarian governments, and democratic ones for that matter, also engage in these practices.

CHAPTER OUTLINE

Developing an Argument

Four methods of inquiry—political theory, field observation, comparative case studies, and statistical analysis—will be used in this book. Chapters 1 and 2 will demonstrate why an alternative approach to the comparative study of political culture, specifically Islam, is necessary. A review of the literature on political culture and politics and Islam and politics in chapter 1 will show that:

- Little has been done to confirm or disconfirm, using broad cross-national samples, the notion that shared belief systems and ideologies influence policies

- Evidence supporting arguments regarding the relationship between Islam and politics has been largely anecdotal, has focused on individual countries, and has not accounted for competing variables or explanations
- Most work on Islamic political resurgence has focused on predicting the consequences of this phenomenon while little attention has been given to evaluating what has already transpired

I complete the development of my argument as to why and how Islam could have an effect on democracy and the protection of individual rights in chapter 2. First, I will search for answers in Islamic political doctrine and traditions. I will then consider various notions of politics and economics—Islam's basic sources. I will also examine briefly the work of several modern Muslim political theorists, whose writings have influenced contemporary Islamic political groups. Finally, I will add universal factors that have been thought to play a significant role in political developments and transitions to democracy. In short, because Islam can facilitate a wide range of political systems and, by itself, does not determine whether countries are democratic, an inquiry into Islamic precepts and law will not suffice. Consequently, it is necessary to identify variables that interact with Islamic political culture, such as wealth, ethnic cleavages, and the modernization process, to produce political outcomes.

It is also essential to consider how regimes respond to the challenge of growing Islamic political opposition. Regime behavior, as will be seen in the differing experiences of Egypt, Algeria, and Morocco, is often an undervalued consideration. Also, what is the nature of the ideologies offered by these opposition groups? Events in Jordan have shown that some groups offer programs that allow them to participate in largely secular governments. At the same time, the foresight of King Hussein, who opened the political system to the Islamic Brotherhood, was also essential. In short, I will be looking for the type of consensus that is discussed in elite theories of democratic transition (O'Donnell 1986; Rustow 1970; Dahl 1971). The political systems that result from the challenge of political Islam are not just the results of ideology or uncontrollable social forces. As will be seen, political actors, in the Islamic world (like everywhere else), are also important.

Case Studies

Chapters 3 through 6, through comparative case studies, illustrate the argument that was developed in chapter 2. It is important to note that the eight countries—Egypt, Jordan, Syria, Tunisia, Saudi Arabia, Morocco, Algeria, and Iran—to be analyzed in the case studies have been included because they represent differing relationships between Islam and politics. By investigating the considerations discussed in the previous paragraph across these eight nations, a general theory of the relationship between Islam and democracy will be produced. Particular attention will be given to Morocco, Tunisia, and Jordan because, when compared with the other five nations, secular and religious cultural forces appear to co-exist and interact with relative ease. Although these three nations are only marginally to somewhat democratic, the same is also—at best—true of the other five countries in this study. Since none of the cases can serve as an example of an Islamic democracy, it important to consider carefully the combinations of factors that have produced the potential for representative government.

Egypt and Jordan will be considered in chapter 3 because modest openings of their political systems corresponded with the growing power of the Muslim Brotherhood. Hence, these cases suggest that Islam may be able to play a part in the growth of democracy. This assertion will be further supported in chapter 4, where I will look at Syria and Tunisia. The current regime in Syria is highly authoritarian but, also, secular based. In fact, some of the worst human rights offenses committed by the Assad regime and the Bourghiba and Ben Ali regimes in Tunisia have involved the repression of religious groups. Tunisia, however, took a more moderate course regarding religious political groups and, subsequently, has seen some improvement in its human rights record, but the ban on religious-based political parties remains, and these organizations continue to be repressed.

Chapter 5 will analyze two Islamic monarchies, Saudi Arabia and Morocco. King Fahd's official title includes "Guardian of the Holy Places" and King Hassan II, in addition to being head of state, is also "The Commander of the Faithful." Is it Islam that allows these and other monarchies to survive up to the approach of the twenty-first century, or is it other factors? Finally, chapter 6 will discuss two nations, Algeria and Iran, where the rise of political Islam has been associated with violence and turmoil. These nations are included because, at face value, their recent histories contradict that notion that Islam and democracy are compatible. However, it might be that authoritarian regimes would exist in these countries regardless of the influence of Islamic political culture. At this point, hypotheses regarding the relationship between Islam, democracy, and human rights will have been developed that can be tested across all countries with predominantly Muslim populations and a matching sample of non-Muslim developing countries.

An Indicator of Islamic Political Culture and Statistical Tests

Chapters 7 and 8, where I will evaluate the propositions developed in the case studies, are the greatest leap into the unknown and will be the most controversial part of this study. This is because I have created a numerical index of Islamic political culture that will be used in quantitative analysis. In essence, I will be concentrating a system of belief, legal tradition, and way of life into two dimensions that can be assumed to apply to all Muslim societies.[1] As will be seen, others have classified Islam political ideologies into categories and placed the groups that espouse these ideologies on two-dimensional graphs (Shepard 1986). However, to my knowledge, I am the first to attach numbers to these placements. It is my belief that what is lost in detail is more than compensated by the ability to test hypotheses regarding Islam across a large sample of nations while controlling for the influence of other variables.

Criticism of this type of methodology has been of three general varieties. The first claims that this type of activity is simply wrong, of little value, and that such a broad and abstract notion of Islamic political culture cannot be successfully captured in two dimensions or enumerated. There is little use in responding to this type of polemic because it is rooted in disciplinary or methodological prejudices. The only way to please this critical group would be to abort the project. However, the classifying and placing of numbers on broad and abstract topics is widely accepted in contemporary political science as indexes of democracy, human rights, and even Liberalism have been developed. Finally, this group of critics engages in the activity that they are condemning every time they construct and grade essay exams for their courses.

A second group of critics claims that I, as a Westerner, am imposing my own hegemonic meaning on Islam and that, furthermore, I cannot truly understand or evaluate objectively Islamic political culture. Of course, to some degree, both of these assertions are true. However, I do not believe that they invalidate the findings to be produced in this study. I have engaged many Muslims in the coding process and have had at least one citizen of each of the countries included in the sample review my coding of their nations. Also the two dimensions utilized in the index are ones that are the most often mentioned in the writings and speeches of contemporary Muslim political theorists. As mentioned, I am building on previous literature that classifies and places Islamic political ideologies on two-dimensional scales. My residence in Morocco—experiencing life and Islamic political culture and numerous discussions regarding religion and politics with Moroccans from all strata of society—has supported my confidence in the index. The alternative is not only to abandon this project but also the study of Islam by Americans and other Westerners. This, I believe, would only serve ignorance and misunderstanding.

The third group of critics has already been of great assistance in this project—that is, those who either disagree with the dimensions that I have chosen to represent Islamic political culture, the coding methods and procedures, or the rankings assigned to individual nations. As a result, I have rethought and reformulated basic assumptions, methods, and the assigning of numbers to various countries. A survey that I sent to other scholars was an attempt to gain as much input from as many sources as possible for this project. The construction of the indicator of Islamic political culture, assigning of scores, and statistical methods for ascertaining the reliability of the index will be taken up in greater detail in chapter 7 and the appendices. I, of course, take full responsibility for all of the coding and assigning of numbers.

Chapter 7 will outline the methodology to be used for the hypothesis testing, discuss how key indicators (including the development of the scale of Islamic political culture) will be measured, and test propositions regarding the relationship between Islamic political culture and democracy. Chapter 8 will use similar statistical analysis to take up the question of Islam's influence on individual rights. Chapter 9 will summarize the findings of the study and provide the foundations of an answer to the question of the relationship between traditional political culture, form of government, and government policies. Appendix I explains how the indicator of Islamic political culture was developed, how coding of the indicator was completed, and how the reliability of the coding process was tested. Appendix II includes the Islamic political culture scores for the countries in the sample of predominantly Muslin countries. Appendix III provides an explanation for the Islamic ideologies mentioned in the case studies in chapters 3 through 6.

It is also hoped that this book will serve the normative purpose of demystifying political Islam.[2] Too often Islam is viewed as a monolithic, irrational, and other worldly phenomenon that is beyond comprehension. Consequently, everything that cannot be explained or that we find disagreeable about Muslim nations or societies is simply attributed to Islam. One way to overcome this oversimplification is to spend a long period of time in a Muslim society. After a year in Morocco and visits to Tunisia, Jordan, and Egypt, it is hard for me to believe that Islam is always the primary motivation for political behavior in these countries. A second method is to use the methodologies of political science to compare and contrast systematically Muslim societies with each other and non-Muslim societies to determine if the outcomes that we attribute to Islam are really caused by Islam. Having developed an assertion using the first method, I will now proceed to test it using the second.

NOTES

1. It is important to note that I am only considering and attempting to capture the key dimensions of political Islam and not Islam in its entirety.

2. This is not to claim that political Islam can ever be completely understood through academic inquiry, particularly by an American non-Muslim. Also, one of the most important aspects of Islam is its rich mystical tradition.

1

The Need for a New Approach

OVERVIEW

The question of the relationship between Islam and politics must be viewed as a function of national politics as well as the influence of doctrines, beliefs, and legal codes. As the following discussion will demonstrate, research that has not included both of these factors has not been successful in answering this question of relationship. In other words, methods that view everything as being unique, incomparable, and unclassifiable are of little value in trying to understand political phenomenon that manifest themselves across national borders. At the same time, methods that do not account for regional differences are equally problematic, especially when they have been applied to Islam and the Middle East. In short, it is important to try to bridge the gap between political science and area studies.

The purpose of this chapter is to demonstrate why the approach to analyzing the nature of the relationship between Islam and politics outlined in the introduction is necessary. I will trace the literature regarding the role of traditional political culture, specifically religion, in developing nations. From this discussion, I will begin the development of an argument as to why a political culture, such as Islam, might have an influence on important political outcomes such as democracy and the protection of the individual. I will also show how this study will help fill a hole in the literature on political culture, that is, the shortage of cross-national studies that investigate if and how shared attitudes, values, and beliefs affect government policies.

I will also consider how the relationship between Islam and politics has been studied in the past. Although, my primary focus will be on political science, I will also mention briefly the approaches of other disciplines such as anthropology, sociology, literary criticism, and psychology. Here I will seek to demonstrate that, although there has been significant progress in collecting information on Islam as a political force, too much strength is automatically attributed to religion as a determinant of political outcomes in the Middle East and the Islamic world in general. I will also argue that too much effort has been exerted in trying to predict what form political Islam will take in the future, while little has been done to analyze systematically its consequences.

POLITICAL CULTURE AND DEVELOPMENT

Max Weber

Weber's (1958) contention that reformation Protestantism was conducive to the growth of the spirit of capitalist productivity and accumulation sparked a controversy over whether political culture has a significant influence on political and economic systems. Weber's critics have claimed that other factors such as geography, wealth, and historical circumstance are of greater importance (Eisenstadt 1968). Hence, began the debate between advocates of cultural, structural, and rational choice theories. Advocates of the importance of political culture have been left with the difficult tasks of:

1. showing that political culture is not simply a concept that is used to account for everything that remains an anomaly in a given society,
2. showing that differences in political culture can explain differences in political behavior across governments and changes in political culture across time result in changes in political behavior and,
3. codifying and identifying different variants of political culture.

Because Weber (1958) argued that only capitalist societies were modernized, rationalized, and bureaucratized, the first generation of development theorists placed great emphasis on the third task and focused on the division between tradition and modernity. According to Weber (1958), it was the influence of certain tenets of Protestantism that helped facilitate a transformation in the shared beliefs and attitudes of a society. This new ideological foundation, subsequently, led to new modes of economic production. Consequently, the transformation from religious-based ideology to "secular-rational" ideology became a cornerstone of the liberal theories of the late 1950s and early 1960s. At the same time, it also appeared that the role of religion in politics was declining across the world, just as it had in the United States and Europe (Jurgensmeyer 1993).

Liberal Theory

Lerner (1958), one of the first researchers who emphasized the importance of the change from traditional to modern political culture, focused on the Muslim Middle East. Lerner, using the example of a Turkish village and then a cross-national sample, identified a number of factors—such as urbanization, literacy, and communication—which break down traditional society and stimulate political and economic development. According to Lerner (1958), these forces permanently destroy the old relationships and world-views that supported these societies. Once communities become connected to the modern world and all that it has to offer, patterns of thought (in this case, those of Islam) that prevent the enjoyment of the benefits of modernity cannot survive.

Lerner's work was followed by seminal works by Lipset (1959), Deutsch (1961), and Inkeles (1974), who identified factors that were associated with the process of social mobilization and democratization. The general theme of these works was that as people moved to the city, learned more about the outside world, and came in contact with a wider variety of people, they would develop the skills necessary to take part in a participatory society. Concurrently, the belief that people, not the uncontrollable forces of nature or God, for that matter, controlled human destiny resulted in rising levels of education and technological progress. Subsequently, religion's role as the set of principles and the value system that ordered societies was bound to decline (Smith 1970).

W. W. Rostow's (1958) *Stages of Economic Growth* outlined a series of four stages through which nations proceed as they modernize. The catalyst for this process is the introduction of an "outside force" into a traditionally based society that begins to break down the primordial ties that were the foundation of the social and political order. It is important to note that Rostow (1958) emphasizes that these bonds are regressive and work against development and modernity. This line of thought became dominant in the study of political development and comparative politics and was emphasized in the textbooks of the late sixties, such as Almond and Powell's *Comparative Politics: A Developmental Approach* (1966). In short, development was to take place at the expense of traditional forces such as religion.

This process is largely what had transpired in Christian-dominated Europe and North America. Of course, there is no better example than Weber's Puritans. It was the spirit of capitalism and its associated behaviors which were inherent in the Protestant ethic, that, ironically, weakened religion's hold on the Puritan communities (Weber 1958). These same values, when introduced into an Islamic society, should have had the same affect. However, Weber never finished a volume on Islam in his sociology of religions, and his writings suggest that Islam was antimodern and that its value system might not facilitate modern capitalism (Turner 1974). The work of Orientalist scholars and Marx's Asiatic Mode of Production also suggest that Islam was different from Puritan Protestantism and repressed, rather than facilitated, modern vales (see Said 1978; Binder 1988).

RELIGION AND DEVELOPMENT

Liberal Theory

The proposed differences between Islam and Protestantism were smoothed over in Smith's (1970, 1974) two works on religion and development, which both strongly echo the liberal paradigm in that the spiritual will eventually become separated from the temporal. Smith (1970) wrote that religion's influence on politics in developing states goes through a four-step process similar to Rostow's stages of economic growth: separation of religion and politics, the expansion of the secularized polity into areas previously dominated by religion, secularization of political culture and, finally, polity domination of religion. In another volume, Smith (1974) predicted that Egypt's political system was in the midst of a transformation that would take it from traditional Islam to socialism. This prediction, however, was soon to be proved wrong by the events of the late 1970s.

Marxist Theory

The subordination or adaptation of religion to economics and politics theme is also prevalent in Marxist and dependency theory (Cordoso and Faleto 1979). For example, in *Islam and Capitalism* (1978), Rodinson wrote that even in purely traditional Muslim societies, religious belief did not significantly affect economic practice. According to Rodinson (1966), when religious doctrine stood in the way of gain and profit, it was either ignored or interpreted liberally. The theme of the irrelevance of Islamic doctrine in regulating economic practice is also reflected in the works of Gran (1979) and Amin (1978). This theoretical orientation viewed the importance of political culture as, primarily, being its growing irrelevance. Had this been true, the cross-national and regional study of political culture would not be necessary because all modern political cultures would be relatively similar. However, the study of political culture would remain important because modernity was not necessarily the final stage in the temporal progression of political cultures.

POSTMODERNISM

The continued relevance of political culture is evident in the growing body of literature on postmodernism of the last decade. The Kaas and Barnes (1979) project showed that a new culture of political activity might be developing in Western democracies. Wildvasky's (1990) article in the *American Political Science Review* outlines how changes in the nature of political cultures within nations might affect institutions. However, Inglehart's *Culture Shift in Advanced Industrial Societies* (1990), which proposes a change from modern to postmodern political culture in Western Europe, has been the most significant development in the field of political culture. Identifying the values that are postmodern, how they manifest themselves across generations, and how this transformation will affect political systems and policies will provide a full plate for the temporal analysis of political culture for years.

This line of research helps fulfill the fourth objective of political culture research—the codification and identification of different variants of political cultures, such as modern, postmodern, and traditional. This research can also lead to the examination of the question of whether variances in political culture across nations and subnational units result in different public policies. Recent studies (Hofferbert and Budge 1990) have shown that political parties follow the planks of the platforms they submit to the public before elections. At the same time, research is placing the political parties of democratic nations on the traditional/modern/postmodern continuum (Klingemann, Budge, and Hofferbert 1994). Consequently, it may be seen if differences in spending across nations or subnational units are related to the political cultural orientation of ruling parties.

CONSERVATIVE THEORY

The Developing Nations of the Muslim World

An important limitation of the temporal evolution of political culture and postmodernism literature is its irrelevance to many developing nations, particularly those in the Islamic world. The study of Islamic political culture and the political culture of the Middle East has not been able to achieve this fundamental task of identifying and codifying political culture among populations because of the difficulty of survey research in most Islamic and Middle Eastern countries (Binder 1976; Tessler 1987b). As will be seen, this has caused serious problems for research on Islam and politics. At the same time, the lack of true electoral competition and the presence of one-party states prohibits the use of political parties as indicators of political culture. As my own experience in Morocco demonstrated, it is difficult to study systematically political culture in authoritarian political systems.

Another limitation on the study of Islam's influence on politics is that the traditional/modern dichotomy does not appear to fit the political cultures of Islamic countries (Gellner 1981). This is largely a result of the current, and possibly never ending, conflict between things deemed "traditional" and those deemed "modern" in many of these nations. Of equal importance, in some nations, particularly Jordan, Morocco, and Tunisia, a co-existence and integration of these two forces appear to be coalescing. Consequently, the traditional/modern dichotomy may not be relevant to Islamic nations, which would signify the existence of a unique variant of political culture that should influence politics and policies. This is the crucial assumption about Islam that is accepted at face value but that has not been placed under rigorous examination.

The Resilience of Tradition

The notion of a universal culture of modernity actually came under attack in the late 1960s from a group labeled by Binder (1988) as conservative development theorists. It must be remembered that the liberal theorists themselves (Pye 1965) cautioned that tradition would never completely be eliminated from the realms of politics and economics. This thinking was represented in what are still the seminal works on political culture, Almond and Verba's *The Civic Culture* (1963) and *The Civic Culture Revisited* (1980), where it is claimed that tradition plays an important role in strengthening bonds and allegiances to participatory political systems. As mentioned, this raises the possibility that the ideological foundations of democracies may vary beyond those that are found in the West.

The concept of traditional political culture playing an important role in developing political systems can be found in the work of Huntington (1967), who wrote that traditional forces are important stabilizing elements in countries that are undergoing rapid political, economic, and social change. The use of tradition, according to Huntington, can maintain loyalty to regimes during these trying and turbulent times. Consequently, Huntington, along with Apter (1968) and Weiner (1966), called for the strengthening of traditional institutions, such as religious-based monarchies. The liberal development paradigm has also been criticized for its assumption that there are universal starting and ending points for all nations. Bendix (1967) argued that modernization could take place in some spheres of life in some countries but not in others. This leaves open the possibility that religion may be one of the "traditional" forces that affect politics in some modern nations. Hofferbert and Sharkansky (1973), in conjunction, found that it may be that, in some segments of society, industrialization proceeds separately from another developmental process, integration. In other words, some geographical locations remain isolated from the development that is taking place in neighboring areas.

These works all suggest that political culture not only varies significantly along the temporal domain but also along the spatial domain. This is the other half of the Weber thesis. Capitalist practice developed much faster in predominantly Protestant areas than in Catholic ones because of the different dogmas of the two churches. However, the Catholic-dominated areas eventually caught up to those of the Protestants. Thus, the question becomes whether differences in political culture can endure. Research on specific countries has provided evidence that these partitions might be long term or even permanent. It was also found that the traditional caste system in India is actually a factor that has aided the social and economic mobilization of the lower castes, which has facilitated the growth of democracy.

There is also evidence to suggest that political culture continues to affect policy in developed nations. King (1973) concluded that a uniquely American political culture is a cause of the small amount that that country spends on social programs and the slow development of its social programs. Also, Fried (1971) found that, within Italy, the existence of two political cultures may be a factor that affects variation in spending across cities. A basic assumption, for many years, in research on politics and public policy across American states was that a fundamental difference existed between Southern and Northern states (de Tocqueville 1956; Key 1984; Dye 1990). If various countries are unique and political cultures have been shown to vary within nations, it is essential that we investigate variance across a number of countries.

THE RESURGENCE OF POLITICAL CULTURE

The nature of the relationship between political culture, form of government, and public policy, as mentioned, has resurfaced in the study of politics. In addition to the previously discussed postmodernism research, there have been efforts to evaluate political culture in developing nations. One of the most noteworthy is Pye's work on China (1988). Several of the articles in a recent edited volume on the state of comparative politics (Rustow 1992) focus on political culture in the Third World. Also, another recently published collection of essays (Diamond 1993) focuses specifically on the relationship between traditional political culture and democracy. However, with the exception of the theme of political culture, the authors' focuses and methodologies vary greatly. Hence, the production of cross-national studies, which investigate the influence of a specific political culture on politics and policies while controlling for other factors is the next logical next step.

Recent events in international politics have also strengthened the arguments of those who advocate the importance of political culture. At the end of the cold war, many of the enduring conflicts are rooted in religious, ethnic, or linguistic partitions (Mazrui 1990). At face value, the conflicts in Bosnia, Israel/Palestine, the former republics of the Soviet Union, Kashmir, and elsewhere suggest that culture is important enough to cause wars between nations and destroy existing states. Huntington (1993) has gone as far as to argue that clashes between "civilizations" with conflicting value and belief systems might be the cause of the great wars of the twenty-first century. Huntington (1993) specifically points to the incompatibility of Islam and the West as a potential cause of conflict. This same concern with the relationship between Islam and the West, although to a less extreme extent, can also be found in the work of Lewis (1993).

ISLAM: TRADITIONAL OR MODERN

Early Works

The previously discussed literature raises the question whether Islam—specifically—hinders modernization and democracy. Can we find differences in levels of democracy and public policies between Islamic and non-Islamic developing nations? Also, do differences in the level of influence of Islamic political culture result in differing forms of governments and policies? Early works within political science that focused on the Middle East were strongly influenced by the liberal paradigm (Rustow 1971). Halpern (1967) wrote that a modern middle class was emerging in the Middle East that would lead the process of modernization in that region. Halpern (1967) went on to argue that Islam was an irrational and very dangerous threat to this process. Various studies undertaken during this period, of the political systems of various Middle Eastern nations, reach the same conclusion.[1] Generally, the mobilization of a middle class that had received a Western-style education would lead to the modernization and the secularization of political culture. However, events such as the Iranian Revolution, the Lebanese civil war, and the murder of Egyptian president Anwar Sadat soon proved otherwise. Consequently, political scientists and other area specialists were forced to reconsider Islam's role in politics and society. The resulting literature can be placed into four categories:

1. The study of Islam in the West is distorted by its relationship to Islamic societies. The West has always approached the study of Islam from a position of power and dominance, the colonizer and the hegemon, which has prevented Western scholars from gaining an accurate understanding of Islam and Islamic societies.

2. Islam is a very mysterious and irrational force that overwhelms societies. This trend attributes almost all behavior in Islamic societies to Islam. In other words, Islam is used to explain everything and is the most important

variable in understanding these societies. Changes in behavior are attributed to cyclical fluctuation in the influence of Islam.

3. This most basic approach has been an effort to collect information on Islamic political groups, the chains of events that have been associated with the rise of political Islam, and the nature of the ideologies being offered.

4. Realizing that Islam's role in society was not weakened as much as originally claimed by the writers of the 1960s and 1970s, this strain of literature attempts to understand the relationship between Islam and politics by applying the methods of the social sciences while, at the same time, recognizing that Islam might produce a political culture that varies from those of the West.

Postmodernism/Deconstructionism

The first response was important as it threw a red flag in front of Western Middle East specialists and caused them to rethink their methods. Most noteworthy in this body of literature are the two works of Said. The first, *Orientalism* (1978), takes scholars to task for the reasons discussed. The second, *Covering Islam* (1981), documents the unfair treatment of Islam in the media and government funding of Middle East research. Of interest to this project, Said (1981) suggests that innovative methods, such as quantitative studies and those that emphasize similarities between the Western and Islamic worlds, would be of value. This appears to match my earlier stated goal of demystifying Islam and going beyond attributing all that is unknown about the politics and societies of the Muslim world to Islam.

Islam Is Everything-Orientalism

The work of Said and other deconstructionists, although important as a criticism of methodology, does not attempt to produce new knowledge, specifically, evidence that political culture affects important political outcomes. We are told that political culture is important but that we, as Western analysts may not be able to discover how (Binder 1988). This view is, in part, a response to the second type of explanation of Islamic political resurgence, "Islam is everything." This approach predates the most recent rise of "Islamic fundamentalism" and is associated with Orientalism. In short, Orientalist research is based on the premise that Islamic societies can be understood through the deciphering of Islamic texts. A major shortcoming of this approach is that many of the fundamental precepts of Islamic societies are not contained in texts or are not even related to texts (Gellner 1981).

The second problem with recent versions of this orientation, and more central to this book, is that they can only explain temporal variances in

Islam's influence on politics but not spatial ones. For example, Lewis (1976), a highly esteemed contemporary Orientalist, writes that periods of Islamic revival are based on a sense of decline and decay in Islamic societies. This feeling is caused by the realization that the Islamic world is not keeping pace with rival civilizations, such as the West, which leads to a turning inward and, very often, irrational and self-destructive behavior. Islam, in short, can be viewed as a dark storm cloud that periodically overwhelms societies (Lewis 1976).

The "Islam Is Everything" explanation is also prevalent among journalists, commentators, and nonarea specialists. Huntington's two recent works (1991, 1993) are very prominent examples of works by nonarea specialists. Skocpol (1994), in her analysis of social revolutions, resorts to attributing the Iranian revolution to Shia extremism. As for the first two groups, one need only look as far as the titles. Journalist Robin Wright's (1986) book on Islamic political resurgence is titled *Sacred Rage: The Wrath of Militant Islam.* Hiro (1989) attributes conflict in the Middle East to *Holy Wars: The Rise of Islamic Fundamentalism.* Newspaper headlines have warned unsuspecting Americans that "The Muslims are Coming" and to be aware of "The Sweeping Tide of Islamic Fundamentalism." Area specialists (Kramer 1996; Dennis 1996) also still warn of the great threat presented to the West by a monolithic and hostile Islam. In short, Islam is something to be feared and stands in opposition to America and the West.

The "Islam Is Everything" explanation, both in its popular and Orientalist forms, is problematic for several reasons. First, this theory only explains temporal changes in Islam's influence on society but not cross-societal differences. If the period from the late 1970s to the present is a period of societal decline and Islamic resurgence, how does one explain the variance in the influence of Islam across countries with large Muslim populations? What about those that were religiously oriented prior to 1970 and those that have been less affected by the current resurgence of Islamic sentiment? This leads to a second shortcoming—the lack of consideration of other factors such as economic and social structures. Perhaps behavior that is being attributed to Islam is really being caused by something else? Islamic countries, of course, are not the only developing states experiencing turmoil and authoritarian rule.

A third problem results from the difficulty of survey research and other issues relating to social science research in most Muslim countries (Binder 1976; Tessler 1987b).[2] Hence, we do not really know if people have become more religious in the past twenty years or if their opinions regarding the proper relationship between religion and politics have changed as few methodologically sound surveys have been completed in the Muslim world. Perhaps, as Eisenstadt (1973) argues, they simply have begun to articulate long-held beliefs. It might also be that a small segment of society is attracting a lot of attention through acts of violence and sabotage. Finally, this argument is based on the assumption that Islamic political ideologies are irrational and cannot be successfully merged with those from the outside, which simply is not true (Shepard 1986).

Information Collecting

The third group of literature, and by far the largest, has been largely an information collecting exercise. First, there are numerous monographs detailing the rise of political Islam in a number of nations. The chapters on various countries are usually contributed by different authors and describe the events that led to Islamic political resurgence and the nature of important Islamic political groups (e.g., Hunter 1986; Piscatori 1983). I counted over fifty of these works in the library at Binghamton University. A second variant examines the thought of prominent Islamic political theorists (e.g., Esposito 1983; Donohue and Esposito 1982; Davis 1997). The third and final category in this group is in-depth studies of specific Islamic political groups (e.g., Keppel 1985). In short, most of these works have provided a significant amount of important information on political Islam and factors associated with its increasing strength; they have served to refute the "Islam Is Everything" explanation. However, few have rigorously analyzed the consequences of Islam's influence on politics across a large number of countries.

New Approaches

The fourth group of literature has used the theories and methods of academic disciplines to understand the relationship between Islam and politics, at the same time, however, acknowledging that analysis must precede with caution because Islam may, indeed, cause unique political outcomes. A good example of this type of research is Binder's (1978) analysis of the origins of regional elites in Egypt under the Nasser regime. Of interest, one of the central themes of *In a Moment of Enthusiasm* (1978) is that a traditionally oriented class, the rural nobility, played a crucial role in Nasser's campaign to modernize. Thus, the conclusions of both Crecelius (1970) and Vatikiotis (1983) that the rapid modernization and secularization of the Nasser era did not severely weaken the influence of Muslim political culture in Egypt is not surprising.

Perhaps their conclusions are based on the fact that the classifying of political cultures as traditional, modern, or transitional leaves out a very diverse middle ground. Eisentadt (1973) has warned that Islam cannot accurately be deemed traditional or modern. Gellner (1981), using anthropological case studies from North Africa, has argued that, of the three monotheisms, Islam best facilitates modernization and democracy. These works suggest that Islam's role in society, in practice, differs from Christianity's and that governments based on Islam and anchored in Islamic societies may produce outcomes that are significantly different from those of secular-oriented governments. However, this does not mean that the methods of political science and other social sciences are irrelevant to Islamic studies because of the uniqueness of Islam and Muslim societies.

Jerrold Green's (1982) analysis of the Iranian revolution discusses universal processes such as social mobilization, political mobilization, and pseudoparticipation, while accounting for the particularities of Iran. The same methodology has also been successfully used by Norton (1987) in his book on the growth of the Shia militia, Amal, in Lebanon during the early 1980s. Both of these works utilized the previously discussed liberal development theories to discover why modernization led to authoritarianism or anarchy rather than democracy. Binder's *Islamic Liberalism* (1988) used deconstructionist techniques to evaluate the compatibility of Islam with liberal democracy. However, in regard to the relationship between Islam and politics, most recent works have been largely descriptive and few have tested theories through comparative case studies or quantitative analysis.

An interesting and very useful body of literature, based on the realization that it is impossible to classify Islam as a traditional or modern force, has focused on developing typologies of Islamic political ideology (Shepard 1986). This type of research is invaluable to the study of the relationship between Islam and politics. First, it goes beyond claiming that Islamic political culture is different and identifies important aspects of Islam, which might cause the policies produced by Islamic governments to be unique. Second, it helps provide a better understanding of Islamic society than the Orientalist approach because it encompasses ideas and beliefs that are found outside of Islam's core texts. Finally, the categorizing and placing of ideologies on continuums in relationship to each other facilitates the rigorous cross-national analysis that is absent in research on political Islam.

One of the most sophisticated of these typologies is that of Shepard (1986), who collapses Islamic political thought into two dimensions: "totalism" and acceptance of outside ideas, institutions, and technologies. Totalism represents the extent to which strict adherence to Islamic law, *Sharia*, is required. The second realm, acceptance of outside ideas, institutions, and technologies can be succinctly labeled *authenticity*. These two indicators, in my opinion, provide a reliable tool to measure the "Islamicness" of the types of political cultures advocated by Islamic political groups and governments, which claim to rule in the name of Islam. I will discuss the appropriateness of these two indicators and the quantification of Shepard's typology in chapter 7.

THE CURRENT STATE OF THE STUDY OF ISLAM AND POLITICS

The quantity of literature being produced on Islam and politics has continued to increase exponentially in the late 1980s and early 1990s. Approaches to this problem have ranged from psychoanalytical (Mernissi 1992) deconstruction of deconstructionism (Binder 1988) and analyses of civil society (Norton 1995); Orientalist research also continues (Sivan 1990). However, most work continues to debate whether "Islamic fundamentalism" is a threat, is going to spread to more moderate countries such as Morocco and Tunisia, and whether Islam is compatible with democracy. At the same time, scholars continue to ask whether political Islam should be seen as a primarily religious or primarily political process (Shahin 1997; Ayubi 1995). In short, the recent resurgence of political Islam has endured for twenty-five years, but scholars, journalists, and commentators are still trying to predict what shape this phenomenon will take in the future and are still trying to decide how to study it.

It can be concluded that political science has yet to provide a sufficient answer to the question of the relationship between Islam and political outcomes. It has been found that Islam may not be traditional or modern and, most likely, represents a unique political culture. It is now a given fact that Islam is a fundamental element of political discourse in Muslim countries to which all political actors must pay credence or suffer severe consequences. However, we cannot be quite sure of what this political culture and social system are because of the difficulty of completing survey research in many Muslim countries. These unknown factors and the continued tension between Islam and things Western in some countries has led to the previously mentioned cottage industry of speculating about the future of political Islam.

The last twenty-five years have also provided a large enough database and storehouse of information to examine systematically the consequences of the political resurgence of Islam. As mentioned earlier, much information has been gathered regarding the role of Islam in politics in individual countries, various Islamic political groups, and different variants of Islamic ideologies. At the same time, we also have access to the speeches and statements of political officials as well as to the legal frameworks and constitutions of Muslim nations. Finally, the basic principles and values of Islamic society are recorded in core texts, such as the *Quran* and Islam's four legal traditions, and have been passed down orally through the *Sunna* and *Hadith* (examples of the behavior of the prophet and his oral statements).

These sources will allow me to see if the differing influence of Islamic political culture on governments is, subsequently, represented in forms of government and public policy. Are Islamic countries more or less demo-

cratic than non-Islamic developing nations? Have Islamic-based governments treated their citizens any better or any worse than secular-based
governments? Rather than speculating, I will evaluate twenty-five years of
performance. At the same time, I will be helping to fill a gap in the literature
of comparative politics and policy analysis by providing evidence that either
supports or disconfirms the significance of political culture as a determinant
of major political outcomes.

The next step is to determine how and why Islam should affect forms of
government, public policies, and the protection of the rights of citizens. I
will look at what the *Quran, Sunna*, and *Sharia* say about the political. In
this discussion I will be highlighting the obtuse and amorphous nature of
references to politics and policy in Islamic textual sources and traditions.
A look at the ideas of some of the influential modern Islamic political
theorists will show that contemporary variants of political Islam reflect the
practical objectives of the writers. Based on these sources and work on
transitions to democracy, I will then produce my own theory of the conditions under which Islam can facilitate transitions to democracy and, subsequently, influence public policies. Of course, I will also consider the
current social, political, and economic realities in several Islamic countries.

NOTES

1. For examples, see, Lewis (1961), Safran (1961), Cottam (1964), and Moore
(1965).

2. My own experience in Morocco is a good example of this problem. First, my
request to do survey research was refused by the Moroccan government. Second,
people—even on an informal basis—were reluctant to express their opinions regarding political matters. Third, it is impossible to obtain random samples where
nobody is exactly sure how many people there are.

2

How and Why Islam Should Influence Politics

The first step in rigorously evaluating the consequences of Islamic political resurgence is the development of an explanation, which will lead to the development of testable hypotheses, as to how and why Islam should influence forms of government and public policies. Otherwise, I run the risk of falling into the trap of attributing all political outcomes, behaviors, and policies in predominantly Muslim countries to Islam. In developing such hypotheses, I will first look to the basic sources of Islam, the *Quran*, the *Hadith*, the *Sunna* (words and deeds of the prophet), and the *Sharia* (Islamic law). A brief discussion of Islamic economics and notions of democracy will illustrate the lack of a clear and readily usable political program in the previously mentioned sources. I will then proceed to examine the works of four twentieth-century political theorists who have had a strong influence on current Islamic political movements. Finally, given the obtuse and contradictory nature of these texts, traditions, and theories, I will develop propositions regarding Islam and democracy based on both Islamic doctrine and tradition and research in political development, specifically, transitions to democracy.

The notion that political Islam can be the dominant influence on political systems and public policies in late twentieth-century nation-states is based on the problematic assumption that there is a defined set of principles, ideas, beliefs, and rules that are accepted by most Muslims as the basis of political Islam. All Muslims do, at base, accept the sanctity of the *Quran* as the word of God, the *Hadith* and the *Sunna* as being infallible, and the *Sharia* as the regulator of society and daily life. However, this is where uniformity in the realm of political Islam stops. Indeed, the diverse and amorphous nature of political Islam is rooted in the lack of a defined and readily usable political program in these sources. Instead, they primarily provide a vague set of guidelines for a society that existed over 1,000 years ago.

THE FUNDAMENTAL TEXTS AND TRADITIONS

Only about 270 of the 65,000 *sura* (verses) in the *Quran* discuss matters of governance or public policy (most of which deal with economic transactions and criminal punishments). It is also difficult for the examples from the prophet to serve as concrete prescriptions for matters of governance in the twentieth century, as the dilemmas arising from his small community of believers bear little resemblance to those confronted by the leaders of modern nation-states. Finally, Islamic law (*Sharia*), which must serve as the foundation of an Islamic state, was finalized over 800 years ago and has not been significantly altered since. Consequently, as will be discussed later, the application of *Sharia* is usually dependent on the interpretations and, subsequently, political purposes, of individual *alim* (religious judges/scholars). Even if the *Quran* did include lengthy discussions of political practice, contemporary Muslim rulers reigned over nomadic tribes rather than modern nation-states, and had *Sharia* been updated over the years, a unified Islamic political program would still remain an illusive concept.

Those who give the entire Muslim world a set of political characteristics or deem it inherently hostile to democracy also ignore the fact that Islam is in no way a monolithic religion. First, practice, tradition, and doctrine vary between Sunni and Shia. Second, within both Sunni and Shia, there are various sects, which also maintain different interpretations of Islam. Third, within the Sunni tradition, the existence of four different legal approaches also affects matters related to public policy (Enayat 1982). Fourth, theorists and *ulama* (religious scholars, plural of *alim*) representing the government and opposition forces interpret Islam according to their objective of either maintaining power or bringing down a political order. Finally, within opposition forces, traditional, modernist, and radical solutions are offered for society's ills.[1]

It is not surprising, given the preceding, that interpretations of the *Quran, Sunna, Hadith*, and *Sharia* vary widely. This is best represented in the *fatwah* (edicts) that the *ulama* issue on a regular basis. During the 1960s, the rector of the Al-Azhar University in Cairo issued a *fatwah* that ascertained that socialism was compatible with Islam (Shaltut 1982).[2] Under Anwar Sadat, a different rector declared that the new president's *infitah* (opening of the economy) policy was sanctioned by Islam. In 1979, Al-Azhar declared that the Camp David Accords were also in accordance with Islam (Keppel 1985). At the same time, clerics in other Muslim countries were issuing *fatwah* declaring Anwar Sadat an apostate (Ajami 1982). These conflicting *fatwah*, of course, are possible because of the previously mentioned amorphous and diverse nature of Islamic texts that deal with politics. To further illustrate this point and the absence of a singular widely accepted Islamic political program, I will briefly consider Islamic notions of economics and democracy.

AN ISLAMIC ECONOMIC SYSTEM

One of the apparent threats of government based on Islam is that it would not facilitate capitalism. If Islamic governments do not respect free trade, open markets, and the sanctity of private property, then they are unlikely to integrate into the current international order.[3] Islamic economics might best be summarized as a capital mode of production and a socialist mode of distribution (Mazrui 1990). Because Mohammed's second wife was a merchant, the prophet was strongly in favor of an open market and fair competition (Mazrui 1990). Private property is also part of the foundation of an Islamic economic system. Market competition is supported because individuals, who work hard, should enjoy the fruits of their labor. Labor is an important aspect—but only one component—of self-development, and those who are not willing to work or who are lazy are not entitled to the benefits of the Islamic state. These capitalistic tendencies are strengthened by the writings of one the most renowned Islamic sociologists and thinkers, Ibn Khaldun. Khaldun's (1958) theory of economic practice represents Mazrui's capitalist mode of production, as Khaldun emphasizes the importance of an atmosphere in which business and economic activity can thrive. Khaldun also writes that the primary duty of a political leader is maintaining order, which should be achieved at almost any expense. At the same time, governments should avoid overtaxation and should allow citizens as much economic liberty as possible.

Islam, however, places more stringent restrictions on market competition and how labor may be utilized than Western capitalism does. Natural resources that are vital to the functioning of state and society are to be controlled by the government so that these resources will be equally available to all citizens. Also, private property must be used in a manner that will provide some benefit to the society as a whole, not just its owner. Finally, land or other essential property that is not being exploited is to be transferred to the community (Abd al-Kadr 1983). This is a function of the communitarian nature of Islam, where the rights of the community, generally, have precedent over those of the individual. This ethic could easily lead to an interventionist state that would define the economic good of the community and protect (or enforce) that public good.

Profits, along these lines, are also to be regulated by the Islamic state (Abd al-Kadr 1983). Eventually, the government would determine and regulate these excess profits. Possible methods of implementing this policy could include high income and property taxes or a rigid system of price controls. The state might also have the authority to certify that both parties benefited from a business transaction. Another restriction on profit is the stipulation that profit must be reinvested to provide more goods for the community. In short, a successful merchant would have to charge a fair price for his or her goods and would be able to keep enough of his or her earnings to lead a comfortable but not extravagant lifestyle. A final restriction is that goods produced or sold should be useful for the betterment of society and not purely for enjoyment (Abd al-Kadr 1983).

In addition to regulating the accumulation of profit, the Islamic state would also redistribute excess wealth to needy members of society who cannot earn a living. In an Islamic state, the *Waqf* (charitable foundation) is to be administered by the government and could levy a tax to provide alms (*Zakat*) for the poor. Also, Islamic law calls for an equal distribution of inheritance among male dependents. Finally, there is also a form of property tax from which the proceeds are also to be used for the poor (al-Maamiry 1983). In short, all citizens of Islamic states, who are willing but unable to work, are to be provided with the necessities for basic subsistence. Given the strong redistributive ethic, a high level of taxation to support an extensive welfare system might be expected in an Islamic state (al-Maamiry 1983).

Other economic regulations in a Muslim state would prevent *ribah* transactions, the charging of interest. Also, workers are not to be exploited in order to make a profit and are to be treated humanely, forgiven for stealing, and paid a fair wage. On one hand, the Islamic economic system is designed to encourage hard work, competition, and the quest for profit. An uneven distribution of wealth is not only tolerated but, rather, expected. However, after profit has been made, the state has the right to garner whatever it believes is necessary to provide for the community as a whole (Abd al-Kadr 1983). The state could also determine what are moral and ethical business practices. In short, there is nothing, except the ban on interest, in Islamic economics that is foreign to the economic systems of Western nations. At the same time, the "capitalist mode of production" and "socialist mode of distribution" appear to contradict each other. Consequently, it is reasonable to predict that individual regimes, according to their needs, would determine whether to emphasize the socialist or capitalist elements of Islamic economics.

It is important to note that it is the ban on interest that is particularly troublesome to non-Muslim commentators (Turner 1974). However, works by Gran (1979) and Rodinson (1978) have found that this ban, historically, has not been an impediment to economic growth in Muslim societies. Rodinson (1978) argues that when religion has stood in the way of profit in Muslim societies, it has either been ignored or liberally interpreted. Gran's

(1979) study of eighteenth-century Egypt reaches roughly the same conclusion. Today, nations such as Saudi Arabia, which ban *ribah* (usury) transactions are, of course, active participants in the global economy. A common method of circumventing the ban on interest is the use of joint development schemes between banks and developers rather than loans (Springborg 1988). The development of a strong banking network that adheres to *Sharia* is illustrated in Moore's (1990) study of the growth of Islamic banks in Turkey and the Middle East.

ISLAM AND DEMOCRACY

Many works have focused on how democracy has been represented in Islamic political doctrine, how it has been viewed by Islamic political theorists, and whether Islamic civil societies can facilitate democracy.[4] Rather than rehash the particulars of this debate, I will briefly mention factors within Islam that work for and against democracy. A notion of democracy, *shura*, which translates into consultation, is found in the *Quran*. In short, Islamic leaders must consult with the citizens before instituting policies or taking major actions. Consultation, however, does not necessarily translate into representative government and free elections, as it could mean anything from direct democracy to consulting with a small group of elites selected by the regime to represent the citizenry.

A second democratic principle inherent in Islam is *ijma*, consensus, meaning that important policies should have the support of a significant segment of society. Once again, consensus could translate into the support of a majority of the populous through referendum or monarchs who claim that because their rule is ordained by God, the people naturally agree with their policies. The possibility that leaders or regimes can use the communitarian tendencies of Islam to rule in the name of the community is a possible hindrance to truly representative government, because democracy is impossible without a degree of individual autonomy from the state. Islam, *does* have such a provision, *ijtihad*. *Ijtihad* means that Muslims have autonomy in interpreting Islam when there is no clear precedent from the *Quran, Sunna,* or *Hadith*. The gates of *ijtihad*, however remain closed for *Sunni* Muslims (Piscatori 1986).[5]

Other important components of democracy, such as equality and participation, are also inherent in Islam as all Muslims are partners in the community of believers and are equal before God. Gellner writes: "By various obvious criteria—universalism, scripturalism, spiritual egalitarianism, the extent of full participation in the sacred community not to one, or some, but to all, and the rational system of social life—Islam is, of the three great Western monotheisms, the one closest to modernity and best facilitates democracy" (Gellner 1981, 7). Finally, the *Quran*, especially many of the early verses, contains many favorable references to democracy, individual autonomy, and the desirability of universal participation by all members of the community in matters of governance and policy. However, because the *Quran*, like the Torah, is often vaguely worded and uses poetic language, verses can be interpreted to suit one's political objectives (Rosenthal 1962).

The primary factor that is inherent in Islam, which might hinder democracy, is the primacy of *Sharia*. Many of the political groups, which are currently calling for an Islamic state, claim that the nature of the state is of secondary importance to the implementation of *Sharia*.[6] Consequently, authoritarian government would be acceptable if it results in the application of *Sharia*. This is the case because many of the groups and individuals that call for an Islamic-based government believe that the implementation and following of *Sharia* will lead to a just society (al-Bannah 1981). Islamic law itself may be problematic as it extends into spheres of life that liberalism dictates as being left to individual discretion. Most notable are the restrictions on women relating to dress and personal conduct and religious control of matters of personal status, such as marriage and divorce (Mayer 1991).

Another area of concern is what the role of non-Muslims would be in an Islamic democracy. Traditionally, Jews and Christians were given protected status (*dhimmini*) and were allowed to regulate the social and religious affairs of their communities. However, they were forced to pay tribute and were usually denied political rights (an-Naim 1987). Also, the quranicaly justified fulminations against Jews and Christians by some spokesman of political Islam are quite unsettling.[7] The lack of a historical tradition of democracy is also a factor that works against the establishment of representative government in today's Muslim nations. During the two Islamic empires (*Abasaid* and *Ummayid*) and the Ottoman Empire, which covered much of the Muslim world, a tendency developed among the *ulama* to support authoritarian rule. Religious scholars and judges, generally, claimed that order and security were preferable over the disorder that might follow a revolt against authoritarian rule (Hourani 1991). Hence, the religious establishment often became the defenders of authoritarianism.

The preceding discussions of Islamic economics and Islam and democracy have briefly explained how Islamic texts and traditions do not provide a clear political program, concrete guide for governance, or a public policy that can be labeled authentically Islamic. I, of course, have only scratched the surface but that was purely intentional. As mentioned, others have investigated these topics in a more in-depth manner and have reached the same conclusion. Before moving on to discuss influences that shape the various manifestations of political Islam in modern nation states, I will detail the ideas of four contemporary Muslim political theorists. It might be that we can find some common themes and similar interpretations of Islamic texts and tradition in their responses to the problems that face contemporary Muslim nations and communities.

NOTIONS OF GOVERNANCE AND PUBLIC POLICY IN THE WORKS OF FOUR CONTEMPORARY MUSLIM POLITICAL THEORISTS

Sayyid Qutb

Qutb's (1981) political thought is marked with socialist and humanist themes. His goal is for all individuals to feel that they are integral parts of society and humanity. He, at the same time, criticizes communism for its denial of any spiritual component and capitalism for its acceptance of great disparities in wealth and exploitation. Although Qutb supports the use of modern science and its achievements in God's service and has no qualms about incorporating technology from the West, he argues against the desirability of unrestricted progress as a societal goal (Qutb 1974). This notion is very similar to the postmaterialist values that have surfaced in the politics of Western nations in the last twenty-five years. However, we do see the state being responsible for the possible contradicting goals of advancement and development versus spiritual and personal fulfillment (Qutb 1975).

Qutb's (1974) economic theory is based on an equitable distribution of wealth. All citizens should be guaranteed employment, and crucial natural resources that are essential for human subsistence are to be controlled by the state. Although private ownership and an open market are tolerated, methods of accumulating wealth must be justified to society, and private property must be used for the common good. Finally, the state must provide for those who cannot work. However, the lazy and those who are not willing to contribute their labor to the state are to receive nothing (Qutb 1981). Qutb, it appears, favors a large state apparatus because of the strong redistributive ethic and broad definition of what is to be shared by the community. Although the market and private property are protected, the moral component of Qutb's (1974) political program also points to a strong and possibly coercive state apparatus. How would it be interpreted as to which uses of science and technology are in the service of God? What standards would be used to justify the accumulation of wealth? According to Qutb (1981), following the principles of the *Quran* and adherence to *Sharia* would lead to the answers to these questions. However, given the vague nature of the former and the need for constant interpretation of the latter, political expediency would also have a strong influence.

Mawlana Mawdudi

Mawdudi (1967) feared that Indian Muslims, much to their own detriment, were being seduced by secularism. Because Muslims are a minority in India, he was concerned that a secular democracy would result in a tyranny of the majority, which would discriminate against Muslims. He wrote that Indian Muslims should turn their primary allegiance toward the Muslim community rather than the secular nation, which would foster increased self-fulfillment (Mawdudi 1967). Again, this is because the precepts of Islamic law, which are designed to provide self-development, extend into all areas of life. Mawdudi (1967) does not discuss public policy at length but rather the end result, his ideal society that would be based on equality and social justice. This ideal society would be achieved through the election of scholar-rulers who, in addition to forming legislation, would regulate religious and moral behavior (Mawdudi 1967).

As was true for Qutb, it appears that a powerful governing apparatus would be necessary to formulate and implement proper conduct. However, Mawdudi (1967) does add the qualifications that matters not covered in the *Sharia* would be left to the individual and that private property would be protected. It is also important to note that Mawdudi (1967) writes of the need for strong leadership that would properly guide society. However, based on Mawdudi's writings, it might be that he is advocating a system similar to that of the United States, where trustees are elected to represent the people and, for the most part, formulate policy, while only periodically consulting the populous. Pragmatically, Mawdudi was scornful of wealthy Indian Muslims and the power that they wielded in local communities. It might be that he simply wanted to replace an economic ruling class with a theocratic one.

Ali Shariati

The concept of the ideal society, once again, is the prevalent theme in the writings of Ali Shariati (1979), whose nickname is "The Ideologue of the Iranian Revolution." The work of Shariati is of interest because it is an amalgamation of Islam and concepts taken from the Western social sciences. His primary concern was eliminating the exploitation of the Muslim world by the West through its ideas and institutions. However, in order to reach the secularized Iranian students, his Islamic alternative is couched in secular and Western notions of liberation, social justice, and a classless society. But, the spiritual component of Islam would provide the fulfillment for the soul that is absent in communism, which contends that the proper relations of production are the only necessary condition for self-fulfillment.

Shariati (1979), as was the case with Qutb and Mawdudi, does not concern himself with the formal structure of the Islamic state or matters of public policy. At the same time, there is a desire for social justice and the release of the individual from an oppressive political system. The new order will bring about equality and self-fulfillment simply because it will be based on Islam. Once again, there is the notion that public policy will be just in an Islamic state because that policy is rooted in *Sharia*. Given that the purpose of Shariati's writing was to motivate Iranians to rebel against the

Shah, it is understandable that he makes his appeals based on a complete restructuring of society. Perhaps those who analyze the prospects for government in an Islamic state based on the works of these theorists forget that, after the revolution, lofty ideals and utopias are discarded for the nuts and bolts of day-to-day governing. This is exactly what is happening, today, in Iran following the death of the Ayatollah Khomeini (Esposito and Piscatori 1991).

Mohammed Iqbal

The final theorist under consideration, the Indian poet, Mohammed Iqbal (1964), presents a vivid description of God's will for mankind. This includes the intertwining of religion and state, which will lead to democracy with a spiritual component. According to Iqbal (1964), an Islamic democracy, in contrast to secular democracies, which encourage individuals to exploit others for their own purposes, would further freedom, equality, and brotherhood. Why? Simply because citizens would be acting according to Islamic precepts, which call for them to work for the betterment of the whole community. At the same time, the individual's sense of self-worth would also be elevated. As was the case with the other three theorists, we see a natural convergence between the happiness of the individual and the overall welfare of the community. However, unlike the other theorists, Iqbal (1964) specifically mentions democracy as the preferred form of government.

Iqbal (1964) also does not discuss the kinds of public policies that would bring about this transformation of society. He does write that the interpretation of the *Sharia* should change with the times and that tradition should be adapted to accommodate modern conditions. However, he does not state whether the individual should be able to perform this task through *ijtihad*. On the other hand, the importance of a strong leader to interpret and implement the law is emphasized. This statement supports the notion of a legislator or executive chosen by the people, based on his knowledge of the *Sharia*, to rule on their behalf. Iqbal (1964), like the other writers, seems to be perplexed as to the role of the individual. All call for the individual to have some part in the political process and decisionmaking. However, it is assumed that individuals will agree on most important matters and think of the community first because the precepts of Islam guide their actions. It is also agreed that a strong scholar-ruler is needed to guide the community.

Multiple Political Islams

This discussion of the works of four contemporary Muslim political theorists has strengthened the earlier reached conclusion that Islamic doctrine can facilitate a variety of political systems and public policies. In the writings of each ideologue, there have been ideas that would appear to support both democratic and authoritarian government as well as both market- and state-centered economies. The one area where they are consistent is the need for a spiritual component in government and politics. However, this spiritual component is not the *result* of a specific type of political system or set of policies but rather it is their *cause*. People behaving according to Islamic principles and following *Sharia* would bring about spirituality and morality, which would naturally produce Islamic governments and policies. As this final product had not actually occurred since the time of the prophet, it is impossible for the theorists to be specific about the results. Consequently, they, like the sources that their works are based upon, must be vague.

The preceding conclusion contradicts the notion that government based on the framework of the *Quran, Hadith*, and *Sunna*, in conjunction with adherence to *Sharia*, will lead to a predetermined outcome known as political Islam. Of course, as we see today, the government and politics of countries such as Iran, Saudi Arabia, and Sudan, which all claim that their polities are founded on Islamic principles and, to a significant extent, utilize Islamic law are, indeed, quite different. This leads to the question of what, if not the influence of Islamic political culture, causes these differences? Previous studies and my own preliminary investigation have led to factors related to politics, economics, society, and foreign relations. The case studies in the chapters to follow will provide the beginnings of an answer to this question. However, it is first necessary to discuss the variables to be analyzed in these case studies, which is the focus of the final section of this chapter.

CASE STUDY RESEARCH DESIGN

Overview

The purpose of the case studies is to identify factors that influence (1) whether political Islam gains a foothold in political systems and (2) whether a rise in the influence of political Islam leads to an opening of the political system. Once these factors are identified, they will be operationalized and tested in chapters 7 and 8, which use statistical analysis to evaluate the relationship between Islam and democracy and Islam and human rights. I will be looking at factors that the literature in political science relating to transitions to democracy has found to be significant. In general, these factors can be put into four groups: political, historical, societal, and economic. I have chosen eight Middle Eastern and North African countries (which have all seen a rise in political Islam in the last twenty years) to compare and contrast across these four groups of variables.

Cases

The eight countries selected for the case studies have been chosen because they represent different relationships between Islam and politics. The inclusion of a variety of countries and relationships is essential, because I am seeking to identify variables that influence the form in which political Islam manifests itself and the type of affect that it has on political systems. Consequently, it is important to know how the four groups of factors (political, historical, societal, and economic) vary across states with different relationships between Islam and politics. For example, if I were to examine only Algeria, I would conclude that opening the political system to Islamic groups leads to anarchy. However, if I add Jordan to the analysis, this conclusion is challenged as the same process in that country helped maintain political order. As a result, I would need to compare and contrast the two countries in regard to other variables.

The eight countries that I have selected are Algeria, Egypt, Iran, Jordan, Morocco, Saudi Arabia, Syria, and Tunisia. They can be categorized into the following four relationships between Islam and politics:

1. Egypt and Jordan, where a growing Islamic influence was facilitated by regimes and accompanied by modest pluralization

2. Syria and Tunisia, where Islamic opposition has been suppressed by secular-based government, which has resulted, to varying extents, in continued authoritarianism

3. Saudi Arabia and Morocco, where Islam has continuously influenced government and politics and regimes have remained, to varying extents, authoritarian

4. Iran and Algeria, where the rise of political Islam has strengthened authoritarian tendencies

The analysis in the case studies will, generally, begin with the period following the Six Day War because that event is often credited with stimulating the rise of political Islam (Ajami 1982). However, I will concentrate on the years, in each nation, which saw the greatest amount of activity by Islamic political groups and a growing influence of political Islam. These periods, of course, will vary from nation to nation with the exceptions of Morocco and Saudi Arabia, where secularizing regimes have never ruled. For those two countries, my inquiry will center on the past twenty-five years. Each case will begin with a brief history of political Islam in that country, proceed to an analysis of the factors that will be detailed in the remainder of this chapter, and briefly consider what has transpired since the critical period when political Islam challenged secular-based authority.[8]

Political Leadership

Many discussions of the resurgence of political Islam have focused on three important factors: (1) economic and cultural dependency on the West, (2) inequalities caused by modernization, and (3) ineffective government.[9] Although these factors are all of great importance, they deal with processes and relationships that are relevant to almost all developing countries, both Muslim and non-Muslim. Morocco's government probably has been almost as ineffective as Algeria's and has gone through the same process of modernization, yet political Islam has taken a much less virulent form in Algeria. All of the countries in the case studies, except Saudi Arabia, were penetrated by Western colonialism and all, today, are influenced by Western culture.

These explanations, in short, only account for increases in the demand for a more influential role for Islam in politics. Of course, because Islam does not play an active role in the politics in all nations with predominantly Muslim populations, other factors must account for the varying results of this demand. The three previously mentioned explanations may have labeled the necessary conditions for an increase in the influence of Islam on political systems but not the sufficient ones. The factor that has yet to be adequately explored is the role of political leadership and the nature of its interaction with Islamic political groups. In the last twenty-five years, most leaders of secular-based regimes in countries with large Muslim populations, particularly those in the Middle East and North Africa, have been faced with the growth of an Islamic opposition.

This challenge should not be looked at as an extraordinary event or a step backward, as implied by early liberal and Marxist theory. The demand for Islam playing a role in politics did not disappear, as liberal theory predicted but, rather, it declined or was repressed.[10] As stated, because religion and politics are intertwined in Islamic law and doctrine, Islam *should*, as a majority of Muslims still believe, play a significant role in the politics of Muslim countries. It is also important to note that most nations with large Muslim populations have gone through a long period of interaction with the West and its secular ideas. Naturally, many of these ideas have taken hold with the elite, which have had the most exposure to the West. The Muslim world has easily and freely adapted Western ideas, institutions, and technologies for over 500 years (Piscatori 1986).

It might be expected, given the preceding, that healthy competition between Islamic and secular-oriented political forces would take place if democracy was achieved in predominantly Muslim countries. Perhaps, as in the case of Israel, some spheres of public life would be controlled by religious law and others by secular law, or a "modernist" Islam similar to that proposed by Abduh (1966) and al-Afghani (1969) 100 years ago would develop into the dominant political culture. This "mixed" political culture is supported by history, as much of the Islamic world was only penetrated, but not dominated, by the colonial powers. England and France, without full control of government and administration, were forced to rule in concert with local leadership (Brown 1984). Consequently, local traditions endured.[11] However, the question still remains as to whether this Islamic component can tolerate and co-exist with the secular component. At this point, the evidence is mixed.

One reason for the tension between these two forces is that the reassertion of political Islam, naturally, comes at the expense of the existent, and usually reluctant, secular—authoritarian—regimes. Consequently, their reaction to the Islamic challenge is crucial. The important but often overlooked part of the equation is that these leaders do have viable options, and the choices they make do matter. They, as those who warn about the sweeping tide of "Islamic fundamentalism" claim, are not simply overrun by an uncontrollable force. Leaders decide whether they have no choice but to provide entry for the Islamists into legitimate politics and attempt to form coalitions with them or whether resistance is the best option. They consider whether there is a significant convergence of interests to facilitate a deal or whether ideology and other cleavages leave them no choice but to resist. These interactions—the options chosen and their consequences—will be the focus of the case studies and are of great significance to the process of democratization in the Islamic world.[12]

Factors Affecting Regime Choice

The Regime's Grip on Power. It is no surprise that Islamic opposition groups usually rise at a time when regimes appear to be losing their grip on power. Consequently, I will be looking to determine whether the regime in power has control over key segments of the state apparatus such as the leadership's inner circle of confidants, the bureaucracy, the military, and the internal security forces. Also, has there been significant rioting, demonstrations, or other events, which would demonstrate that the regime is losing its hold on power? Another concern is a loss in a war or other military embarrassments, which are signs that a regime is enervated.

The Strength and Ideological Orientation of the Islamic Opposition. A regime, naturally, has little reason to believe that it needs to accommodate an Islamic opposition that does not appear to pose a significant threat. Consequently, leaders would opt for forcible oppression. It can be expected that the regime would take into consideration the approximate size of the Islamic groups and whether they are based in social strata (e.g., the military, rural landholders, or industrialists) whose support is essential for regime maintenance. Also, is the opposition geographically isolated where it can be contained or is it a presence in central areas and major cities? It is important to note that the regime can miscalculate, as was the case in Iran, both in evaluating its own strength and the power of the opposition.

The nature of the Islamic groups is also a factor the regime takes into consideration. Obviously, compromise is more likely to be reached with moderate than extremist groups. For example, no government is likely to seek accommodation for a group that calls for the immediate implementation of *Sharia*. It is also unrealistic to expect that the hand of reconciliation be extended to a group that calls for a violent *jihad* (a struggle or campaign waged for God) to install an Islamic government. Shepard's (1986) two dimensions of Islamic political ideology are most relevant here. If Islamic political groups are not adamant about the immediate implementation of *Sharia*, are somewhat acceptant of ideas that originate in the West, and do not use violence as a means of increasing Islam's role in government, then cooperation is possible.

The Regime's Islamic Credentials. The ideological orientation of the regime and its "Islamic credibility" are also important considerations. A regime with a strong Islamic orientation may be less likely to negotiate with Islamic opposition because that would weaken its legitimacy. In short, an Islamic regime cannot recognize the authenticity of another group that claims to represent "true Islam." On the other hand, a regime seeking to enhance its "authenticity" may try to bring moderate Islamic groups into legitimate politics. Finally, regimes and oppositions at opposite ends of the secular-Islamic continuum are likely to clash.

Supporting Cleavages. There are often factors relating to societal divisions, in addition to the secular-religious divide, that shape political Islam's affect on political systems. When these cleavages support the breach between Islamic-based opposition and regimes, the probability that political Islam will take a more virulent form increases. First, the supporting cleavages usually heighten the animosity between the regime and the opposition. Second, this animosity, which has usually developed over a long period of time, weakens the trust and good faith that are necessary for accommodation. These cleavages include:

1. Sectarian. The divide between the regime and the Islamic-based opposition often falls along sectarian lines, usually Sunni/Shia. The differing interpretations of Islam and historical tensions between the two sects makes accommodation less likely.

2. Class. Large disparities in wealth and class divisions, as was the case in the Islamic communities of Mawdudi's India, often fuel the growth of Islamic political opposition. Once again, this is a factor that could lead political Islam to take a more virulent form.

3. Geography. The physical location of the Islamic political groups is also a significant consideration. Animosity can result when a regime favors a

particular region of the country or the cities over the countryside (or vice versa). Also, the isolation of the opposition in rural areas or away from important cities and population areas affects the extent to which it is seen as a threat to the regime.

4. Ethnicity. A final cleavage that can widen the gap between regimes and Islamic political groups is ethnicity. For example, the populations of three of the nations to be discussed, Morocco, Tunisia, and Algeria are divided between Berber and Arab.

Contextual Factors

These previously mentioned variables (supporting cleavages, the regime's Islamic credentials, the strength and ideological orientation of the Islamic opposition, and the regime's grip on power), of course, are not the only factors that are related to the growth and consolidation of democracy. Contextual variables such as wealth, social development, and modernization, which have been shown to influence levels of democracy in past studies, will be considered in the case studies and added as control variables in the statistical analysis in chapters 7 and 8. It is precisely these processes and variables, which are cited as causes of political Islam, that are often undervalued in the explanation of political outcomes in Islamic countries. This point is important to emphasize because, as will be determined in chapter 7, these countries might well be authoritarian regardless of the influence of Islamic political culture. Another crucial contextual consideration is the legacy of Western colonialism and the nature of contact with the non-Islamic world. This factor is significant because the countries in the case studies have had different experiences with Western colonialism and cultural penetration. It is not logical to expect countries that have had little contact with the outside world to accept readily Western culture and ideas. At the same time, one would also expect hostility from societies that were most adversely affected by colonialism.

Government performance is also a factor that affects the nature of political Islam. Of interest is that the regime to be considered in the case studies that historically has best provided for its citizens is the Saudi monarchy, which also maintains the least democratic political system. At the same time, the strong influence of Islamic political culture is often listed as a cause of Saudi Arabia's authoritarian government. Even with the high level of services and standard of living in Saudi Arabia, Islamic-based opposition still exists. Perhaps it is the wealth and services that have enabled the Saud family to be successful in fighting off challenges from its Islamic opposition. All of the governments to be considered have been accused of corruption, favoritism, not providing equally for all of the people, abusing human rights, and not being able to deal with social and economic problems. However, poor government performance is not a complete constant across the eight countries in the case studies. It might be that the popularity of Islamic groups seeking to alter radically systems of governance is dependent on the extent to which people are satisfied with their politicians. With that in mind, I will proceed to analyze the interactions between these groups and the governments that they seek to alter or replace. The result will be an idea as to what shapes the nature of political Islam.

NOTES

1. Gilles Keppel's *Prophet and Pharaoh* (1985), which discusses the political programs of Islamic political groups in Egypt during the mid-1980s, provides a good example of the variance in ideology across Islamic political groups.

2. Al-Azhar is the state-sponsored and supervised Islamic university in Egypt. Consequently, the *fatwah* issued from the university's *ulama* almost always support government policies.

3. This concern is reflected in scholarly work, where a whole body of literature has developed surrounding the relationship between Islam and capitalism (see Binder 1988 for a review). Journalists have also frequently pondered this question in their assessments of the threat of "Islamic fundamentalism" (e.g., see the pullout section of *The Economist* (August 6–13, 1994) on political Islam.

4. Some recent examples can be found in the collection of essays in the fall 1994 edition of *PS*. Of course a full listing of such works produced in the last five years alone would go on for countless pages. For such a list, see the bibliography in Peretz (1994).

5. In the course of the past 100 years, several reformers, most notably Mohammed Abduh and Jamal al-Afghani, have called for the reinstitution of *ijtihad*. Also, Shia Muslims have always been free to practice *ijtihad*.

6. For example, see the writings of Sayyid Qutb (1981) and Hassan al-Bannah (1981). Qutb's works are particularly influential with militant Islamic groups in Egypt. Al-Bannah was the founder of the Muslin Brethren, the largest Islamic political organization in the world.

7. See the essay by the late Ayatollah Khomeini in Esposito (1983).

8. All of the cases that I have selected are from the Middle East and North Africa. I made this choice because the relationship between Islam and politics has been best documented in these countries, my own expertise is greatest in this region, and the process of Islamic political reassertion began the earliest in these nations. In the future, it certainly would be interesting to do an analysis of the predominantly Muslim nations in Asia located outside of the Middle East and North Africa.

9 For examples see Green (1982), Lewis (1976), Norton (1987), and Ajami (1982).

10. This point will be illustrated further when individual nations are discussed in chapters 3 through 6.

11. For an interesting case study of how a local political culture survived colonial occupation, see Waterbury's study of Morocco (1970).

12. Here I am following the logic of the "elite theory" model of democratic transition, which contends that democracy is most likely to develop in countries where a coalition of elites agrees to share power. See Dahl (1971), Rustow (1970), and O'Donnell (1986).

3

Egypt and Jordan

GOVERNMENTS ON THE BRINK?

The political systems of Egypt and Jordan, since the Six Day War, have shared an important characteristic—a constant appearance that their regimes are hanging on to power by the slimmest of margins. However, the only changes of power that have occurred in either country have been in Egypt following the death of Gamal Abd al-Nasser and the assassination of Anwar Sadat. At the same time, the strength of Islamic political groups has increased in both these countries. Finally, in correspondence with these processes, there has been modest pluralization in both countries' political systems. This chapter will focus on Egypt and Jordan as cases where a rise in the influence of political Islam and Islamic political culture on government may have facilitated the growth of democracy. Of equal importance, these countries are also important examples of one way in which regimes respond to their own weakness and the appeal of political Islam as an opposition force.

The analysis for each country will begin with a brief history of Islam's role in politics and the course political Islam's resurgence has taken. I will then proceed to discuss the variables relating to regimes, oppositions, and contextual factors, which were detailed in the previous chapter. After discussing Egypt and then Jordan, I will compare and contrast the two cases in the concluding section of this chapter. For Egypt, I will focus on the Mubarak regime because, by the time of Sadat's assassination, Islamic political groups had become a significant force in Egyptian politics, and it was clear that Islamic political culture, in some fashion, was going to influence government and politics. For Jordan, I will primarily be considering the 1980s, because that is when Islamic political groups posed the greatest challenge to King Hussein's regime and when he was forced to take action. Finally, I will also look at the 1990s to see whether the gains of the 1980s were maintained.

EGYPT

Islam and Politics Under Nasser

During the years following the Officers' Coup in Egypt up to the Six Day War, it appeared that the predicted course of modernization was taking place in Egypt in regard to the role of religion in government and politics. First, Egypt was undergoing polity secularization and the religious authorities, such as Al-Azhar, were brought under the control of the state.[1] Second, religious law was relegated to the area of personal status.[2] Third, the power of the Muslim Brotherhood in Egypt was harnessed by the Egyptian government (Dekmejian 1971). These processes were facilitated by Nasser's tight grip on the army, security apparatus, and state bureaucracy. Neither of his successors enjoyed this luxury and were forced to rely on the cooperation of outside forces to remain in power (Springborg 1988). After the Officers' Coup, Nasser was slowly able to eliminate all competitors for power within the Free Officers group. At the same time, he replaced the senior personnel in the army from the previous regime with lower ranking officers, who were loyal to him and filled the top levels of the bureaucracy with his supporters. In contrast, both Mubarak and Sadat had to deal with officers and bureaucrats whose loyalties remained with the previous leader or who had created their own semiautonomous fiefdoms (Hinnebusch 1988).

Nasser, with the government and army firmly under his control, was able to eradicate his external opposition, including the Muslim Brotherhood. The Free Officers, when they came to power, had received assistance and cooperation from the Brotherhood. As a result, it was the only independent political organization allowed to exist after the coup. However, the Brotherhood continued to agitate for an Islamic government, the implementation of *Sharia*, and to criticize the socialist policies of Nasser's government. After a failed assassination attempt by a Brotherhood member, the organization was outlawed, and many of its activists were either executed or imprisoned. This process of Brotherhood agitation followed by regime repression was to continue throughout Nasser's rule (Israeli 1984).

A factor that supported Nasser's near eradication of the Brotherhood was his tremendous popularity. According to Vatikiotis (1978), the Egyptians adulated Nasser and viewed him as their savior. At the beginning of his reign, he appeared to be wiping out the corruption of the previous regimes and mild agrarian reform gave the populous the impression that he was a man of the people. Finally, the fact that he had been shot at six times by an assassin and survived further enhanced his larger than life persona. This combination of power and charisma enabled him to denounce the previously popular Muslim Brotherhood as anti-Egyptian traitors and Saudi lackeys (Vatikiotis 1978). Nasser's popularity was further strengthened by successes in the international arena when he forced the British out of Egypt and nationalized the Suez Canal. Then in 1956 he turned the military defeat in the Sinai into a victory over the French and British imperialists and the hated Israelis when the occupying forces were compelled to withdraw by the superpowers. Finally, Nasser moved Egypt back to the leadership position in the Arab world and to the forefront of the nonaligned movement. Dekmejian (1971) writes that Nasser was able to take these victories in international crises and use them to gain support for the new Pan-Arab and Arab-socialist ideologies that he was installing at the expense of Islam.

It is important to note that Islam did not disappear while Nasser was in power. Rather, it was under his control and was utilized for his purposes. Students continued to be instructed in Islamic practice and history in the public schools and the state religious institutions continued to function (Crecelius 1970). However, the *ulama* were aware of the consequences of falling from Nasser's favor and continued to act in their traditional roles of regime legitimizers (Hopwood 1985). As mentioned in chapter 2, the sheik of Al-Azhar could be counted on to produce a Quranic verse to justify Arab socialism (Shaltut 1982). Nasser also frequently pointed to the Islamic character of his reforms. After all, they were based on equality, social justice, and the spirit of cooperation, all of which are at the heart of Islamic doctrine (Israeli 1984). During this period, there was no Brotherhood, or any other viable Islamic opposition, to contend this position.

The Six Day War and Reassesment of Political Islam

The temporary and incomplete nature of Egypt's secularization became apparent after the disastrous Six Day War. Vatikiotis (1983, 68) writes: "Despite all the economic and social changes that had taken place in the past fifteen years of continuous development, religion had not yet been rejected by a vast section of the population and the vast majority of Egyptians still identified with religion and not the secular nation." Israeli (1984, 64) calls this a period of "elites pursuing massive modernization while the masses still maintained faith in tradition and religion." Finally, Binder's (1978) study of Nasser's Egypt found that the regime was built on the foundation of a traditionally oriented stratum of society, the rural landholders. Consequently, it is not surprising that following the rout by the

Israelis and the exposure of all the other failures of the Nasser regime, a large number of Egyptians turned to religion for the solution to their country's problems.[3]

Nasser, following the war, tried to strengthen his own Islamic credentials through the frequent use of Islamic terminology and the framing of policies in Islamic themes, when addressing the people. He portrayed himself as a believing Muslim, made the pilgrimage to Mecca, and often gave the sermon during Friday prayers at the Al-Azhar mosque. The agelong conflict between Muslim and Jews often appeared in his diatribes against Israel, the loss in 1967 was attributed to the will of *Allah*, and the government press frequently used anti-Semitic terminology in its descriptions of Israel (Harkabi 1971). However, at this point, a competing Islamic perspective surfaced in the writings of members of the Muslim Brotherhood, such as Sheik Kiskh, who blamed the results of the war on the regime (Kiskh 1969). Given the Islamic sentiments that prevailed in society, it was no longer expedient to imprison the Brotherhood. Political Islam now had to be accommodated.

Kiskh wrote that Egypt had lost the war because it had worshipped a false God, Nasser. The soldiers, lacking the spiritual inspiration of Islam, had fought poorly, and God did not come to their rescue because they had ceased to follow his law (Kiskh 1969). Kiskh (1969) also criticized the regime for selling out to the Godless Soviets, who turned their back on the Egyptian Muslims in their time of need. The same type of criticism was also reflected in Sayyid Qutb's *Milestones* (1981), which railed against Nasser for abandoning Islam and portraying himself as a deity. The corruption and inequality in Egyptian society had resulted from the abandonment of *Sharia*. As was the case with Kiskh, Qutb's prescription for reforming Egyptian society was the implementation of *Sharia* and ridding the country of corrupting Western influences (Qutb 1981). The works of both men became popular with educated Egyptians.

Islamic Resurgence Under Sadat

Anwar Sadat, who ascended to the presidency following Nasser's death in 1970, was faced with the task of replacing a popular leader who had left a government, military, and bureaucracy filled with loyalists and protégés. In addition, the nation was still reeling from the Six Day War, and the population was generally disgruntled over the lack of social and economic development. In short, Sadat was a weak leader in a fragmenting polity. Consequently, he was in search of allies, legitimacy, and national unity, and Islam had the potential to provide all three. Accordingly, in Egypt, it was the regime that helped give rise to political Islam. At the same time, Sadat, by inviting new actors and ideologies into the political arena, helped to produce a more competitive political system. The ensuing discussion of the choices made by Sadat and his successor, Hosni Mubarak, will help explain how political Islam has manifested itself in Egypt.

Sadat's first objective was to separate himself from the legacy of the secular-socialist Nasser regime.[4] First he emphasized his own personal piety and traditional village upbringing. Second, he frequently denounced socialism and eventually threw the Soviets out of Egypt. Finally, he framed the 1973 war with Israel in a religious context by labeling it a *jihad* to regain Islamic lands by launching the war during Ramadan and comparing Egypt's success with Islamic military victories of the past (Heikal 1983). He also appealed to religious passions by frequently clashing with the Coptic pope, who was concerned about the growing Islamic overtones in Egyptian politics (Ansari 1984a). Sadat, by these actions and by his frequent statements about building a society based on faith, religion, and cultural solidarity, was clearly trying to appear to be leading the resurfacing of Islamic sensibilities that had actually preceded his rise to power.

Another strategy for consolidating power, the active mobilization and support of religious political groups, produced consequences that still affect the Egyptian political system today. Sadat granted amnesty to the imprisoned members of the Islamic Brotherhood; he allowed the group to legally reorganize, and he gave it permission to resume publishing its newspaper, *Al-Dawah* (The Call). He also gave financial support to the growing Islamic *Ga'amat* (cells) on Egyptian university campuses and fixed student union elections so that the Islamic Student Associations would win.[5] These groups were encouraged to hold public prayers in university facilities and to spread their activities to the neighborhoods near the universities (Keppel 1985).

Sadat was hoping that the new Brotherhood, which had renounced violence, would serve as an ally in his battle against the Nasserists and the communists. The university graduates, who belonged to the *Ga'amat*, would provide a pool of loyal future state employees who shared his desire to move away from Nasserism (Heikal 1983). At the same time, the Egyptian populous was constantly being reminded that Egypt was an "Islamic" country and that *Sharia* would soon be the basis of the country's government and legal system (Heikal 1983). However, actual policies soon caused the Brotherhood and other Islamic groups to believe otherwise. Of greatest importance, Sadat never went any further than making symbolic gestures— such as banning alcohol in some public places and calling on judges to take *Sharia* into account when making rulings—when it came to implementing Islamic law (Hinnebusch 1988).

Committees were formed to codify *Sharia* into a modern legal code, but they never produced a finished product. At the same time, personal status laws were being liberalized through Sadat's personal directive. Also, the peace treaty with Israel was signed, and American culture and money began to permeate Egyptian society. As was the case with his predecessor, Sadat could count on a *fatwah* from the state *ulama* to support his policies. The peace treaty with Israel was justified by the example of the prophet entering into treaties with his defeated enemies and by a ruling that the *Quran* states that *jihad* is only to be used for defensive purposes (Rahman 1983). However, both Sadat and his *ulama* had lost credibility with the leaders of the Brotherhood, the neighborhood preachers, the students, and of course extremist Islamic political factions. The growing inequality in the distribution of wealth, increasing American influence, Egypt's marginalization in the Arab world following the Camp David Accords, and the regime's hedging on Islamic government drove a wedge between Sadat and his former allies. When they began to criticize and protest, he responded with repression and imprisonment (Heikal 1983).

Mubarak's Dilemma

Hosni Mubarak was left with the predicament caused by the increasing strength of political Islam, as Sadat was assassinated before decisive action was taken. Given that Sadat's killer was a member of the military and from a radical Islamic group, which had also instigated insurrection in the city of Asyuit, Egypt appeared to be "on the brink."[6] Mubarak's grip on power was even more tenuous than that of his predecessor. Consequently, he had to develop an approach for dealing with the Islamic political groups and sentiments that had been encouraged by his predecessor. His strategy, as discussed by Springborg (1988), was threefold. A low-key leadership, a less extravagant lifestyle (than Sadat), and a conservative approach toward the peace process with Israel made him less of a target of personal resentment than the maverick and opulent Sadat.

Mubarak attempted to marginalize the radical groups, such as the *Jihad* (the group responsible for Sadat's murder), *Takfir wa al-Hijra*, and the violent *Ga'amat*. This was done through infiltration by the state security forces and imprisonment. At the same time, Mubarak, starting with the trial of Sadat's murder, waged a propaganda battle to discredit the radicals as not being "true Muslims." This campaign involved sanctioning the Muslim Brotherhood and other moderate Islamic groups as voices of authentic Islam. Because the regime and the state religious apparatus had lost credibility, these groups were used to speak out against violence in the name of Islam and the need for a gradual approach toward Islamic government. In turn, the Brotherhood was allowed to join with other political parties in the 1984 and 1987 elections and field a list of candidates. Next, I will consider the factors that led to this decision.

Contextual Factors: Perpetual Social and Economic Malaise

It is important to emphasize that economic and social problems were important causes of Mubarak's precarious position. First, Egypt was a poor and overpopulated country. Consequently, the government had been strained to provide basic services (e.g., housing, health care, and education) at subsistence level existence and maintain the country's infrastructure. In addition, much of the government's revenue had been eaten up by the tremendously oversized bureaucracy, which was infamous for its ineffectiveness. These problems were compounded by high population concentrations in urban areas, particularly Cairo, and declines in three important sources of Egypt's revenues—tourism, remittances from workers in the Gulf countries, and oil (Springborg 1988).

Egypt's high illiteracy rate, which would usually be considered undesirable, was actually beneficial to the regime. This indicator symbolized the large segment of Egypt's population, which was primarily located in rural areas and the poorest quarters of Egypt's cities, that is politically irrelevant, because it was too concerned with the struggle to survive to pay attention to politics. Its lack of a formal education also facilitated the belief that politics was something that they could not influence and that their condition was the will of a higher power (Keppel 1985). However this economic and social malaise did influence the relationship between the government and political Islam, as groups such as the Muslim Brotherhood have stepped in to provide social services (health care, welfare, and education) that the government had not. The provision of such services bolstered the popularity of the Islamic groups at the expense of the government (Sadowski 1989).

Regime Strength

It should be apparent, by this point, that Egypt, under Mubarak, was (and continues to be) a fragmented polity.[7] In addition to the inefficiency, corruption, and inability to provide for a majority of citizens that have characterized all Egyptian regimes, Mubarak suffers from additional weaknesses. As mentioned, the Brotherhood and other Islamic groups have surfaced as credible rivals in providing social services. At the same time, the Egyptian government has been under constant pressure from the World Bank, International Monetary Fund (IMF), and the United States to cut subsidies, to reduce the size of their bureaucracy, and to privatize. The flip side of these reforms is that they took power from the regime because:

- Subsidies permit even the poorest Egyptians to eat. When Sadat cut the wheat subsidy in 1979, three days of riots took place. In short, these subsidies were a means of keeping a lid on discontent.

- Higher education in Egypt is free and admissions, for the most part, are open. As a result, the universities produce far more graduates than the economy can absorb. The government bureaucracies serve as a safety valve

by providing employment. Of course, a large number of unemployed college graduates is a threat to stability.

• State agencies and industries also provide positions that can be given as
rewards to political supporters.

Mubarak, like Sadat, faced the task of distancing himself from the legacy
of his predecessor. Although Sadat was held in high esteem in the West,
his popularity had plummeted in Egypt. In short, he was viewed as being
arrogant, extravagant, and a tool of the Americans. Sadat was also criticized for the growing American influence in Egypt and the appearance that
a small group had become wealthy at the expense of the rest of the country.
Many Egyptians were also angered by the peace with Israel that led to
Egypt's pariah status in the Arab and Islamic worlds (Heikal 1983). Finally,
Sadat had resorted to imprisoning and torturing his critics. Consequently,
Mubarak faced a very disgruntled country when he took power. As mentioned, a low-key, moderate, and low visibility leadership style was used
to alleviate this national discontent.

Another legacy of the Sadat era that weakened the Mubarak regime was
the *infitah* (opening of the economy) policy because this created a powerful
new interest—owners and capitalists—that had to be contended with. This
group's autonomy increased as it grew to control a large amount of wealth
and exert influence over the Egyptian economy. It also grew at the expense
of the state-sponsored sectors, which, naturally, were easier to control. In
addition, much of the important state apparatus that had been firmly controlled by Nasser, such as the military, the rural landholders, and the bureaucracy, had also developed independent power bases and patronage
networks. Finally, the international financial organizations and donor
countries that were helping to support Egypt's economy were another independent force to be appeased from time to time (Springborg 1988). Consequently, although Mubarak was clearly at the top of Egypt's power
hierarchy and the political system remained, for the most part, authoritarian, his control was limited.

The Islamic Opposition

This precarious situation led Mubarak to the same group as his predecessor, the Islamists. However, because the Islamic political groups were
already established and their popularity was growing, a more cautious approach was necessary. Before going on to discuss Mubarak's strategy, I will
briefly detail the major Egyptian Islamic political groups during the mid-
1980s. The groups will be categorized according to the scheme developed
by Shepard (1986).[8]

Modernists. This tendency is best represented by the Egyptian Brotherhood, which renounced violence and accepted the legitimacy of the gov-

ernment after Sadat released its activists from prison. They claim that Islam should be spread through preaching, education, and "setting an example." Their activities have included publishing a newspaper, *Al-Dawah*, setting up educational, social, and health institutions and joining forces with secular parties to run for the People's Assembly in 1984 and 1987. The new Brotherhood approach has often been described as "legalist." They do not believe that government institutions should be avoided because they are controlled by secular forces. Rather, they should be used to transmit the Islamic message, which explains the frequent appearance of Brotherhood spokesmen (and women) on government-controlled television (Sadowski 1989). Some, within this camp, have argued that Islamic law, indeed, must be updated before it can be implemented. Others claim that Islam and modernity are compatible because Western science and ideology were predated in Islam (Sadowski 1989). Even Islamic garb has been updated to correspond with the latest fashion trends.

The Modernist constituency is predominantly from the middle-class and upward. Many have benefited greatly from the secular state's free-market oriented economic system. A good example of this tendency is Egypt's "Islamic banks," which claim to follow *Sharia* while participating in international financial markets (Springborg 1988). This group fears the takeover of a radical Islam, because it would threaten the already shaky foundations of Egypt's economic system. Consequently, the goal of the Modernists has not been a violent overthrow of government that would lead to the immediate institution of *Sharia* but, rather, to "redress the existing structures and institutions in Islamic garb" (Binder 1988, 388).

Radicals. A variety of radical groups have been active in Egypt for the past twenty-five years. During the mid-1980s, the most prominent were *Takfir wa al-Hijra*, Islamic *Jihad* (also referred to as "The Video Group" and *Tanzim*) and various university *Ga'amat* (cells). All trace their roots to the writings of Hassan al-Bannah (1981) and Sayyid Qutb (1966), who both wrote that, for a true Muslim, *Shahada* (professing to Islam) and following Islamic precepts are insufficient. Rather, one must fight (violently, if necessary) to create an Islamic state with the *Quran* as its constitution and *Sharia* as its legal system. No compromises may be made with outside forces (e.g., the United States or Israel) or domestic secular governments. These ideas were reiterated by *Jihad* and *Takfir* members when they were interviewed in prison. They viewed Sadat as an apostate because he had not implemented *Sharia* and had permitted the United States to spread its anti-Islamic culture. Consequently, it was their duty to bring down the regime that was transforming Egypt into a *Jahiliyah* (pagan) society (Ibrahim 1980).

These groups, with the exception of *Takfir*, are of further danger to the regime, because they move freely within society and use modern media and technology. Supposedly, under their rule, science, technology, and progress would all be desirable if they were in the service of *Allah* (Ibrahim 1980). It is important to note that the radical groups are not unified and that there are major differences in their ideologies, tactics, and interests (Keppel 1985). The university cells maintain *Jihad*'s "*Sharia* now" objective but are less likely to use violence. They are also concerned with university issues, such as overcrowding, banning the mixing of the sexes in classrooms, and the showing of Western films (Keppel 1985). Gilles Keppel's (1986) study of these groups also found a greater emphasis on universal themes such as social justice, freedom, and democracy than in the nonuniversity groups. Finally, *Takfir* prefers to isolate itself from society so that they may remain pure until the time for revolt and Islamic government is known. A majority of the members of these groups are newcomers to the city who have degrees in engineering and the sciences. In general, they are alienated by the foreign influences in the city and the large gap between the wealthy and the rest of society. These poorly prepared graduates work at low-paying government jobs with no opportunity for advancement. In short, they were thrown into modern society but still maintain traditional values (Ibrahim 1980). Despair, which is the common element in these groups, turns people to radical solutions for society's ills.

Neotraditionals. This orientation is held by wide segments of Egypt's lower middle class and lower classes, which, as discussed, do not participate in politics. An overwhelming majority shun the organized violence of the radical cells but have turned to rioting when their immediate interests appear to be threatened by cuts in subsidies, inadequate salaries, or rumors that Copts have been trying to convert Muslims (Ansari 1984). Sometimes these riots have taken religious overtones, but they are not a sustained campaign for the imposition of *Sharia* or Islamic government. Neotraditionalist Islam, in Egypt, is best represented by the television preacher, Mohammed Shah-Rawi, and the National Democratic party's (the government party) newspaper, *Al-Liwa* (The Banner). A review of letters to the editor found that a majority dealt with traditions and superstitions, such as protocol for visiting the dead and the nature of the *jinn* (spirits) (Sivan 1987).

The review also found that the newspaper advocated a rigid interpretation of Islam regarding matters such as women's rights, the treatment of minorities and foreign cultural influences. As would be expected, the paper supported the government's call for a gradual switch to *Sharia* and other government policies, such as the continuation of privatizing the economy (Sivan 1987). An analysis of Shah-Rawi's sermons found the same theme, a disdain for the West and its culture but a call for patience. According to Shah-Rawi, the West was in decline and Egypt, if it held to Islamic values, would, once again, become the center of civilization. He also turned folklore into pseudoscience by saying that it could be proven that angels built the *Kaba*. As was the case with *Al-Liwa*, he preached a conservative Islam and called for the implementation of Islamic punishment (Sivan 1987).

Mubarak's choice of action should now be clear. There was a clear union of interests, primarily economic, between the regime and the Modernist groups. At the same time, the Modernist's ideology could co-exist with the secular state, while a radical takeover would threaten their growing wealth. Thus, they were willing to participate in elections and strengthen Mubarak's Islamic legitimacy. The Radicals were a clear threat to the regime and had to be weakened and marginalized. In this endeavor, the regime has been uncompromising. Finally, the largest group, the Neotraditionals, were not politically active. It must also be pointed out that Neotraditionals generally hold that the change to Islamic government will be the work of God, not man. They also would accept secular government over an Islamic government that altered *Sharia*, and they prefer the strict implementation of Islamic law in some areas rather than the rapid leap proposed by the Radicals. Finally, Mubarak appeased both the Modernists and Neotraditionalists by allowing them to freely criticize the United States, Israel, and Western culture.

Supporting Cleavages

The accommodation between the regime and Islamic opposition in Egypt during the mid-1980s was also facilitated by a lack of supporting cleavages. First, Egypt's Muslim population is almost entirely Sunni. Thus, the historical animosity between Sunni and Shia and their different interpretations of Islam did not come into play. This rift, as is the case in Iraq, Saudi Arabia, Bahrain, and Syria, can be a strong barrier between regime and opposition. Second, the Islamic group with the most political and economic power, the Modernists, are primarily in the middle and upper classes and share the regime's desire for an open economy. At the same time, a majority of the lower classes adhere to an Islam that calls for political passiveness.

Geography is also a factor that forced Mubarak's hand in reaching out to the Muslim Brotherhood. Given their strength in Cairo and in other major cities, he had no choice. Ethnicity works both for and against a moderate political Islam and accommodation. On one hand, Egypt is entirely Arab. However, the presence of the Copts and their disproportionate political and economic power has served to fuel the power of the radical groups and the xenophobia of the Neotraditionals. However, these conditions helped facilitate Sadat's opening of Egypt's political space to include an active Islamic component and Mubarak's opening of the political system to Islamic groups. As a result, Egypt's political system became more competitive, democratic, and open. I will take up the durability of these gains in the closing section of this chapter.

JORDAN

A Traditional Monarchy

The recent history of religion and politics in Jordan differs from that of Egypt. The most important divergence was that Jordan did not experience a period of Arab socialism and rapid polity secularization. Instead, Jordan has always maintained a traditional monarchy with a ruling family that claims that its roots can be traced back to one of the prophet Mohammed's daughters, Fatimah, and has emphasized its past role as guardian of the Islamic holy places in Jerusalem (Robbins 1991). Islam has always been Jordan's official state religion and the prime minister must be a Muslim. In fact, the traditional nature of the Jordanian regime kept it at constant odds with Egypt and its allies up to the Six Day War. Thus, Jordan's defeat in this war did not induce a rethinking of religion's role in society and politics because the regime had never tried to relegate Islam to a secondary role and had used Islam to help provide a sense of national identity in a country that had none. Unlike Egypt, it was difficult for political movements to organize on the claim that the regime had turned away from Islam. In addition, another cleavage, ethnicity, was soon to push the Hashemite monarchy to the brink.

The Bedouin Hashemites are a minority (6–10 percent) in their own country as a majority (60 percent) of Jordan's population is Palestinian.[9] The first wave of refugees came in 1948, after Israel was established in western Palestine and many Arabs fled or were forced to depart. This group was primarily well educated and primarily middle class, so it was easily absorbed and integrated. The second wave, which came from the West Bank after Israel captured that area during the Six Day War, was much larger and poorer. This group was put in refugee camps, where it has since lagged in economic and social development (Day 1986). Subsequently, the Palestinian nationalist movement established itself in these camps and began to use Jordan as a base for raids into Israel, which brought swift retaliation. These raids and the Palestinians' brazen challenges to the regime led to a civil war in September 1970, which resulted in the PLO's leadership fleeing to Lebanon.

The defeat of the Palestinians in "Black September" finally entrenched Hussein's regime in power; however, the Palestinian issue remained at the forefront of Jordanian politics throughout the decade of the 1970s. Consequently, ethnicity, integration, and the creation of national identity pushed religion to the background (Sayigh 1991). Also, King Hussein still faced a strong threat from communist and other secular-radical groups as the Palestinians' nationalist movement did not take on Islamic overtones until the 1980s. Among the non-Palestinian population, Islam was a regime supporting function, because it was intertwined with the traditional bonds of clan and tribe (Sayigh 1991). Ultimately, almost all of these groups were tied to the monarchy and their members filled the top positions in the government and the military. Hussein, at the same time, provided ample financial support for the clergy and the state religious institutions to ensure their loyalty. He has also publicized his personal piety and was often seen on television at prayer or performing other rituals (Sayigh 1991).

The king, like Mubarak, also made efforts to co-opt the Muslim Brotherhood. This was particularly important during the 1960s and 1970s, when he needed a unifying force to counter the pro-Nasser Pan-Arabists and the Palestinian nationalists. The Brotherhood was also of use in attempts to destabilize the Syrian Ba'athist regime, which had supported the Palestinians during Black September. Hussein permitted the training of activists, who were sent to Syria to stimulate Islamic-based opposition to the Assad regime (Satloff 1986). The government's support of the Brotherhood has included funding, facilities, and permission to propagate the message of Islam on behalf of the regime. At the same time, the Brotherhood has influenced the operation of the country's mosques, the Ministry of Islamic Affairs, and religious education (Morris 1993).

The Brotherhood, in turn, has supported the government and has called for a gradualist approach to the implementation of Islamic law. Thus, with the exception of an attempt to assassinate Hussein in 1969 by a member of *Tahrir*, a more extreme Islamic group, political Islam, up to the late 1970s, was largely government controlled or manipulated. However, it has been a relationship of mutual dependence, because Islam is an important source of the regime's legitimacy and authority. Consequently, the support of this independent Islamic voice is essential. Hussein's desire to co-opt the Brotherhood is best illustrated by the fact that it was the only legal political party in Jordan from 1955 up to the most recent elections (Nevo and Papp 1994).[10] Thus, in a sense, Hussein made the same deal as Sadat. However, as will be seen, he made the choice to go further as political Islam in Jordan began to develop independently of the regime.

The Growth of Political Islam as an Opposition Force

The growth of an Islamic political opposition in Jordan was, to some extent, stimulated by the Iranian revolution. First, many Jordanians were angry that the king had supported the Shah up to the Iranian revolution. Second, the decision to favor secular-oriented Iraq in the Gulf War between Iran and Iraq was also troublesome. Third, Khomeini's polemics against Israel and his linking of the Iranian revolution with the liberation of Jerusalem appealed to the Palestinian population. Finally, Jordan was affected by three events in neighboring countries such as the murder of Sadat, the violent eradication of Syria's Islamic opposition by Haffez al-Assad, and the rise of radical Islamic groups in Lebanon such as *Hizballah* (Satloff

1986). All three events served as examples of Islam serving as a rallying point for opposition to unfair government. Given that fact that the Jordanian parliament had been closed since 1971 and that an advisory council was dismissed every time it disagreed with the monarchy, the king felt the need to appeal to Islamic sentiments.

Hussein, like Sadat, took actions to give the impression that the monarchy was not only in tune with the growing appeal of political Islam but also its leader. As a result, the amount of religious programming on state-run television and radio increased. The government also encouraged payment of *Zakat* (charity) and enforced bans on smoking and alcohol during Ramadan (Day 1986). Another response was the creation of the Jordanian Islamic Bank for Finance and Investment, which does not charge interest. The bank also offers clients the opportunity to participate in building low- and middle-income housing and to invest in small businesses (Wilson 1991). However, *imams* (preachers) and Islamists who were too outspoken in their criticism of the regime (such as those who vocally supported Iran in the Iran-Iraq War and continued to agitate against the Assad regime while the king was attempting reconciliation) were imprisoned (Day 1986).

The Brotherhood, despite the king's efforts, became more independent during the early 1980s and began to challenge the regime's commitment to Islam. The group's leader Mohammed al-Khifa commented: "This is an Islamic government but it is not wholly Islamic. We would like to see the teachings of the *Quran* followed much more closely. This government can stop us from publishing, but they cannot stop our tongues. If they try to close our offices we would go to the mosques. They cannot shut those" (*Sunday Times*, December 8, 1980). During this period, the strength of Islamic student groups surpassed that of Palestinian and nationalist organizations as they gained control of student government at Jordan's two largest universities, Yarmuk and Jordan University in Amman. As in Egypt, they began to expand their influence into the neighborhoods surrounding the campuses. Many of the people joining these groups were Palestinians, who were frustrated by the PLO's defeat in Lebanon in 1982 and its failure to make any real progress toward achieving a state (Satloff 1986).

The increasing appeal and independence of Islamic political groups was only one of several forces that were squeezing the monarchy. First, the economic growth and subsequent social development that had taken place in the 1970s and early 1980s began to slow. Also, economic development and modernization led to the decline of tribal and clan identity, which had tied the rural population to the regime (Wilson 1991). Second, three foreign policy decisions—the reestablishment of relations with Egypt, the reconciliation with Syria, and the tacit acceptance of the Reagan Plan—were all unpopular (Garfinkle 1993). Third, the government was frequently criticized for its poor human rights record, its repression of dissent, and its failure to democratize. The last consideration also served to strengthen the

Muslim Brotherhood, because it was the only legal political organization in the kingdom. Consequently, it gained many new members, who did not necessarily agree with its ultimate objective (Islamic government), but were looking for a venue to express their opposition to the monarchy (Robbins 1991).

The Decision to Democratize

The regime continued to try to manipulate Islamic sentiments by playing up its role as the defender of Jerusalem by claiming the Iranians had to be defeated because they were "idolaters and fanatics," and by the frequent use of Islamic rhetoric (Satloff 1986). However, as economic conditions continued to worsen, it became apparent that the king's balancing act could no longer be achieved through words and patronage. Consequently, in 1984, he decided to reconvene the parliament. The first step was to hold runoff elections to replace the eight deputies who had died since the parliament was closed in 1971. Islamic candidates won three of the eight seats and also swept municipal elections in the city of Irbid. As Jordan's economic situation continued to decline and the demand for government reform increased during the late 1980s, the regime seemed vulnerable. The breaking point was three days of riots in South Jordan, an area that had few Palestinians and that historically had supported the monarchy. This upheaval occurred in April 1989 in response to an IMF prescribed austerity program. Hussein then called for national parliamentary elections, which took place in November. The Islamic block of candidates took thirty-four of eighty seats and became the largest faction in the parliament. As is par for the course, many were warning that Jordan was about to be overrun by Islamic fundamentalism.[11]

King Hussein's decision to let the Islamists participate in legitimate politics paid off as the group served as a loyal opposition. First, the Islamist MPs (members of parliament) went to great lengths to emphasize their support for the regime during the campaign as well as after they were elected. Second, they did not actively protest when they were not given any portfolios, despite being the largest block in the parliament. Third, in 1990, they signed an annex to the constitution accepting the legitimacy of the monarchy (Robbins 1991). In return, the Islamists and other opposition groups were permitted to criticize the country's foreign policy, human rights record, and its responsiveness to the needs of the Palestinians in the refugee camps. The Islamists were also free to call for the implementation of *Sharia* and were almost successful in passing a law that would have segregated schools and government offices by sex (Nevo and Papp 1994). Finally, the king permitted the organization of political parties. The most significant sign that the Brotherhood and other Islamists were going to play by the rules was their acceptance of electoral defeat in the 1993 elections.

I will further detail the results of the entry of the Islamists into legitimate politics at the end of this chapter, where the experiences of Egypt and Jordan will be compared. Next, I will analyze the factors that facilitated this strategy.

Contextual Factors: Vulnerability to Events in Neighboring Countries

Jordan's economic woes, although significant, are not nearly as crippling as Egypt's problems because of Jordan's small population (roughly 4 million). Although Jordan is not blessed with natural resources and does not have a well-developed industrial base, it does have one of the best educated populations in the Arab world. Consequently, many Jordanian university graduates found employment in the Persian Gulf states during the oil boom.[12] The remittances sent home by these workers and the aid given by the Gulf states stimulated the economic growth of the 1970s and early 1980s. Subsequently, the government spent heavily on constructing housing, expanding education, and developing social welfare programs (Gubser 1983). Thus, the regime, although authoritarian and plagued with corruption, alleviated discontent by taking care of its population. Consequently, the despair syndrome that was detailed in the discussion of Egypt was not as devastating in Jordan.

It was Jordan's vulnerability to events in neighboring countries that caused a downturn in the economy and social unrest. The decline of the world oil market during the mid-1980s led to the repatriation of many Jordanians and a decline in aid from the Gulf states. Then, the Palestinian uprising in the West Bank and the king's decision to sever legal, administrative, and financial links with the occupied areas instigated criticism and reminded the Palestinian population of its dual loyalties. At the same time, the end of the Iran-Iraq War hurt Jordan's economy, as much of the supplies being sent to Iraq had passed through the port of Aqaba. Finally, the Iraqi invasion of Kuwait and the subsequent Gulf War of 1991 provided the most crippling blow. The king's decision to take a conciliatory posture toward Saddam Hussein and not to join the coalition against Iraq led to the termination of aid from the Saudis and other benefactors. Those countries also expelled most of their Jordanian and Palestinian workers, which caused Jordan's population to increase by 300,000 in six months (Morris 1993). However, the Gulf War followed Jordan's 1989 parliamentary elections and the conciliatory stance toward the Iraqis further bolstered the king's popularity.

Regime Strength

The Hussein regime, despite its historical vulnerability to its neighbors, remained stronger than its Egyptian counterpart. Several factors, in addition to the country's small, well-educated population and developed infrastructure contributed to the stability of the monarchy.

Longevity. The Hashemites have ruled Jordan since its birth, and King Hussein has reigned since 1952. This has led to a psychological mind-set that Jordan should be under the guidance of King Hussein. As several Jordanians told me during a recent visit, the nation and the ruler are one and the same. His long reign is also interpreted as a sign of God's favor (*baraka*). Of greatest important, it has allowed the king to co-opt important segments of the population through patronage and the development of long-standing personal relationships with tribal leaderships (Jureidini 1984).

Affection. Most Jordanians, especially the non-Palestinians, feel a genuine affection for the king. This phenomenon is emphasized in most of the literature on Jordan. In contrast, few Egyptians feel the same emotional attachment to Hosni Mubarak. Of course, few Jordanians would take the risk of publicly stating their opposition to the king, but most of the favorable remarks made to me about the king appear to be genuine.

A Solid Base of Support. King Hussein's grip on power is strengthened by a solid base of support among the Bedouin and Hashemite populations. The "minority" status of the native Jordanians and members of the king's clan in their own country has closely tied these groups to the regime. Of course, they all, especially up to 1970, have feared a Palestinian takeover. Consequently, the king staffed the military, internal security forces, and key positions in the state apparatus with members of these loyal tribes and clans. As mentioned, almost forty-six years of patronage have solidified this support. It is also important to emphasize that the military is highly loyal to the monarchy (Sayigh 1991). However, urbanization and modernization have begun to weaken these primordial bonds.

Skillful Leadership. A final factor that has allowed King Hussein to remain a ruling monarch at the turn of the twenty-first century is his political adroitness. Some examples of his acumen are:

- A conciliatory stance toward Iraq in the 1990–1991 Gulf crisis, which helped maintain domestic stability. Subsequently, he quickly returned to America's favor by supporting the peace process and, ultimately, signing a peace agreement with Israel.

- Investing heavily in Jordan's infrastructure, education system, and social welfare programs during the boom years of the 1970s and early 1980s.

- Making efforts to integrate the Palestinian population into the nation by encouraging them to take a prominent role in business, industry, and the economy but keeping them out of sensitive government positions.

- Opening legitimate channels for political participation to those with grievances through parliamentary elections. This move also created another target (parliament) for citizens to blame for Jordan's declining economy.

> Finally, the opportunity to participate in running the government led the
> Islamists to moderate their ideology.

One needs only to look at neighboring countries such as Iran, Iraq, and
Egypt to see what has happened to kings who lack skill in governing.

The Islamic Opposition

Modernists. The Modernists, as in Egypt, are best represented by the
Muslim Brotherhood and its political party, the Islamic Action Front
(IAF).[13] The Brotherhood, as discussed, has long accepted the legitimacy of
the monarchy. The IAF's platform calls for the implementation of *Sharia*
but under the monarchy, it was also pointed out, the Brotherhood has had
access to government institutions and influenced their operations. Thus,
their approach, like that of the Egyptian Brotherhood, can be labeled "legalist." "A middle approach between the extremes that embrace most Arab
states today is characterized by less overt hostility and an orientation towards learning from the West and adopting the tools of the West so the
Islamic world might triumph. They are not pro-western but, rather accul-
turated to the West as cooperation is sometimes necessary for the success
of Islam" (Jureidini 1984, 25). Consequently, moderate Islamists have used
parliament, chambers of commerce, and professional associations to push
for Islamic law. When in control of the parliament from 1989–1993, they,
indeed, attempted to ban alcohol, segregate the schools by sex, and pass
laws requiring Islamic dress for females (Robbins 1991).[14]

The Modernist trend in Jordan also has taken a hard line regarding foreign policy in its attempts to destabilize Syria, its support for Iraq in the
Gulf War, and its opposition to any compromise with the Israelis. However, the king has imprisoned leaders and preachers who actively interfere
(not oppose) with government foreign policy (Nevo and Papp 1994). The
leadership of the Brotherhood is predominately middle and upper class and
non-Palestinian. Like the Egyptian moderates they have an interest in stability. However, a growing percentage of the rank and file are Palestinians
looking for a channel to vent their frustrations with the regime and see
Islam as the best hope for regaining Palestine (Garfinkle 1993). However,
the Brotherhood and the IAF, up to 1997, continued to be a loyal, if vocal,
opposition to the king. Although the king most likely did not anticipate
the Islamist candidates' strong showing in 1989, they are a group whose
participation in government strengthened the monarchy rather than threatened it.

Radicals. The radical tendency is not nearly as significant a force in Jordan as it is in Egypt. A small radical group, *Tahrir*, existed from 1967
through the early 1980s. However, outside of the attempt on the king's life
by one of its members in 1969, it caused little disruption (Day 1986). In

recent years, two new radical groups have appeared. The first is centered in the Palestinian refugee camps and combines militant Islam with Palestinian nationalism. However, the groups's primary objective is the destruction of Israel rather than the Hashemite regime. The other is similar to the Egyptian *Takfir wa al-Hijra* in that it seeks to isolate itself from corrupt, secular society until the time arrives for the creation of the Islamic state (Nevo and Papp 1994). This group also does not pose a threat to domestic peace. As mentioned earlier, the conditions of despair that have fueled the popularity of radical groups in Egypt are not nearly as severe in Jordan. However, many of the 300,000 Palestinians who entered the country during the Gulf War remain unemployed. Also, the strength of militant Islam in the West Bank could influence the politics of the Palestinian community in Jordan.

Neotraditional. The Bedouin and other rural tribes are the primary Neotraditional groups in Jordan. As discussed, these groups are the primary support base for the monarchy. These societies are hierarchically organized with the tip of the triangle being the king. Clearly, tribe and clan are the primary considerations that influence voting, not which party will make the country more Islamic (Robbins 1991). As is the case in Egypt, this population is more concerned with ritual and practice than politics.

Supporting Cleavage

It should now be quite clear that ethnic cleavage is a crucial influence on Jordanian politics, but the Palestinian-Jordanian divide has not translated into a secular-religious division. If anything, the Palestinian issue has served as a moderating influence.

- The Palestinian threat put Islam, as a political factor, in the background until the late 1970s.

- Jordan's ethnic fractionalization caused the king to use Islam to unify the country and to create a Jordanian identity.

- Hussein's search for allies led him to the Muslim Brotherhood, which resulted in its legal status and its subsequent co-optation and moderation. As mentioned earlier, the Brotherhood and the Islamic Action Front are composed of both native Jordanians and Palestinians.

The potential, however, for a radical Islamic movement to develop within the Palestinian community, as has been the case in the West Bank, exists and is dependent, once again, on the behavior of a neighboring country, Israel.

No other cleavages separate the regime from its Islamic-based opposition. Almost all of Jordan's Muslim population is Sunni. The country does have a small Christian minority (6 percent), but the Christian-Muslim cleavage has not been politicized as is the case in Egypt. Even the decision to reserve 12 percent of the seats in the parliament only produced a mild letter of protest from the IAF (Robbins 1991). Class and geography, as discussed, also do not affect the relationship between the regime and the Islamic opposition. In all, despite the external forces and economic woes that squeezed the monarchy in the late 1980s, it was strong enough to relieve some of these pressures by taking real steps toward democracy. Because of his own Islamic credentials and his history of cooperation with the Brotherhood, the king was able to bring the Islamists into the forefront of legitimate politics in Jordan. At the end of the chapter, I will discuss what has taken place in Egypt and Jordan since the process of pluralization began.

THE FUTURE OF ISLAM AND DEMOCRACY IN EGYPT AND JORDAN

Divergent Paths?

The move made toward a more democratic political system in Egypt slowed during the 1990s. First, the results of the 1987 parliamentary election were voided by the Supreme Court because of improper restrictions on opposition and independent candidates. The Muslim Brotherhood boycotted the subsequent elections to replenish the assembly because they could not organize as an independent political party and because of alleged harassment by government officials. Clearly, Mubarak had set a limit on how much influence the Islamists could wield. This was partly due to the increased terrorist activity of the radical groups, particularly the radical *Ga'amat*, which Mubarak claimed were receiving support from the Brotherhood (*Al-Ahram*, December 2, 1992). These activities included a massacre in a Coptic village, an assassination of the speaker of the assembly, and attacks on tourists that took the lives of sixteen Greeks in 1996 and eighteen Germans in 1997. The regime has responded with summary arrests, execution, raids, martial law, and human rights violations. In short, the definite priority is to "win the war" against *Jihad* and other radical groups. At the same time, the Islamification of society continues as more women wear Islamic garb, "improper" entertainment is decreasing, and mosque attendance remains high.

The transformation that took place in Jordan has been more enduring. Following the 1989 elections, political parties were legalized, the government loosened its reign on the press, and human rights practices improved. Also, in 1990, three Islamists were named to the cabinet. Then, in the 1993 elections, the Islamic Action Front only won sixteen seats but accepted the results as legitimate and continued to participate in the parliament. One of the reasons for their failure was the redrawing of districts to overrepresent rural areas, where the monarchy is most popular, and Christians, who are weary of the increased influence of the Islamists (Robbins 1991). Another cause was the poor performance and corruption of the ministries given to the Islamists. Many Jordanians also blamed the Brotherhood for the regime's support of Iraq in the 1991 Gulf War and Jordan's subsequent fall from favor with the West and the Gulf states (Garfinkle 1993). It may be that the appeal of political Islam is weakened when Islamists are permitted to run the government. The process of pluralization received a setback in the 1997 elections when the Islamists and four other parties boycotted because of alleged unfair election practices.

The Importance of Regime Strength and Contextual Factors

It should now be clear that, in Egypt and Jordan, weakened, authoritarian regimes were in search of allies to bring into the political system to buttress their grip on power. In both countries, the search led to the Muslim Brotherhood, because Islam is the most comprehensible and popular way for Muslims to express their discontent regarding politics and government. Again, the intertwining of the sacred and the temporal in Islamic doctrine, texts, and tradition is more extensive than in Christianity. The enduring strength of Islam as a political force was made evident by its resurgence in Egypt following the secular-socialist period in Egypt and its constant role in Jordanian politics. However, the degree to which Hosni Mubarak and King Hussein were willing to open their political systems to Islamists was related to the differing extents of their weaknesses, which were strongly influenced by factors over which they had little control.

Egypt, under Mubarak, was a more fragmented polity than Jordan under Hussein, as Mubarak took over a country where the authority of government was weakening. As discussed, the military, the state security apparatus, the middle and upper classes, and the bureaucracy were becoming more autonomous. He was also left to deal with the increasing strength of political Islam, which had been unleashed by his predecessor. Also, because of Sadat, the Egyptian population was skeptical and distrustful of government. At the same time, rapid population growth in an already overpopulated nation made it harder for the country to provide for its citizens. Declines in important sources of revenue hurt a weak economy, which has always been on the brink. At the same time, the universities continued to produce far more graduates than the economy could absorb, which forced the state to underemploy them in the bureaucracy. This condition of malaise and despair fostered the growth of the radical groups. In short, Mubarak's very tenuous grip on power caused him to be reluctant to release too much authority out of fear that his regime would fall, which, in turn, has fueled the flames of radicalism and pushed moderates toward the extremist groups.

King Hussein of Jordan, although constantly at the mercy of events in neighboring countries and mindful of the potential threat from the Palestinian majority, had more control over his government and country. This is due to a long reign, personal popularity, a solid base of support in the rural areas and the military, and skillful political leadership. Jordan also has a small, educated population and well-developed educational and social welfare systems. In short, Jordan is far more manageable than Egypt. Finally, moderate Islamic political groups in Jordan have a long history of cooperation with the regime. In Egypt, the relationship was first hostile and then quickly turned suspicious following a brief honeymoon at the beginning of the Sadat era. Given these advantages, Hussein's rule is more secure and, subsequently, he, along with the Islamists, took a bigger step toward democracy. However, attempts to influence the outcome of elections demonstrate the limits that Hussein placed on pluralization.

This chapter on Egypt and Jordan has demonstrated that political Islam is not inherently antithetical to democracy. Rather, the increasing influence of Islamic political groups has coincided with democratization. It was also shown that the relationship between Islam and democracy is highly dependent on other factors relating to regime strength, demographics, economic development, social development, and a country's neighbors. In the next chapter, I will place this assertion under further exploration in my discussion of Syria and Tunisia, two countries where the rise of political Islam was accompanied by continued authoritarian rule. However, both governments are secular oriented and Islamic political groups have been shut out of legitimate politics. Thus, it might be that countries with a predominantly Muslim population cannot be democratic if Islam is not allowed to influence the political system.

NOTES

1. Al-Azhar is Egypt's Islamic university, which plays a key role in determining government policy relating to religion.

2. Personal status reform (secularization) was also later instituted.

3. These failures include continued poverty, corruption, murder and torture of opposition, and the continued existence of a privileged small circle of power-holders.

4. Sadat had been Nasser's vice-president, but he was largely an unknown when he ascended to the presidency.

5. Student politics in Egypt, as in most of the Middle East, focus on national political concerns and issues as much as those relating to the university.

6. The group was hoping that the assassination and insurrection would lead to the overthrow of the Egyptian government. Also, the members of the team that carried out the assassination were all from the military. For an account of the assassination and its plotters, see Youseff (1986).

7. In fact, a study of Mubarak's Egypt in the late 1980s is titled, *Mubarak's Egypt: Fragmentation of the Political Order* (Springborg 1988). Since then, a num-

ber of books and articles have been produced, which have focused on this theme. Springborg's is particularly well done.

8. I have provided a short description of each of Shepard's types of Islamic political ideology in appendix III. For a more comprehensive discussion, see Shepard (1986).

9. King Hussein's grandfather, Abdullah, was given the eastern half of Britain's Palestine mandate after he was forced out of the Arabian Peninsula by the Saudis. This gift was a reward for supporting the Allies during World War II.

10. It is important to point out that there were no real elections for the Brotherhood to take part in from 1971–1987 and that the Brotherhood boycotted the most recent election in November 1997.

11. *New York Times* coverage of the elections provides a good example of this concern.

12. It is estimated that as many as 400,000 Jordanians (10 percent of the country's population) lived abroad during this period.

13. The IAF was created by the Muslim Brotherhood for the 1993 elections after political parties were legalized in 1991.

14. An interesting development has been that women's groups in Jordan have worked with the Brotherhood to develop a clear set of guidelines regarding women's rights.

4

Syria and Tunisia

SECULAR AUTHORITARIANISM

The governments of Syria and Tunisia, like those of Egypt and Jordan, have faced significant challenges from Islamic opposition groups. However, the current regimes in both of these countries chose a different strategy for meeting these challenges—repression. Islamic political groups in both Syria and Tunisia have not been allowed to participate in legitimate politics, and Islamic political culture has not been as important an influence on politics as it has in Egypt and Jordan. At the same time, both countries maintain, to varying extents, authoritarian, one-party political systems. The cases of Syria and Tunisia also appear to support the assertion that the increasing strength of political Islam and Islamic political culture on political systems does not impede democratization as both countries are secular-based polities, but they are not democratic. Perhaps a cause of the lack of democracy in these countries is that authoritarianism is necessary to shut Islam out of the system, and, subsequently, repression is keeping the political systems of these countries out of balance with their political cultures.

This chapter is organized along the same format as chapter 3. For both nations, I will provide brief histories of the rise of political Islam, analyze the variables relating to regime strength and contextual factors, and compare and contrast the two cases to better understand Islam's role in politics in Syria and Tunisia. Once again, I will demonstrate that Islam is only one of many forces that shapes political systems in predominately Muslim countries. For Syria, my analysis will center on the period between 1975 and

1982, as that is when the Muslim Brotherhood rose to threaten the Assad regime and then was destroyed in the Hama massacre. For Tunisia, I will focus on the period from 1985 to 1990 as that is when it became apparent that Bourghiba's years were numbered and, concurrently, the strength of the Islamic Tendency movement (MTI) increased. From 1987 to 1990, following Ben Ali's ascendancy to the presidency, the regime decided how to meet MTI's challenge. Finally, the consequences of both regimes' decisions will be considered at the end of the chapter.

SYRIA

The Ascendancy of Ba'ath Secular Arab Socialism

The marginalization of political Islam and the Muslim Brotherhood in Syria took a course similar to that in Egypt. During Syria's first sixteen years of existence (1946–1963), the Muslim Brotherhood operated legally and took part in the country's periodic elections.[1] However, in 1963, the Ba'ath (Arab Socialist Renaissance) party took power through a military coup. When a new secular-oriented constitution was unveiled in 1965, which did not make Islam the religion of state, the Brotherhood protested and instigated disturbances. The organization, subsequently, was outlawed, and its leaders were jailed or executed, but it continued to be a serious threat to the government through 1982 (Olson 1982). However, in contrast to Egypt and Jordan, Islam has remained at the margin of government and politics, and the Islamic opposition has been repressed rather than invited into the political system.

Another crucial contrast between Syria and Egypt and Jordan is that the Assad regime successfully consolidated power and then tightened its hold on the organs of government and society. A look at the choices made by Haffez al-Assad and the factors that helped shape them will show that the marginalization of political Islam was necessary for the survival of his reign. Assad came to power in 1970 after he led a coup by the military wing of the Ba'ath party over the Marxist-oriented progressive faction. It is important to note that Assad took over a country with a legacy of instability, a country that was still reeling from its devastating loss of the Golan Heights in the 1967 war with Israel. However, unlike Sadat (who took power in the same year), Assad was not as desperate in his need for allies. Assad already was a faction leader within his party and was not replacing a beloved legend. At the same time, the Syrians' expectations had not been raised and dashed like the Egyptians. When Assad took power, his regime, seemingly, was just another in a long line of regimes, as the country had already experienced twelve coups d'état and six constitutions in its twenty-four year history (Olson 1982).

The Importance of the Military and Sect in Assad's Rise

Haffez al-Assad, like King Hussein, also assumed power with an important power base, the military. Since the period of French colonial rule between the two world wars, the army had been the only means of advancement for Assad's *Alawi* sect. The Alawis were primarily a poor and rural group that had been dominated by urban Sunni landlords in the colonial period and the first fifteen years of independence (Batatu 1981). During this period, middle- and upper-class Syrians were able to buy their way out of military service if they could find a replacement. Consequently, a large number of Alawi were paid to enter the military (Batatu 1981). Many Alawi, as they rose through the ranks, helped their relatives and clan members obtain noncommissioned officer positions and entrance to the officer academies.

Following the Ba'ath party's rise to power and subsequent purges of Sunni officers, most of the key positions in the army were held by Alawi. After Assad took control of the government, he further closed the circle of power by placing only members of his specific tribe, the *Qamari*, in high-ranking positions. He created a praetorian guard, which was responsible for protecting the regime, that was almost entirely Alawi and placed it under the command of his brother Rifaat (Batatu 1981). Consequently, the Assad regime had always rested on the solid foundation of a large and loyal military. Assad further consolidated his hold on power by appeasing the traditionally oriented Sunni merchants of Damascus by loosening state control of the economy and by improving the infrastructure and standard of living in Damascus. The Islamic opposition was limited to outlying urban areas, such as Homs, Hama, and Aleppo (Roberts 1987). Also, Assad's popularity was bolstered by the army's improved performance in the 1973 Arab-Israeli war.

The Islamic Challenge

The use of force, in spite of Assad's consolidation of power, was still needed to control the Islamists. In 1973, the Brotherhood rioted again because Islam was not designated the religion of state in a new constitution. Several hundred demonstrators were killed, and many Brotherhood leaders were executed, exiled, or imprisoned (Hinnebusch 1990). A Brotherhood campaign of assassinations of Ba'ath leaders was followed by the dragging of the corpes of executed conspirators through the streets of Hama (Drysdale 1982). This cycle of agitation and violence by the Muslim Brotherhood, followed by regime repression, continued until 1982. In Syria, there was no union of interests as Islamic government was unacceptable to a secular-socialist regime and, as will be seen, additional cleavages furthered the divide between the regime and the Islamic opposition.

Assad, like Nasser, frequently paid lip service to Islam and used Islamic terminology by claiming that he was leading the Muslim world's campaign to rid Jerusalem of its Jewish occupiers (Seale 1986). In order to enhance his own status as a Muslim, Assad obtained *fatwah* from Iranian and Lebanese religious scholars ruling that Alawi are, indeed, Muslims.[2] He also went on the *haj* during his first year in office and even went as far as having an edition of the *Quran* printed with his picture on the cover (Olson 1982). Like Nasser, Assad found a number of Sunni *ulama*, who were willing to claim that Arab socialism was compatible with Islam and to denounce the Brotherhood as criminals who were using the name of Islam to corrupt the youth, instigate sectarian conflict, and murder innocent civilians (Drysdale 1982). However, according to Ba'ath ideology, the Islamic culture, spirit, and call for unity—but not faith—are pillars of Arab society (Roberts 1987). In short, Islam could serve as a guide for society but not politics, government, or economics, which, of course, was unacceptable to the Muslim Brotherhood.

The battle between the Assad regime and the Islamic political groups continued through the 1970s. Outside of the army, the Ba'ath party, and the Alawi (7–10 percent of Syria's population), Assad remained unpopular as he lacked the charismatic personality of Nasser and the majestic aura of King Hussein. As mentioned, he, because of his rural Alawi background, was always viewed suspiciously by Sunnis and residents of urban areas (Humphreys 1979). The regime came under further attack from the Islamists in 1975–1976, when it intervened on the side of the Christian Phalange in the Lebanese Civil War. Syria's refusal to allow Palestinian forces to relieve the Maronite siege of Tel-al Zatar, which resulted in the death of between 2,000 and 3,000 Palestinians, opened his regime to charges of being a tool of Israeli, Maronite, American, and Saudi interests (Dekmejian 1985).

This was a considerable mistake given the crucial issues in Syrian politics. "Among the most important [issues] in Syrian political culture are internal stability, social justice, government consistent with Islam, Arab unity, Palestine, economic development, and political participation. Syria's government must deliver on all of these issues with special emphasis on its fidelity to the Palestine and Arab causes" (Hudson 1982, 84). The support of the Christians and the subsequent retreat when the Israelis advanced to Lebanon's Litani River, in 1982, was evidence, that Assad had failed in all of these areas.

- The secular nature of the regime, its refusal to implement Islamic government, and its repression of the Brotherhood was obvious.
- Social justice and political participation were nonexistent.
- Support of the Lebanese Christians over the Muslims and their Palestinian allies was evidence that the Alawi were, indeed, non-Muslims.

- Obviously, the claim to be the defender of the Palestinians was now deflated.

- The continued occupation of Lebanon damaged Assad's pan-Arab credentials.

The Muslim Brotherhood, in the late 1970s, began a *jihad* of assassination against Ba'ath party officials, institutions, and Assad, himself, that was designed to instigate and embolden opposition to the regime (Van Dam 1981). This campaign included the murder of sixty-three Alawi cadets at a military academy in Aleppo in June 1979 and almost daily bombings in Damascus. It is important to note that the literature produced by the Syrian Islamic opposition was aimed more at arousing opposition to Assad than the reformation of society, which was called for in Egypt (Syrian Islamic Action Front 1981). Their primary goal was not a *Sharia*-based polity but, rather, the toppling of the regime. Consequently, a variety of oppressed groups—Sunni, urban lower and lower middle classes, and clerics—came together under the ideological force that could lead the widest segment of the Syrian population to action—Islam. The program of the Islamic Revolutionary Front stated:

> This is the beginning of a long journey in the way of establishing the desired Islamic society and demolishing the despicable rule of governance. . . . The Ba'ath Party is a total disaster. It squashed freedom, abolished political parties, nationalized the press, threw people in prison, and hanged those who voiced their disapproval. We hope that followers of the Alawi sect—to which the people's affliction, Haffez Assad and his brother, belong—will positively participate in preventing the tragedy from reaching its end (Syrian Islamic Action Front 1981, 83–84).

They further demanded that Assad honor the International Human Rights Charter, end the state of emergency, and hold free elections (Syrian Islamic Action Front 1981).

Assad's Response: The Destruction of the Brotherhood

The near civil war intensified as the Brotherhood attempted to assassinate President Assad in June 1980. The regime responded by killing between 600 and 1,000 Brotherhood prisoners and conducting weekly roundups in the Brotherhood strongholds in Hama, Aleppo, and Homs. Finally, in February 1982, Assad decided to end the Brotherhood opposition by literally attacking the city of Hama with his army. After a three-week battle—in which the city was destroyed and between 10,000, and 30,000 were killed—the Islamic threat to the Assad regime was finally ended. Thus, the question surfaces as to what factors caused Assad to believe that accommodation with the Brotherhood and other Islamic groups was impossible and that their destruction was necessary for the maintenance of his regime? The next task is to answer this question using variables related to contextual factors, regime strength, Islamic opposition, and supporting cleavages.

Contextual Factors

Syria has faced, to a lesser extent, many of the same economic, social, and demographic challenges as Egypt. The first is a rapidly growing population as the country's population has tripled from 4.5 million in 1960 to 13 million in 1992. This has strained the government to provide for the basic needs of the population as it has been constructing housing constantly, as well as schools, and health facilities. As usual, infrastructure is worse in the rural areas, which has led to migration to the cities. As is the case in the other countries being considered, most of the new arrivals are undereducated and have difficulty finding employment. Many, in this group, are drawn to political Islam as a means of taking action on their grievances. Ironically, Syria has an abundance of land for farming but the only option for peasants available, in most of the country, is tenant farming. The subsistence level existence that accompanies tenant farming drives peasants to the cities. Also, the government's inability to provide irrigation facilities causes farmers to be dependent on unreliable rainfall (Perthes 1995).

Syria's economic woes were exacerbated by several factors. First, its numerous regimes had never produced a clear economic strategy. Throughout the country's history, there has been a vacillation between nationalization and privatization, modest land reforms, which have often been rescinded, and an ambivalent posture toward foreign investment. Second, the state-controlled sectors are plagued by corruption and are largely inefficient. Third, the country earmarks a large amount of its GNP (25 percent) for defense, which was particularly problematic during the late 1970s and early 1980s for three reasons:

1. The intervention in Lebanon and the subsequent cost of occupation of that country was a tremendous economic burden. The Lebanese civil war also brought about the return of 500,000 Syrians who had worked as unskilled laborers in Lebanon, who all needed housing and employment.

2. The damage from the 1973 war was estimated at $2 billion, with most of the country's ports, key industries, refineries, and power plants being incapacitated by Israeli bombing. Syria spent most of the 1970s recouping from these losses.

3. After Egypt signed a peace treaty with Israel in 1978 and Jordan effectively removed itself from the Arab-Israeli conflict, Syria was left alone to face

Israel, which served to further increase Syria's defense burden (Perthes 1995).

However, Syria's need for a large army has helped to alleviate unemployment and provided an important group of supporters for the president.

Assad's response to Syria's economic malaise was to liberalize decisively and open the economy in order to encourage foreign investment. The result of this move was the same as in Egypt, a widening gap between the rich and the poor. First, the high defense spending and privatization of the economy led to inflation. Second, as was the case in Egypt, a small group of Syrians—capitalists, importers, and owners—benefited the most from the open economy. It is important to note that many of these beneficiaries were supporters of the regime or employees in the public sector who used connections to their advantage in the private sector. The new, affluent neighborhoods sprouting up in Damascus furthered the impression that a small elite was making it at the expense of the rest of society (Perthes 1995). Of course, this all flew in the face of the regime's socialist and egalitarian slogans, which helped to lead many of the disenfranchised to a competing ideology that is also centered around social justice—Islam. Again, the Brotherhood and other Islamic groups attracted many of the first generation migrants to the cities as well as others left behind by the privatization of the economy.

Regime Strength

A principal cause of Assad's decision to violently resist the challenge from the Muslim Brotherhood and the Syrian Islamic Action Front was his belief that his regime was strong enough to resist. As mentioned, Assad's regime was built on the solid foundations of tribal loyalty and a military stacked with supporters. By 1982, Assad had installed supporters in all of the top military positions, and members of his Alawi sect also dominated the officer corps and the elite units. In addition, the praetorian guard and two divisions guarding the capital from internal threats were from his specific tribe. Of course, a Sunni or Islamic Action Front takeover would mean an end to their lofty and lucrative status. The same is true of the Mukhabarat (the intelligence agency) and the internal security apparatus, both of which were predominately staffed with Alawi and other loyal supporters.

The regime's sectarian roots are equally important. As discussed, the Alawi are a small minority (7–10 percent) in Syria. They are widely distrusted by the middle and upper classes because of their rural impoverished roots. Their unorthodox practice of Islam, which blends Shia, Ismaili, and Christian traditions, is viewed by many Sunni as being heretical (Batatu 1981). This spiritual uniqueness, their rural backgrounds, and their impoverished status, historically, have alienated them from the rest of Syria.

Also, the mountainous terrain in which they reside has enabled them to resist being conquered and has preserved their distinctive characteristics (Devlin 1983). This isolation and alienation has resulted in a tightly knit community that has benefited greatly from Assad being in power. Naturally, they have an incentive to defend it against an Islamist, Sunni revolution, which called for representative government. In short, the intertwining of the Alawi, the Ba'ath Party, the military, and the internal security has provided a solid foundation for the regime.

A third source of stability, as in Jordan, is the longevity of the Assad regime. However, this factor was not as significant in Syria, psychologically, because it was not until after Assad had squashed the Islamic-based opposition that firm entrenchment of the Assad regime became the common mind-set. However, Perthes (1995, 4) comments that during the first ten years of the Assad regime, "institutions were developed, the bureaucracy expanded, and corporatist structures bringing large parts of society under the umbrella of the state were consolidated. Though flawed in some respects, a comparatively stable authoritarian, or authoritarian-bureaucratic state came into being." In short, the expansion of the bureaucracy and state industries created a large group of workers that was dependent on the regime for their position and status. In contrast to Egypt, they were relatively well compensated. Most state workers believed that they would not fare as well following an Islamist takeover (Olson 1982).

It is also important to note that Assad made efforts to expand the regime's base of support. As mentioned, he appeased many in Damascus by spending heavily on improving the city's infrastructure and raising its standard of living. The opening of the economy and pursuit of foreign investment appealed to the capital's traditional trader and merchant classes (Perthes 1995). Thus, a large segment of the country—rural poor, urban industrial workers, government employees, and most residents of the capital—were supportive of the regime. As will be seen, the various constituencies of the Syrian Islamic Front were not essential for the survival of the regime. Finally, Assad kept a tight hold on the university campuses, which in other countries, are hotbeds of radical Islam (Olson 1982). Thus, despite a declining economy, another military embarrassment at the hands of the Israelis in 1982, corruption, abuse of human rights, and harsh authoritarian rule, Assad correctly concluded that he still had a firm grip on the reigns of power.

The Islamic Opposition

The crucial difference between the Islamic opposition in Syria and those in Egypt and Jordan is that the regimes in the latter two countries created and, to varying extents, controlled them. In Syria, their primary function and raison d'être of the largest Islamic political groups was bringing down the regime. After a brief honeymoon when Assad took power, the relationship between Assad and the Muslim Brotherhood and, later, the Syrian Islamic Action Front became confrontational and increasingly violent.[3] Therefore, from the beginning, Assad made the decision that Islamic political groups had to be controlled and, ultimately, destroyed. After the Islamic opposition united to form the Syrian Islamic Front in 1975–1977, it became the only viable Islamic political group in Syria. Hence, it will be the only one discussed here. However, as is the case in Egypt and Jordan, there is a large Neotraditional constituency that does not engage in politics.

The ideology of the Islamic Action Front was pragmatic because it was an umbrella for a variety of individuals, and its primary objective was to bring down the Assad regime. Consequently, the creation of an Islamic state was of secondary importance. As a result, their program was an amalgamation of concepts taken from Islam, liberalism, and capitalism. Included in their manifesto are calls for:

- the separation of powers
- individual dignity and human freedom
- a government that respects all of Syria's religious and ethnic communities
- free trade, private ownership of land and industry, and economic justice
- immediate *jihad* against the Syrian government

Missing from the program is a call for the immediate installment of *Sharia* as the law of the land (Syrian Islamic Action Front 1981).

The program is also void of the abstract idealism that marks the ideology of the radical groups in Egypt and Jordan. There are also few references to Islam's glorious past or calls to dislodge *jahiliyah* from Syrian society (Syrian Islamic Action Front 1981). Given the preceding, the Syrian Islamic opposition can hardly be labeled as inherently anti-Western. Here, we begin to gain a clear picture of one of the important functions of Islam in politics—mobilization. It is important to reiterate that orthodox Sunni Islam was the thing that the various groups that opposed the Assad regime had in common. Thus, Islamic terminology and themes are common in the Front's Manifesto, and the eventual implementation of *Sharia* was mentioned in order to appeal to the more religious factions (Syrian Islamic Action Front 1981). However, their goal as Islamists was more democracy—not less. It was Assad that was defending authoritarianism. Consequently, it is hard to argue that political Islam and Islamic political culture are monolithic or inherently antidemocratic.

It has already been stated that the minority status of the Alawi and the antiregime orientation of the Islamic Action Front made accommodation, which would lead to more representative government, impossible. Indeed,

the Front was composed of groups that have been hurt the most by Assad
and the Ba'ath socialist party:

- Sunni Islamic scholars and clergy
- Large landholders who were hurt through redistribution schemes
- Petty artisans and merchants, especially outside of Damascus, who, traditionally, are more religious and who have suffered from Ba'ath policies that
  have favored industrial workers and peasants
- University-trained professionals who advocated democracy, railed against
  corruption, and took the regime to task for its poor human rights practices

Assad's decision to combat the Islamists was influenced by the regime's
ability to survive without the support of these groups. The large landholders were a small group that could not stop the state's modest land redistribution. Also, the regime was popular with the peasants because their lot
had improved. None of the opposition groups had a strong influence on
the nation's economy either. Finally, the active number of participants in
the Islamic Action Front was never greater than 50,000, and it never gained
a foothold in Damascus (Dekmejian 1985). Next, I will consider the final
determinant of Assad's choice, the deep supporting cleavages that strengthened the divide between the regime and the Islamic Action Front.

Supporting Cleavages

The crucial role of supporting cleavages in causing the irreconcilable division between the Assad regime and the Syrian Islamic Action Front should
now be evident. A review of these divides will help illustrate this crucial
factor.

Sectarian. Assad's Alawi origins make him a non-Muslim in the eyes of
many Sunni, which intensified the predominately Sunni opposition's desire
to depose him. As discussed, the predominately Alawi composition of the
regime was frequently mentioned in the Islamic opposition's manifestos. At
the same time, Assad knew that his minority Alawi would lose their privileged position in a democratic Syria or in a government controlled by the
Islamic Action Front. These considerations combined with the historical
animosities between the groups, which resulted from years of Sunni domination of the Alawi followed by a reversing of the tables under Ba'ath rule,
made accommodation impossible.

Rural-Urban. Assad's rural origins also strengthened the breach between
Assad and the Islamists. As mentioned, the Islamic opposition was centered
in various urban areas in Syria, with the important exception of Damascus.
This was, in part, a result of the land reform policies, which had given land
that had formerly belonged to urban landlords to rural peasants. Conse-

quently, rural Sunni also supported the regime. Finally, there was a widespread perception among many urban Sunni that the rural Alawi were using power to gain revenge on the cities.

Class/Profession. Part of the animosity between Assad and the Islamic opposition was a result of class. The Alawi/Ba'ath ruling cliqué was primarily of peasant and lower-class origins, which explains their attraction to Arab socialism. As mentioned, the Islamists were predominately from the middle class. Consequently, the regime was also accused of exacting class-based revenge. The middle-class interests of the Islamic Action Front were seen in their call for an open market and the protection of private property.[4] Finally, as discussed in the sections on regime strength and the Islamic opposition, members of the Islamic Action Front represented, for the most part, professions that had suffered from Assad's policies. In short, the estrangement between Assad and the Islamic Action Front was far greater than a disagreement over whether Islam should have a more influential role in politics and government.

TUNISIA

Bourghiba: The Royal President

Tunisia, of all the countries being considered, is probably the nation that went the furthest in marginalizing Islam's role in society, politics, and government (Hudson 1982). This is primarily a result of the efforts and policies of Habib Bourghiba, who ruled Tunisia from its independence in 1956 until 1987. However, in spite of twenty years of government legislated and propagated secularization and Westernization, Islamic opposition arose to challenge Bourghiba in the late 1970s and continues to pressure the current Ben Ali regime. Both Bourghiba and Ben Ali, like Assad, have resisted, often with force and repression, the Islamists. As was the case in Egypt and Jordan, the rise of political Islam corresponded with an opening of the political system. The government's refusal to recognize the major Islamic political group in Tunisia, *Al-Nahda*, was the beginning of the end of the period of hope for a more democratic Tunisia. Once again, authoritarianism is necessary to keep a political system out of balance with a nation's political culture, and it is the Islamists who call for democracy.

Bourghiba emerged as the clear dominant power in the country after Tunisia won its independence from France. Tunisia's traditional monarch, the *Bey*, had been forced to abdicate and Bourghiba was in complete control of the Neo-Destour party, which had led the struggle against French colonial rule. After the Communist party was banned in 1961, Tunisia became a one-party state with the ruling party serving as a tool to implement Bourghiba's policies. His control over the country was so complete that his regime was labeled a "presidential monarchy" (Moore 1965). Subsequently, Bourghiba was named "President for Life" in 1974. As did Nasser, Bourghiba used his power to marginalize Islam's role in politics and to Westernize Tunisian society. Many, however, have claimed that Bourghiba's campaign to limit Islam's influence to the personal sphere was based on personal disdain rather than on political expediency (Hopwood 1992).

The marginalization of Islam, as in Egypt, was facilitated by popular, charismatic leadership. For most Tunisians, Bourghiba symbolized the struggle for independence and its ultimate success (Hopwood 1992). At the same time, he was in control of a party organization that had been in existence for over thirty years and that eventually controlled the government, the bureaucracies, the state agencies, the trade unions, and the state-owned industries. Bourghiba, throughout his reign, tolerated little dissent, both from within the Neo-Destour party and from external sources. Finally, because Tunisia is a small country and the Neo-Destour party's influence on all national institutions was strong, his reign was of a "personalized" nature (Moore 1965). Through his numerous addresses to the nation and his subordinates, Bourghiba seemed to have a direct influence on everything that took place in Tunisia (Hopwood 1992). He was particularly merciless in fighting both Islamic political culture and political groups, which he viewed as his most dangerous opponents in the creation of a modern, secularized, and Westernized Tunisia (Waltz 1994).

Bourghiba's mission to marginalize Islam was a result of his French education and his long-term residence in France (Hopwood 1992). He, in short, wanted to guide Tunisia on a course of modernization and development that would allow it to achieve the standard of living of many Western nations. For this goal to be achieved, Tunisian society also had to be reformed and modernized as traditional beliefs and practices—Islam—were hindering progress. Among the steps taken were:

- The Al-Zaytouna university, which trained Islamic scholars and jurists, was brought under the control of the secular university system; consequently, its power as an independent actor was eliminated
- The government took control of the mosques, appointed *imams*, and even distributed the sermon to be given at the Friday midday prayer
- A liberal code regarding women's rights, which gave them the right to work, request a divorce, and have access to education, was implemented; also, polygamy was outlawed, females were given an equal right to inheritance, and the age of consent was raised to eighteen
- Religious schools were taken over by the state and their curriculums were secularized; also, girls were banned from wearing veils to public schools
- The government also moved to weaken the *Sufi* mystical orders, which were popular in rural areas

Bourghiba's effort to ban fasting during the month of Ramadan because of the resulting decrease in productivity, however, did fail.

Bourghiba remained popular throughout the 1960s and early 1970s as Tunisia's economy flourished because of tourism, oil revenues, and remittances from workers abroad. At the same time, his independent foreign policy, which led to confrontations with Nasser, Khaddaffi, and the French, was also popular with many Tunisians. However, by the mid-1970s, the regime began to come under criticism. First, a failed experiment with socialism in the early 1970s had caused many to distrust the government. Second, power remained highly centralized, dissent was not tolerated, and the regime was also attacked for human rights abuses (Waltz 1994).[5] Third, the end of the oil boom and other factors led to a slowdown in economic growth. Finally, a growing number of Tunisians were disturbed by Bourghiba's unrelenting campaign to remove Islam from politics and as a guide for social relations. Throughout the 1970s, Islamic sentiment began to increase and several political groups, which will be discussed later, began to form.

Islamic Revival and Reconciliation

It was clear by the early 1980s that Bourghiba had to be removed, as the personalized presidential monarchy had turned into a cult of personality (Zartman 1991). The last glimmer of hope for pluralism was dashed after Bourghiba legalized the formation of opposition parties in 1981 but rigged parliamentary elections so that the Neo-Destour won all of the seats. At the same time, the MTI began to actively call for the reform of Tunisian society through Islam. However, they claimed to be nonviolent and hoped to participate in a democratic Tunisia (Magnuson 1991). The president saw the Islamists as a reactionary threat to all of the change that he had implemented and opposed the MTI and other Islamic groups through mass arrests and torture (Waltz 1986). As was the case in Egypt, Jordan, and Syria, Islam was the political language and force that was the most attractive in a rapidly changing society with an authoritarian government. Once again, it was those that were most adversely affected by the changes—first-generation migrants to the cities—who joined the Islamic movements.

Development and economic growth in Tunisia led to the same problems: social disruption, an increasing disparity in the distribution of wealth, and large-scale migration to the cities, that were discussed in the preceding cases studies. Many members of the MTI and other Islamic groups, like their counterparts in Syria, Egypt, and Jordan, were educated young adults of lower middle-class backgrounds. Surprisingly, females were also strongly represented in the Islamic groups (Hermassi 1991). As was the case in Syria, the Islamic political groups were organized in opposition to the government. However, with the exception of scattered organized demonstrations and sporadic acts of violence, which were condemned by the leaders of the MTI, political Islam remained nonviolent. As will be discussed, this was due to the lack of supporting cleavages between the government and the Islamists, events in neighboring countries, and the inroads made by Bourghiba's drive for modernization and Westernization.

Bourghiba, during the 1980s, became senile and more despotic, eventually driving away most of his inner circle.[6] He also clamped down further on dissent and opposition, particularly the Islamists. In 1986–1987, hundreds of MTI members were imprisoned following demonstrations and the bombing of several tourist hotels. When the leaders of the MTI were sentenced to life in prison, rather than death, Bourghiba demanded that they be retried. Fearing massive violence and more erratic behavior from Bourghiba, Prime Minister Zine al-Abidine Ben Ali had Bourghiba (who was past eighty) declared medically unfit to rule, using a constitutional provision, and assumed the presidency.[7] Ben Ali granted clemency to MTI members and other opponents of the regime and began to open the political system by restoring civil liberties to the press, labor unions, and opposition parties. As for the Islamists, it appeared that Ben Ali was going to apply Mubarak's strategy of trying to bring moderate Islamic political groups into legitimate politics in return for recognition of the secular state (Hermassi 1991).

Ben Ali, like Mubarak, was also faced with the same task of mollifying a discontented populous that was tired of flamboyant, authoritarian rule. He was also similar to Mubarak in that he was a low-key technocrat. Initially, it appeared that he was going to lead Tunisia toward democracy as he called for multiparty elections and invited opposition groups to enter into a "national pact" that would set the ground rules for elections, protection of civil liberties, and more representative government. The MTI expressed its support and its desire to participate. Subsequently, it changed its name to Al-Nahdah (The Renaissance) in order to circumvent the ban on religious-based parties, it reiterated its commitment to democracy, and it declared its willingness to participate in a secular-oriented government. At the same time, Ben Ali took measures that hinted that Islam, indeed, might be permitted to play a more significant role in Tunisian society and politics (Anderson 1991).

- He immediately made the pilgrimage to Mecca after ascending to power to pray for the country.
- The call to prayer was broadcast on the state-controlled radio network.
- The harassment of *imams* and other observant Tunisians by the state security apparatus was ended.
- The president stated that he was for a rebirth of Islamic learning and allowed *Al-Zaytouna* to refocus on religious education.

A Quick Return to Repression and One-Party Rule

It is here, however, that the path taken by Tunisia diverges from that taken by Egypt as Ben Ali eventually chose Assad's strategy of banishment and repression. An important influence on his decision was that he took office as a relatively powerful leader.[8]

- Ben Ali was very popular when he took office as an overwhelming majority of Tunisians were relieved that Bourghiba had been removed. Ben Ali, in addition, was given credit for orchestrating the smooth and bloodless transfer of power.
- He replaced over two-thirds of the members of the central committee of the Neo-Destour party with supporters in his first three years of power.
- He had a solid base of support in the military and internal security apparatus.
- He took over a government and party that had expanded successfully into almost every sector of Tunisia's society and economy.
- Events in Sudan, which was rumored to be training radical Tunisian Islamists, and neighboring Algeria caused many Tunisians to be weary of Al-Nahda. Violent conflict took place in both of these countries when Islamists took, or nearly took, control of power.

The first elections following Ben Ali's takeover were marked by the high expectation that the country was on the path to real democracy. Although Al-Nahda was not permitted to field a list of contestants, candidates who were associated with the group were allowed to run as independents. The religious bloc, despite its organizational disadvantage, garnered the largest amount of votes (17 percent) among the opposition parties. The elections, however, were marred by charges that the opposition parties had not had significant time to organize, vote fixing had taken place, and that the poll monitors from opposition parties had been intimidated (Zartman 1991). Also, the winner take all system guaranteed that Ben Ali's party, the Democratic Constitutional party (RCD), would win an overwhelming majority of the seats.[9] After Al-Nahda's request to be recognized as a legal political party was denied in 1990, it boycotted the Higher Council that was formed to oversee the implementation of the "National Pact" (Anderson 1991). By the time the next elections took place in 1993, relations between the government and the Islamists had soured, and the Islamists were not permitted to run as independents.

Several events served to end Ben Ali's experiment in permitting the Islamists to enter legitimate politics. The first was the Gulf War as Tunisia remained neutral and did not send forces to aid the coalition against Iraq. Here, Ben Ali tried to capitalize on both sides of the conflict. First, he exploited the anti-Saudi feeling in Tunisia by stating that Al-Nahda was a tool of the Saudi government. Then he blamed the Islamists for being the organizing force behind pro-Iraqi demonstrations (Waltz 1994). Most likely, after the success of the independent Islamist candidates and the tremendous support that was organized for the Iraqis by Islamic groups across the Arab world, Ben Ali saw political Islam as a serious threat to his regime.

This threat was heightened in 1991, when an Islamist campaign of insurrection that was intended to overthrow the regime was discovered. However, Al-Nahda and other moderate Islamic groups denied any association with the radical splinter element that was organizing the attacks. Finally, the violence and terror instigated by Islamic groups in Algeria after elections (which the Islamic party, FIS, won) were canceled and most likely had a strong influence on Ben Ali (Waltz 1994).

Ben Ali, following the discovery of the Islamists' planned insurrection, responded with mass arrests and the exiling of Al-Nahda's leader, Rachid Ghanouchi. After the government announced that it had uncovered an Islamist plot on Ben Ali's life, thousands of Al-Nahda activists were arrested and 170 were convicted of sedition. Once again, Al-Nahda denied involvement, but it was still labeled a terrorist organization. From that point, Ben Ali, like his predecessor, has maintained a policy of suppressing all Islamic-based political activity. At the same time, the regime has come under frequent criticism for abusing human rights (Waltz 1994). Restrictions on the press and association have also been reinstated. Finally, the RCD won 97 percent of the vote in the 1993 parliamentary elections but, again, charges of impropriety were leveled by the opposition parties. Clearly, in Tunisia, the rise and fall of democracy has been associated with the opening and closing of the system to Islamic political groups. As was the case in Syria, it was the Islamic groups that were calling for more democracy and the government that was, successfully, resisting.

Contextual Factors

The importance of the civil war in neighboring Algeria has already been mentioned. The violence and anarchy instigated by Islamic radical groups in Algeria following the canceling of parliamentary elections caused many Tunisians to be weary of Islamists in their own country. This feeling was expressed in a number of conversations during my visit to Tunisia in December 1994. In short, many felt that the mixing of religion and politics would also lead to violence and bloodshed in their own country. Even two university students, who said they would like to see Islamic law guide government policy, stated that a struggle for Islamic government would not be worth the suffering that was taking place in Algeria. Ben Ali is aware of this wariness and has used it as a tool in his campaign against Al-Nahda. Despite the group's support of democracy and denial of involvement with the acts of insurrection, Ben Ali still painted them as a dangerous terrorist group. He also claimed that Al-Nahda was receiving support and training from Sudan's Islamic regime, which is rumored to be assisting a number of radical Islamic groups (Hermassi 1991).

The weary reaction to the events in Algeria and the failure of "Islamic fundamentalism" to overwhelm Tunisia is further disconfirmation of a monolithic political Islam that transcends national borders. Al-Nahda's claim to be prodemocracy and its acceptance of secular authority illustrates the shallowness of the assertion. The differences between Tunisia and Algeria, which have caused political Islam to take a more virulent form in the latter country, will be apparent following the discussion in chapter 6. If anything, the violent tactics of Armed Islamic Group and other Islamic groups in Algeria have led Al-Nahda to continue its strategy of moderation in the face of continued government repression in order to reassure Tunisians, who do not want the peace in their own country disrupted. This leads to a second contextual factor, relative economic prosperity, as a majority of Tunisians maintain a decent standard of living.

Tunisia is often referred to as a model developing economy by the IMF and the World Bank. Although it is still developing a strong industrial base and is somewhat dependent on the fluctuations of the world petroleum market, political stability has facilitated a steady increase in Tunisia's GNP over the past twenty years. During the 1990s, this stability has led to the development of a booming tourist industry and a significant rise in foreign investment. These factors, in combination with a relatively small population (8 million), have allowed the government to provide a decent standard of living and develop the country's infrastructure (Vanderwalle 1988).[10] Consequently, the middle class and the well-off are willing to tolerate a less than perfect democracy, because they fear that increased power for the Islamists would lead to turmoil that would disrupt the economy. In addition, the growth of the private sector in the past fifteen years has created another group that has an interest in maintaining the status quo.

A final important contextual factor is Tunisia's well-developed education system. First, the Westernization and secularization of education has caused Western and secular ideas and lifestyles to become popular among some Tunisians. Although Islamic culture still remains an important influence, particularly in rural areas, a significant segment of the middle and upper classes has relegated religion to the personal sphere (Waltz 1986). In short, Tunisia's culture is a mix between religious and secular—hence, the moderation of Al-Nahda and other mainstream Islamic groups. However, Tunisia's education system has also helped facilitate the growth of Islamic groups. The rapid secularization, which was enforced during the Bourghiba era, was offensive to many students in the South and in rural areas (Hermassi 1991). At the same time, these students were led to believe in ideas such as liberty, justice, and equality. When this group realized that they were living in an authoritarian, corrupt, and repressive one-party state, they turned to political Islam.

Regime Strength

Ben Ali, of all the leaders discussed thus far, had the easiest task in consolidating power. To review, he replaced a leader who had become brutally repressive and unpopular. He also took control of a well-developed and organized party structure that controlled all of the country's important governmental and societal institutions. In addition, he enjoyed the loyalty of the military, as he was a career army man who had also directed Tunisia's internal security apparatus. The military's pro-Western orientation also makes it a willing ally in Ben Ali's campaign against Al-Nahda. Ben Ali's public support increased in the three years after he took power when he restored civil liberties, freed political prisoners, and took steps toward instituting multiparty democracy. However, these gains were short-lived, and Ben Ali reverted to the use of the same repressive measures and human rights abuses as his predecessor to stifle serious dissent. At the same time, elections were rigged to guarantee the RCD's domination of the parliament.

It is important to note that associations such as labor and trade unions, professional organizations, and chambers of commerce, which might serve as opponents to the regime, are also controlled by the RCD. Finally, as mentioned, opposition parties are at a severe financial and organizational disadvantage, while the winner take all electoral system also favors one-party dominance. These factors, along with the RCD's control of the bureaucracy and the state-run economy, leave Ben Ali firmly in control of the political system. His authoritarian rule has been further supported by the previously mentioned contextual factors: a fear of an Algerian-style Islamist insurrection, a flourishing economy, and a modestly westernized and secularized society. Consequently, as Ben Ali's reign progressed, it became increasingly apparent that the regime could survive without bringing in Al-Nahda and other Islamic political groups as junior partners.

The Islamic Opposition

Ben Ali's decision to terminate the short-lived period of reconciliation with the Islamic opposition certainly was not a result of radical ideology. Of the Islamic opposition groups being considered in these case studies, Al-Nahda is among the most moderate and willing to accommodate secular-dominated government. The major Islamic political groups in Tunisia fall under Shepard's Modernist classification.

Radicals. A small cell of the Islamic Liberation party (discussed in the section on Jordan in chapter 3) is known to exist but has not been of significance since the mid-1980s. A radical group, the Commandos of Sacrifice (COS), split from Al-Nahda in the early 1990s and a number of its members were convicted of terrorist activities in 1992. However, since then, they have not caused any disturbances. Ben Ali has used COS to stigmatize mainstream Islamist groups by claiming that it was Al-Nahda's military wing. However, both groups denied this allegation. Although COS does call for the replacement of the current regime with a *Sharia*-based government, and its tracts have discussed whether a *jihad* through force could be used to achieve this objective, it denies being associated with the violent acts of 1991–1992 (Waltz 1994).

Modernists. The Progressive Islamic movement is a small group that is primarily dedicated to reforming Islamic thought. Their main contention is that Islamic thought must be brought up to date before an Islamic society can be built. The group's leader, Slaheddine Jorchhi, calls for the integration of Islam with the rest of society. Thus, a flexible, tolerant, and modern Islam, which is open to differences in opinion is necessary in a rapidly developing society such as Tunisia (Burgat 1993). Although the group has put off active involvement in politics until it has developed an appropriate system of modern Islamic thought, Jorchhi has emphasized the importance of democracy and struggle on behalf of the betterment of the masses (Burgat 1993). The Progressive Islamist movement could co-exist with the present Tunisian government.

The primary Islamic political group in Tunisia, Al-Nahda, maintains the objective of using Islam as a tool to reform society. In short, politics, law, culture, and education all must be guided by Islamic principles. This group, during the Bourghiba era, leveled the same charge as the Egyptian Islamists had used against Nasser. Government and society had become corrupt because religion had been removed from public life. Subsequently, the regime had become abusive because a human ruler had claimed to supersede God (Ghanouchi 1986). Although MTI/Al-Nahda has always called for democracy and equality and rejected violence, it did not accept the legitimacy of the Tunisian government until Ben Ali came to power. As discussed, it was then ready to enter legitimate politics and accept pluralism, but its application to form a political party was denied.

Al-Nahda's program is more political than Islamic. Although it calls for an Islamic state and the eventual implementation of Islamic law, the primary concern is social justice. In the speeches and written statements of its exiled leader, Rachid Ghanouchi (1986, 1992), there is frequent discussion of uplifting the oppressed, fighting for worker's rights, and building a government that treats citizens humanely. He also calls for an open society that encourages all citizens to participate in the governing process and permits criticism of rulers. Finally, Ghanouchi (1986, 1992) goes to great lengths to emphasize that secular parties would be free to participate in an Al-Nahda–dominated political system. The Islamic part of the program is that this transformation would take place through the following of Islam. Although specifics are not given, the group has taken a more liberal position in recent years on issues such as polygamy, women's right to work, and social contact between the sexes (Ghanouchi 1992).

It would appear, based on ideology, that accommodation would be possible between the regime and the Islamic opposition. The harsh, rejectionist, and antigovernment rhetoric that was used by the Syrian Islamic Action Front is absent here. However, as in Syria, the Islamic groups do not represent a segment of society that is vital to the survival of the regime. The ranks of the Islamic groups in Tunisia, like those in the countries previously discussed, are filled by people (first generation migrants to the city who have backgrounds in the sciences, technology, and engineering) who are on the margins of society (Zghal 1991). Although they have better jobs and a higher standard of living than their parents, they still lag behind the established urban bourgeoisie. Most are from the poorer southern and internal regions of the country. When they arrived in the coastal metropolitan areas, they experienced corruption and a distant elite, which was propagating a culture of which they strongly disapproved (Magnuson 1991).

The primacy of political issues over religious matters in Tunisian political Islam is further illustrated by Al-Nahda's strength among the young and on university campuses. Like their counterparts all over the world, the students are ideological and committed to abstract notions of social justice. When they leave the university, they find a reified political system that is built to prevent real change. Therefore, they either join the RCD or another state organ or they turn to the ideological pureness of political Islam to express their grievances. An ironic aspect of the composition of Al-Nahda is the strong representation of women (Magnuson 1991). As stated, Tunisia has the most progressive policies regarding women's issues in the Arab-Muslim world. Again, it is a problem of dashed expectations. Educated Tunisian women are taught that they are equal to men and that they should work. However, this is not the social reality, and they turn to Islam for fulfillment. At any rate, the young professionals that chose the path of political Islam over the path of co-optation are neither a large or powerful enough group to threaten the Ben Ali regime.

Supporting Cleavages

The divide between the Ben Ali regime and the Islamic opposition is not exacerbated by significant supporting cleavages. Unlike Syria, where political Islam also represents long-standing animosities between sects, regions, and classes, the conflict in Tunisia is purely over the form of government. Tunisia is almost exclusively Sunni and the divide between Arabs and Berbers has not been as politicized as in neighboring Algeria and, to a lesser extent, Morocco.[11] Also, Tunisia is too small a country to have significant regional divisions. Although members of Al-Nahda usually have southern and rural origins, most now live in urban areas. Finally, the regime is not thought to be rooted in any particular region of the country or favoring any geographic locations over others. In Tunisia, it is the strength of the regime, relative economic prosperity, and the ominous events taking place in Algeria that have kept Islam on the margins of government and politics. The absence of supporting cleavages may be the reason why the competition between the regime and the illegal Islamic opposition has not been as lethal it has in Syria and Algeria.

THE FUTURE OF ISLAM AND POLITICS IN SYRIA AND TUNISIA

Continued Secular Authoritarianism

Little has changed in Syria and Tunisia regarding Islam's role in politics. After the Syrian Islamic Action Front was destroyed along with the city of Hama in 1981, Islamic political opposition has been absent in Syria, as the surviving leadership fled to other countries. During the 1980s, Assad tightened Syria's hold on Lebanon and, for the most part, is now that country's de facto ruler. His rejectionist posture regarding the Arab-Israeli conflict and betrayal of the Christians for the Palestinians and various Islamic groups, such as Hizballah in Lebanon reestablished his Arab nationalist, Islamic, and Palestinian credentials. Also, the Syrian economy has been improving during the 1990s. The previously mentioned factors—continued repression, denial of civil rights, and human rights abuses—and the example of Hama have kept a tight lid on Islamic-based dissent. At the same time, Assad's alliance with Hizballah in Lebanon has strengthened his Islamic credentials. It is almost certain that Islam will be kept out of politics until, at least, after Assad's death.

Islamic political groups in Tunisia have also remained marginalized. In the last five years, the government has continued its crackdown with more arrests and trials of Al-Nahda members. Leaders of legal secular opposition parties also complain of harassment. However, sustained economic growth and the continuation of the violence and anarchy in Algeria help maintain public support for the Ben Ali regime. However, Algeria permitted two moderate Islamists to run in its November 1995 presidential elections. If the Algerian civil war ends with greater pluralization, then there may be pressure on Ben Ali to institute real reform in his own country. On the other hand, the possibility of insurrection of frustrated Islamists and others, as was the case in Algeria, to bring about this change is a possibility. At this point, both scenarios seem unlikely.

It Is Not the Islamic Groups

The evidence presented in this chapter regarding Syria and Tunisia has further supported my assertion that Islam that is not the primary cause of political outcomes in Muslim countries and that Islam can be compatible with democracy. I have shown that Syria and Tunisia maintained authoritarian but secular-based regimes. Some of the most oppressive measures and worst abuses of human rights have been used in repressing Islamic political groups. However, the largest political opposition groups in Syria and Tunisia were not entirely of a radical or extreme nature. The Syrian Islamic Action Front did use violence to oppose the Assad regime but only after continuous repression and denied access to legitimate politics. Al-Nahda in Tunisia favors democratic rule, is willing to accept the legitimacy of the secular Ben Ali regime, and claims that it would allow secular parties to participate in government if it ever became the dominant party. The Islamic Action Front did support democracy and a pluralist political system. Of course, the moderation claimed by both groups may, as Assad and Ben Ali contend, be just a front.

The factor that led Assad and Ben Ali to repress Islamic political groups and marginalize Islamic political culture was regime strength. Both had roots in the military—strong party organizations, which had permeated their respective societies—and both had the support of crucial groups outside of the government. In contrast, the Mubarak and Hussein regimes were continuously threatened and in search of allies. A reason why the latter felt relatively secure in pursuing the Islamists was that they, or their predecessors, had helped cultivate political Islam. Consequently, rules and boundaries had been created. In Syria and Tunisia, Islamic political groups formed to oppose the regimes in power. Thus, the secular leaders felt that they could never trust these groups to play by the rules. In Syria, long-standing ethnic, tribal, class, and geographical cleavages made accommodation out of the question. An analysis of the relationship between Islam and politics in Iraq would reach the same conclusion. In Tunisia, the shadow of events in Algeria and low-level acts of violence overshadowed Al-Nahda's claim that it wanted to play by the rules. Now it is time to consider two Islamic monarchies, Saudi Arabia and Morocco, which appear to contradict the assertions that Islam can facilitate democracy.

NOTES

1. During this period Syria alternated between civilian government, military regimes, and a three-year merger with Egypt from 1958–1961.

2. Many Syrian Sunni Muslims view the Alawi as heretics. In short, the Alawi tradition and practice of Islam is closer to that of the Shia. For a more elaborate discussion on the Alawi, see Guillaume (1954) and Enayat (1982).

3. There was a brief period when there was a split in the Brotherhood caused by what course to take with the Assad regime. A moderate faction supported Assad after he disposed of a more doctrinaire socialist regime. A radical faction called for the continuation of violent opposition to a government that was still secular and socialist. Following the intervention against the Palestinians in Lebanon, the Brotherhood reunited and joined with several smaller groups to form the Syrian Islamic Front (Batatu 1982).

4. Ironically, Assad began to open the economy and facilitate the growth of the private sector following the eradication of Islamic opposition.

5. One of the few independent political organizations in existence was the Tunisian Human Rights League, a predominately secular-liberal group. Interestingly, its most frequent interventions have been on behalf of the Islamic Tendency movement and other Islamic political groups.

6. It was well known in Tunisia that Bourghiba's second wife, Wasilah, wielded great power as she controlled access to her husband. In addition, many other close relatives lived in the palace and served as informal advisors. Most, including Bourghiba's son, were eventually thrown out.

7. The prime minister, under the Tunisian constitution, secedes the president. Bourghiba's removal from power did not involve violence or bloodshed. The former president, who is past ninety, lives in his place of birth, Monastir.

8. These factors are discussed in more detail in a number of articles that appeared in the years following Ben Ali's rise to power. See Anderson (1991), Ware (1988), and Vanderwalle (1988).

9. Ben Ali renamed the Neo-Destour party to disassociate it from Bourghiba's legacy. It was, in reality, still the same party.

10. Tunisia's relative prosperity is quite evident after one arrives from Morocco. There are far fewer beggars in the areas frequented by tourists, and the poorer quarters of Tunis are nowhere near as deplorable as the Bidonville of Casablanca. In fact, many of the Tunisians I spoke to were offended when I even compared their country to Morocco.

11. The Berbers in Tunisia are a small minority, while they comprise over half of the population in Algeria and Morocco.

5

Saudi Arabia and Morocco

ISLAMIC MONARCHIES

Saudi Arabia and Morocco appear to contradict the central argument of this study regarding Islamic political culture's negligible influence on democracy and other major political outcomes. Both countries maintain monarchies, which still dominate their respective political systems, and use Islam to legitimate their reigns. Morocco's King Hassan II, the "Commander of the Faithful" and Saudi Arabia's King Fahd, the "Guardian of Islam's Two Holiest Places," are the spiritual as well as political leaders of their countries. Finally, neither Saudi Arabia nor Morocco is democratic and both have been criticized frequently for their poor protection of human rights and civil liberties. At face value, it would appear that these two cases support the notion that Islam, indeed, is a dangerous and regressive political force. Things, however, might look quite different after we take a closer look at Saudi Arabia and Morocco and analyze other factors that influence their political systems.

Saudi Arabia and Morocco, with the exception of the similarities listed previously and close ties to the United States, have little in common. Of greatest importance, Islam's role in politics varies significantly between the two countries. Morocco's political system is far more open than Saudi Arabia's, and the West is viewed in very different contexts in the two countries.[1] These differences are not a result of the Saudis being more authentic Muslims than the Moroccans. Rather, they are a product of the interaction of religious texts and traditions that leave room for interpretation and are nations with different political cultures. In regard to political matters, the prevailing interpretations of Islam in Saudi Arabia and Morocco are highly dependent on history, geography, demographics, economics, and other nonreligious factors. I will follow the format that has been detailed in chapters 3 and 4. The historical focus will be more of a more general nature, as regimes in both countries have maintained power since independence and have faced consistent threats to their reigns. Subsequently, the question of interest is how Islamic regimes deal with challenges to their authority from religious political opposition and how this "all Islamic" dynamic affects possibilities for democratic accommodation.

SAUDI ARABIA

Desert Tribal Leadership Legitimated by Puritan Wahhabi Islam

Saudi Arabia's Islamic authoritarian government is rooted in the circumstances surrounding its creation and development. Through the beginning of the twentieth century, the Arabian Peninsula was inhabited by nomadic tribes. A majority of the peninsula was outside of Ottoman control and was never penetrated by European colonial powers. Consequently, tribal, personal, patrimonial, and traditional government was the norm up to the founding of Saudi Arabia, in 1932. The first king of Saudi Arabia, Ibn Saud, was able to conquer and unify the tribes of the Nejd region through marriage and the use of Islam as Saud joined forces with the *ulama* of the Wahhabi movement, which adhered to a rigid and puritanical Islam. Saud, as a result, was able to enlist the traditionally oriented Nejdi tribesman in his campaigns, because they believed that they were following God's injunction to spread Islam. The *ulama*, in turn, gained a political force to help them spread the Wahhabi practice of Islam (Helms 1981).

The adoption of the Wahhabi movement by the Saudi family and the legitimization of their rule through defending religion and enforcing its social norms committed the regime to enforcing a rigid and traditional Islam. Consequently, a lapse in this area allows opposition forces to challenge the regime's authenticity. The importance of Islam as a legitimating force was multiplied when the Saudis captured the Hijaz region, which includes the holy cities of Mecca and Medina. Thus, the ruling family has had to ensure that it does not adopt policies that would contradict its puritan Islamic underpinnings, because loss of the support of the *ulama* and the traditionally minded tribesmen could easily topple the regime. This predicament has resulted in an uneasy agreement between the regime and the *ulama* where:

- *Sharia* is the law of the land and prevails in matters of personal status, criminal punishment, and the regulation of social behavior.

- Special government agencies and religious police ensure that proper Islamic conduct is followed. This conduct includes the segregation of the sexes, strict restrictions on the appearance of women in public, the banning of alcohol and decadent Western forms of entertainment, and the propagation of Wahhabi Islam.

- The government ignores the religious establishment in important political matters, such as foreign policy, modernization, the economy, and most areas of public administration (Kechichian 1986).

A second factor relating to the Nejdi capturing of the Hijaz region also helped to solidify Islamic-based authoritarianism in Saudi Arabia. The Nejdis, as mentioned, were nomadic, traditional, illiterate tribesmen, who had little contact with the outside world. The Hijaz, in contrast, were part of the Ottoman Empire and had been exposed to modern ideas, institutions, and technologies (Huyette 1985). The ascendancy of the Wahhabis meant that the influence of a puritanical Islam and a patrimonial regime, which was fearful of outside forces, spread to the entire kingdom at the expense of the moderate Hijazi Islamic political culture. Thus, the key debate in Saudi politics is not whether Islam will play a strong role in government or whether a liberal or conservative Islam will guide Saudi political culture. Rather, it is whether the regime is sufficiently traditional and strict. This contrasts with Morocco, which was in constant contact with other civilizations and where the cities prevailed over the countryside.

Ibn Saud and his successors consolidated their hold on power through marriage, patronage, repression, and the destruction of forces that threatened the regime. The country's small population and the Wahhabi sanctioning of polygamy allowed the ruling family to marry into the important tribes and families in the kingdom. Saudi Arabia's small population also permitted a personal style of rule, where every citizen has access to the ruling family (Yasini 1985). At the same time, the monarchy and the ruling family were the only important political institutions in the country and opposition, such as the armed tribesmen (the *Ikhwan*), who rebelled because they were against modernization and felt the regime had been lax in promoting religious values, were destroyed. However, the discovery of petroleum and the social consequences of the oil boom of the 1970s undermined the regime's claim to represent true Islam and strained its grip on power.

The Disruptive Influence of the Oil Boom

The late 1950s and early 1960s saw the regime face a rare threat from secular opposition forces, as Nasser's pan-Arabism and Arab socialism were introduced into the kingdom by Egyptian and Lebanese guest workers (Abir 1985). At the same time, monarchies were overturned in Egypt, Iraq, and Libya. Finally, a group of princes in the Saud family called for the passing of power from the monarchy to an elected assembly and the granting of civil liberties. The "liberal" princes were quickly rebuked by the rest of the royal family and went into exile, while troublesome guest workers were deported (Huyette 1985). Also, the appeal of secular opposition groups (Nasserists, Communists, and Ba'athist) was limited, because a majority of Saudis favor the use of *Sharia* to regulate society and daily life. However, a more serious threat to the ruling family would arise from Islamic groups, which questioned the regime's commitment to maintaining an authentic Islamic society.

The discovery of oil, the development of the oil industry, and the wealth that was accumulated as a result of the oil boom had a profound affect on Saudi Arabia. Revenues from the sale of petroleum helped support the regime as the government channeled funds into developing infrastructure, housing, education, welfare, and other social services that benefited lower- and middle-class citizens. Also, the growth of a government bureaucracy to administer these services and projects provided well-paying employment for many young Saudis. In addition, members of the royal family, others connected to the royal family, and government officials became wealthy serving as middlemen, agents, and contractors for the foreign interests competing for projects and contracts (Shaw 1982). The oil boom, in short, added to the ranks of those with an interest in the status quo.

A second consequence of the oil boom was that the kingdom was exposed to the influences of the outside world, particularly those of the United States. These influences, however, ran head on into a xenophobic society with a tradition of puritan Islam, which was being encouraged and spread by the government. Naturally, the religious elites railed against the vices and immorality brought by the expatriates who helped the Saudis produce their oil. The *ulama*, which had opposed the introduction of television and airplanes, also disapproved of the country's increasingly close ties with the United States and its dependence on the West for weapons and defense. Finally, they were also weary of the thousands of Saudis who had received their university training in the United States and other Western countries (Wilson and Graham 1994). In sum, the religious elite, along with many common Saudis, felt that the regime was selling its Islamic heritage for oil profits.

This belief was furthered by the ostentatious displays of wealth, particularly by the ruling family, that became quite common. Although oil profits were channeled into social services and public facilities that aided less fortunate Saudis, members of the royal family and those who were well connected clearly benefited the most. Stories abound of gold-plated bathroom fixtures and princes buying new Mercedes when the old ones ran out of gas (Aburish 1994). It is known that many members of the royal family consume alcohol, use drugs, and womanize behind the walls of their residences and when abroad.[2] To many, this immoral behavior was another sign of the regime's abandonment of Wahhabi Islam. The continued abuse of human rights, the denial of civil liberties, and the failure to expand political power beyond the royal family was also an indication of a turn away from the principles of true Islam (Abir 1993).

When faced with a deepening of its enduring credibility problem, the regime's usual response was to grant further latitude to the religious police (Mutawaeen) in cracking down on immoral behavior (Wilson and Graham 1994). It also built three Islamic training colleges, increased religious education in the public schools, and stepped up its campaign to reassure the religious elite that the regime was strongly committed to an Islamic society.[3] As corruption, dependence on the United States, and modernization continued, the royal family appeared to be on shaky ground when the Ayatollah Khomeini took power in Iran, challenged Saudi leadership of the Islamic world, and invigorated Islam as a political opposition force. Then, the decline of the oil market in the 1980s and the subsequent recession in Saudi Arabia further threatened the ruling family.

The Economic Decline of the 1980s and the Rise of Islamic Opposition

The ramifications of the ascension of the Ayatollah Khomeini and the growing strength of Islam as an opposition force throughout the Middle East were felt in Saudi Arabia in November 1979. First, a group of zealots occupied the Grand Mosque in Mecca in an attempt to rid the country of foreigners and other corrupting elements and depose the monarchy. The group, led by a religious student and former member of the national guard, also criticized the *ulama* for supporting the regime. Eventually, the mosque was retaken and the leaders of the rebellion were executed. The event, however, is telling of the role of Islam in Saudi politics. Because the ruling family claims to rule in the name of Islam, enforce *Sharia*, and protect Islamic morals, it is susceptible to attacks regarding its performance in these matters. Consequently, all of the regime's shortcomings can be attributed to its violation of the principles of Islam, which strengthens Islamic-based opposition.

Two days after the takeover of the mosque, Saudi Arabia's Shia population, inspired by the revolution in Iran, revolted.[4] The Wahhabi consider the Shia to be heretics and have maintained a policy of persecution as Shia religious ceremonies are banned, Shia cannot serve in the armed forces, and they are not employed in government agencies. Many Shia, however, advanced through employment with ARAMCO and attended the schools it provided for its employees (Huyette 1985). Motivated by the Iranian revolution and frustrated by their persecution, they violently pressed their case. The revolt was forcibly ended, but King Fahd did promise to improve facilities and services in Shia regions. The Shia insurgency actually galvanized support for the ruling family because of the Sunni/Wahhabi disdain for the *Shia*. Many Saudis also feared that the Shia's Iranian brethren would be a disruptive force in the region, which could hurt the oil industry.

The oil industry went into a long period of decline in the 1980s as a result of decreased demand and the failure of OPEC members to tow the line on production quotas. The consequences for the Saudi regime were quite serious.

- The regime was forced to cut back on the construction of infrastructure and public facilities, which was an important source of wealth for workers, agents, contractors, and middlemen.
- The regime was also forced to consider reducing its generous subsidies on basic products such as bread, water, and gasoline, which caused a public outcry and reduced confidence in the rule of King Fahd.
- Many of the young Saudis who had entered domestic universities and religious colleges because of the generous stipends given to students, for the first time, faced the prospect of unemployment.
- The corruption and extravagant lifestyle of the regime became even more distasteful during hard economic times.
- Traditionally minded citizens were disconcerted by the large proportion of the kingdom's wealth that was being spent on foreign arms and technology.

In addition to the regime's economic woes, it faced a further challenge from the young graduates of the religious colleges who, unlike the older state-sponsored *ulama*, were not easily co-opted. Many saw the woes of the 1980s as God's punishment for straying from the path of Islam. This group was inspired by Islamic political groups in countries such as Egypt, Syria, Sudan, and Tunisia, which, ironically, were all funded by the Saudi government (Kechichian 1986).

The Gulf War

The Saud family, in spite of the previously discussed pressures, remained firmly in power at the close of the 1980s, because, as will be discussed, it still maintained the loyalty of the key segments of the population. Also, there was still enough wealth, especially after the oil market began to recover in the late 1980s and the placing of sanctions on Iraq following the invasion of Kuwait, to keep most Saudis contented. The Gulf War with Iraq in 1990–1991, however, served to place a whole new set of conflicting pressures on the Saudi regime.

- The religious elite saw the presence of hundreds of thousands of American and other Western troops, including women, as a corrupting influence.

- The fact that the "Guardian of Islam's Two Holiest Places" had been forced to rely on America and other countries to defend them was a source of embarrassment to many Saudis.
- Some Saudi women were inspired by the sight of female American soldiers and began to press for greater autonomy.[5]
- Many Saudis pondered why they had launched a war against a tyrant when their own regime was highly autocratic.

Following the war, two opposing groups began to articulate demands for reform. First, a group of liberals published a letter in several newspapers in London and other Arab countries calling for an opening of the political system, increased civil liberties, and reigning in the morality police but also supporting the ruling family. Then, a group of clergy sent a petition to the king calling for a return to the practice of pure Islam in the kingdom. King Fahd responded by dismissing many of the clergy and forbidding contacts with Islamic groups in other countries (Kechichian 1991). In response to the liberals, he created a consultative assembly, which would be appointed by the monarchy and have no independent power and issued decrees protecting the sanctity of the home (Abir 1993). However, as will be discussed, an increasing number of Saudis were still discontented.

Contextual Factors

The continued reign of an Islamic monarchy in Saudi Arabia is strongly related to several contextual factors.

Oil Wealth. Saudi Arabia's oil reserves have been crucial in supporting the royal family's monopoly of political power. A population that is accustomed to authoritarian rule is more likely to tolerate its continuation when material needs are more than accounted for. The overwhelming amount of wealth that poured into the kingdom has made a large number of elites, both inside and outside the government, very rich. Most elites see continued Saudi family rule as the best guarantee of stability and fear the possible results of a radical Islamic takeover (expulsion of foreigners, a state-enforced ban on extravagance, and a less luxurious existence). Oil wealth has also given the regime the means to buy sophisticated weapons for both its external and internal security. Finally, without oil, the United States and other allies would not have such a vested interest in the royal family's survival.

Oil, despite its benefits, might be the factor that brings down the Saud family. As mentioned, internal discontent and Islamic opposition groups surfaced in the mid-1980s when a decline in oil prices damaged the Saudi economy. Harsh authoritarian government may no longer be tolerable when personal fortunes dissipate, unemployment rises, social services are cut, subsidies are reduced, and the expatriate laborers disappear. Rage is likely to be extreme in a country like Saudi Arabia, which has so far to fall. Oil wealth also brought corrupt Western culture and the dependence on the West, which galls the state *ulama* and the Islamic opposition groups. The penetration of Western culture and ideas into Saudi Arabia's traditional and xenophobic society undermines the regime's Islamic credentials (Aburish 1994). A scenario where Saudi Arabia's eventual economic crash is blamed on a regime that introduced Western values and placed itself in the hands of outsiders (who really hate Islam), looms in the predictions of several analysts (Wilson and Graham 1994; Abir 1993; Aburish 1994).

Demography. Another factor that enables the ruling family to resist change is the country's small population simply because there is more for everybody. A small population has also aided the ruling family as it is possible to either co-opt all key elites, such as the heads of important families and tribal groups, with patronage or through marriage. It is also easier to be aware of the activities of the citizenry in a small country. Another factor relating to population that benefits the regime is dispersion. Although most Saudis now live in cities, there are several large urban areas (Riyadh, Jeddah, Mecca, Medina, Dhahran), which makes it difficult for opposition to organize on a national basis.

Geography. Islamic-based authoritarianism is also rooted in Saudi Arabia's isolated desert society. As discussed, most regions of the Arabia Peninsula fell outside of the Ottoman Empire and the interests of the European colonial powers, which facilitated the continued existence of a nomadic, tribal, patrimonial, and traditional society that was shaped by its desert surroundings. The ascendancy of the Nejdi tribes over the more cosmopolitan Hijaz ensured that the political culture of the former would dominate Saudi Arabia. The presence of Mecca and Medina also intertwines the regime with Islam. Finally, the late arrival of the West engendered hostility rather than cultural integration. Islam's influence on politics and the nature of Saudi political Islam would both be different if Western influences had come earlier and the city had prevailed over the desert.

Regime Strength

The strength of the Saudi regime and the royal family is questionable. It appears, at face value, that the regime has bought off, married, or obtained control of all key segments of Saudi society. A large number of officers in the military are members of the royal family or are connected to the Saud family. At the same time, the National Guard, which watches the military, is staffed entirely by tribes that are loyal to the regime. However, there have been at least three attempted coups launched from the air force, uprisings against officers, rumors of infiltration by Islamic opposition groups, and instances of units and fighter pilots being unwilling to fight during the Gulf War (Abir 1993). For safekeeping, all major Saudi military installations are located on the outskirts of the kingdom. The internal security forces, however, are loyal and keep tabs on citizens with the latest computer technology.

The tribal population, which has almost entirely been settled, is largely loyal as it is tied to the regime through marriage, patronage, and patrimonial rule. Any ordinary citizen can gain an audience with the king or other important members of the royal family for assistance in resolving a problem relating to a government ministry (Huyette 1985). The Western-oriented and educated merchants, agents, professionals, and government administrators are also, for the most part, loyal to the monarchy. They view the royal family as a relatively progressive force and a bulwark against the religious elites and traditionally oriented tribes (Long 1991). This group, recently, has begun to urge the royal family to release its monopoly on political power and has tired of the restrictive nature of Saudi society. The regime, however, has an increasingly difficult task of mollifying both the Western-oriented elites and the *ulama* as both groups have pushed their agendas following the Gulf War. Also, various members of the royal family are entrenched in each of the two camps. This and other disputes within the ruling family have proved to be divisive. Familial power struggles, especially those related to succession, are always a threat to a monarchy.

Religion is another double-edge sword for the Saudis as the regime's survival has partly depended on representing, enforcing, and propagating a rigid and puritanical Islam. The regime's Islamic underpinnings help guarantee the allegiance of many Saudis, particularly those of Nejdi origin (Helms 1981). Also, the royal family goes to great lengths to teach its citizens that the monarchy represents true Islam and that part of being a good Muslim is supporting the regime. Finally, the alliance between the regime and the Wahhabis has produced a mutually beneficial relationship that translates into the support of the *ulama*, who usually grant *fatwah* supporting government policies (Bligh 1984).

Islam is also the greatest threat to the Saudi regime. As mentioned, because of the strong Islamic foundation of Saudi society and culture, religion is the primary dimension on which policies are debated. Consequently, regime decisions regarding issues such as modernization, banking, oil production and pricing, relations with the United States, the Gulf War, and women's education are all susceptible to being criticized for being anti-Islamic. Because the regime claims to represent Islam, it must constantly protect its religious flank. This has led to the enforcement of extremely conservative social, personal status, moral, and behavioral codes. It also means that opposition religious voices must be silenced out of fear that they will replace the regime as the authentic voice of Islam. More liberal and Western-oriented critics must also be muted to demonstrate the regime's piety. Hence, religion and authoritarianism go hand in hand (Aburish 1994).

The Islamic Opposition

Islamic political forces in Saudi Arabia fall into two groups, the state-controlled religious elite and groups organized to oppose the regime. Although the state-sponsored *ulama* are largely under control and have seen their influence decline over the years, they remain a crucial semiautonomous force that must be mollified from time to time. This groups fits into Shepard's Neotraditional category as they have reluctantly accepted modernization but maintain a very orthodox and rigid practice of Islam. As mentioned, they usually yield on issues of high policy in return for control of matters relating to education, personal status, social conduct, and public behavior. Thus, they issued *fatwah* supporting the presence of American troops during the Gulf War and watched a secular administration take over much of the Saudi government, but they have been unyielding in demanding a puritan social code (Wilson and Graham 1994).

This relationship has held throughout the nation's history with periodic expressions of frustration, which usually result in greater power for the religious police and tighter control of public behavior. The petition to the king signed by over 100 *alim* employed by the government signaled their growing discontent. However, they are likely to continue to support the regime because it provides them with funds and positions of power and—they also fear the unknown that would follow a radical Islamist takeover. At the same time, radical opposition groups distrust them because of their past support of the regime (Kechichian 1986). Many *ulama*, however, sympathize with the goals of the opposition groups and, as discussed, question the Islamic zeal of the regime.

The Islamic opposition groups in Saudi Arabia are of a Radical nature. All maintain the objective of creating a new society and replacing the monarchy with some other regime that will also use the *Quran* as the constitution and *Sharia* as its legal system. The first group to gain attention was the neo-*Ikhwan*, which was associated with the takeover of the Grand Mosque in 1979. Most recently, a group called the Islamic Awakening (organized in the 1990s) called for a demonstration against the regime, which was subsequently canceled when the security apparatus warned that all participants would be arrested. These groups have been supported by Saudis living in exile in the West. The common theme of Saudi Islamic opposition is that oil has left the regime and society morally bankrupt and led to corruption, anti-Islamic displays of opulence, and social decay. Naturally, the regime's American friends are labeled as enemies of Islam and the root cause of these disturbing tendencies (Juhayaman 1980).

The Islamic groups usually call for an even more rigid and traditional Islam to govern society and are particularly concerned about working women. They are disdainful of the state *ulama* for selling out to the regime and the Western-oriented elites for being lured by the evil of the West

(Juhayaman 1980). Despite their "totalist" and anti-Western ideology, they claim to favor a more democratic form of government and even organized the Committee for the Defense of Legitimate Rights in Saudi Arabia. Also, members living in Western countries are engaged in a campaign to tarnish the regime's reputation abroad. This might signify their acknowledging that the support of the United States is a necessary evil. The membership of the Islamic opposition groups is representative of Saudi Arabia's middle and lower classes. Many, of course, graduated from the religious colleges. The strength of the Islamic groups is difficult to gauge given conflicting propaganda by the regime and the opposition's foreign supporters.

Although the Islamic political groups in all of the countries being considered are organized against current regimes and forms of government, we have seen that their willingness to act as loyal opposition varies. Those in Egypt, Jordan, and Tunisia have sought reconciliation. In Saudi Arabia, like Syria, most do not. It should now be clear that there is no chance for reconciliation between the regime and Islamic political opposition groups in Saudi Arabia. The harsh response to the petition requesting reform sent by several members of the religious elite is evidence of this sharp divide. Given the crucial role of Islam in legitimating the Saudi regime, recognizing Islamic opposition would also be acknowledging that the regime no longer represented true Islam and was in need of corrective reform. The zero sum nature of the conflict and the regime's relatively firm grip on the state and society make Islamic authoritarianism the ruling family's best choice.

Supporting Cleavages

Class. Social class, given Saudi Arabia's tribal heritage, has not been an important influence on social mobility. With the exception of the tribal or family leader, male tribe members are considered equal. Outside of the ruling family, this egalitarian ethic continues to exist in contemporary Saudi Arabia. In short, one's background is not usually a hindrance to advancement (Huyette 1985). After the oil boom, the availability of free university education and government stipends to support students further enhanced upward mobility for Saudi males. Finally, tremendous wealth combined with generous government subsidies, health care programs, and social welfare programs means that there is no real disgruntled Saudi (Sunni) lower class. This lower class position is occupied by guest workers from developing nations. The viewing of foreigners as a threat has strengthened pressure on the regime to enforce a strict Islamic social code and to demonstrate its desire to defend Islam.

Ethnicity. The presence of Saudi Arabia's large Shia minority helps support Islamic authoritarianism. As mentioned, the Wahhabi disdain for the Shia has led to discrimination and persecution. The resulting Shia antiregime activity, which has included both secular and religious-based opposition groups, and support for Iran has had a rallying effect for the royal family (Aburish 1994). The regime has often portrayed itself as defending pure Islam against "the heretics." Democracy, or the granting of equal rights to the Shia, could come at the expense of the Sunni and the possible end of Wahhabi control of the state.[6]

Geography. The threat of the Shia is alleviated by their concentration in the outlying Eastern Province and the government's policy of preventing Shia migration to other regions. Concurrently, in the last twenty years, it has increased spending on infrastructure and public facilities to mollify the Shia population. The old rivalry between the Nejdis and the Hijazis still affects Saudi politics. The latter view the former as uneducated country bumpkins and resent their domination of power. The Nejdis view the Hijazis as being lax Muslims and too Western (Helms 1981). However, the Saudis have employed the more administratively advanced Hijazis in the government and, after seventy years, the groups have mixed. Recent policies to promote the Nejdis have angered the Hijazis, but this regional divide is not strong enough to threaten the regime.

MOROCCO

The Genesis of a Moderate Islamic Political Culture

Morocco's monarchy, although firmly grounded in Islam, has propagated modernization, religious moderation, and tolerance.[7] The relationship between religion and politics in contemporary Morocco, like that in Saudi Arabia, is rooted in the extent of its preindependence exposure to Western influences and the circumstances surrounding its creation. North Africa, in contrast to the Arabian Peninsula, had a long history of contact with Europe and the West, which, in Morocco, culminated in the French Protectorate from 1906 until 1956. During the protectorate, the French completed the ascendancy of the urban central authority over the tribes and the countryside. Also, political parties and other associations organized to oppose the protectorate, and Morocco's ties to Europe were cemented. Consequently, Western ideas, institutions, and technologies are strongly rooted in Moroccan political culture and have been encouraged by Morocco's government. In addition, a tradition of political activism and participation developed among the elite. It is also important to emphasize that Islam remains the lens through which many Moroccans evaluate the state of their country and society.

The current Moroccan dynasty, the Alawis, have reigned, uninterrupted, for close to 500 years.[8] The Alawi family claims direct lineage (*shorfa*) to the prophet Mohammed and the present king, Hassan II, claims to be "God's Shadow on Earth" and "The Prince (or commander) of the Faithful." Thus, Islam, as in Saudi Arabia, is a strong component of the monarchy's legitimacy. Hassan II has gone to great extents to emphasize his role of religious leader through the broadcasting of his performance of important rituals, such as leading study sessions during Ramadan and sacrificing the first sheep on the prophet's birthday (*Aid al-Kabir*) (Combs-Schilling 1989). The leaders of the dominant political force fighting the protectorate, the *Istiqlal* (Independence), were also observant Muslims and grounded the party's platforms in Islamic terminology. In short, despite the strong Western influence on Moroccan society and political culture, there was never a turn away from Islam and move toward rapid secularization, as was the case in Egypt, Syria, Tunisia, Algeria, and Iran.

The "Islamic consensus" in Morocco resembles that of Jordan rather than that of Saudi Arabia (Entelis 1989). In short, most Moroccans accept the value of modernization, are at ease in a society that mixes native and outside influences, and are willing to tolerate "non-Islamic practices" as long as they remain in reason and are done discretely.[9] Given the regime's propagation of Islam, its use of religion as a source of legitimacy, and the relative ease with which Western culture has been integrated, Islamic political opposition in Morocco did not become a significant force until the 1980s and remains weaker than in the other countries being considered. However, the monarchy is always vulnerable as the king's continued domination of the political system, repression, and the abuse of human rights in combination with a stagnant economy and a 20 to 30 percent unemployment rate have produced a growing class of disenchanted Moroccans. Again, grievances and solutions are increasingly being expressed in the context of Islam.

The continued existence of the monarch is a result of the French decision, during the protectorate, to expel the sultan, Mohammed V, a supporter of independence. Mohammed V's association with the nationalist cause and deportation made him a national hero, and his return became the rallying point for the nationalist movement (Ashford 1963). Subsequently, the monarchy was retained after independence. The Istiqlal and other parties envisioned a constitutional monarchy, but Hassan II, upon ascension to the throne, enervated the political parties, turned the parliament into a debating society, and centralized power in the monarchy.[10] Since then, the king has carefully employed a strategy of rewarding supporters with positions in the government and the private sector, while imprisoning, torturing, and even murdering those who refuse to play by the rules.[11] He has also encouraged the factionalization and splitting of political parties to ensure that they remain weak and beholden to him (Mossadeq 1987).

The king, after the failure of two coups launched from the military in 1970 and 1971, achieved control of the country's political system and economy. The threat of one of Morocco's socialist parties had been terminated by the murder of its leader in France and a campaign to portray it as unislamic. Since then, the king has relied on his status as religious leader (the carrot and the stick), luck, and a high profile in world affairs to maintain power. However, following the attempted coups and the weakening of political parties, the king found himself isolated. Fortunately, the Spanish announced their intention to withdraw from the Western Sahara in 1973. The king, playing on overwhelming nationalist sentiment regarding Morocco's claim to the region, led a march of civilians (the Green March) into the disputed area in 1976. All of the political parties rallied behind the monarchy and supported the ensuing war against the POLISARIO for control of the region (Price 1979). Nationalism was furthered by saber rattling with Morocco's neighbor and rival, Algeria, who was supporting the insurgents.

The Sahara campaign deflected attention from the lack of progress toward true democracy (the parliament was suspended for five years during the 1970s) and the failing economy. However, as the army failed to achieve a quick victory—the phosphate (Morocco's primary export) market collapsed and the shock waves of the Iranian revolution and the resurgence of political Islam reached Morocco—opposition began to coalesce. It is important to note that, unlike Saudi Arabia, there are outlets in Morocco for political participation, such as political parties, trade unions, professional associations, and student groups. The parliament was eventually reinstated and elections take place on a regular basis.[12] Lively political debate and commentary is now permitted in the press as long as it does not specifically criticize Islam or the king.

The Limited Appeal of Islamic Political Groups

Limited participation, repression, and the rewards for playing by the rules served to weaken Islamic political opposition in Morocco. In addition, almost half of the population remains illiterate and most literate members of the rural and urban lower classes are apolitical. Most see politics as a matter beyond their control, accept the legitimacy and religious nature of the monarchy, and are preoccupied with economic survival (Eickelman 1987).[13] All of these factors limited the appeal of the various illegal Islamic political organizations that began to surface in the 1980s. Also, King Hassan II does not have to maintain the standards of a strict, rigid, and puritanical Wahhabi Islam in a xenophobic society, as do the Saudis. However, like King Fahd, Hassan II cannot permit the emergence of Islamic voices opposing the regime because they would challenge the legitimacy of the monarchy, the notion that his rule is blessed by God (*baraka*), and his claim to be God's Shadow on Earth.

Islamic opposition forces began to surface in the late 1970s as study groups and youth clubs were formed. The king, as usual, attempted to co-opt these groups by offering them financial support in return for acknowledgment that the regime represented "true Islam" and the avoidance of politics. Some groups, such as the Islamic Youth, which was a becoming a force on high school and university campuses, continued to rail against the regime (Munson 1993). The largest Islamic political group, the Islamic Charitable Association, was led by a former government employee, Ahmed Yasin, who sent the Hassan II a letter detailing the king's unislamic actions and abuses of power (Yasin 1974). Subsequently, Yasin was sent to a psychological hospital and many of his activists were arrested or fled the country. As is the case in the other countries under consideration, these groups are a product of economic stagnation, a rapidly changing and modernizing society, urbanization, authoritarian government, and resentment caused by the unequal distribution of wealth. Many of the members, again, are from the lower middle class and are educated, new arrivals to the city.

It has appeared, at several points in the last twenty years, that the monarchy was at the brink of being toppled. Approximately every five years, there have been large demonstrations in the poor quarters of one of Morocco's large cities in response to announced cuts in government subsidies, unemployment, corruption, or general social malaise. The government then responded with force and things returned to normal.[14] Islamic activists usually participated in these demonstrations, and Islamic slogans were shouted. However, it is widely accepted that the demonstrations were not organized by the Islamists but, rather, were spontaneous displays of rage by Morocco's underclass. It should also be noted that Marxists and other groups were also present at the demonstrations and that the violence was usually instigated by the military and police. In short, these protests cannot be seen as organized militant Islamic insurrections (Munson 1993).

The Moroccan political system remains, for the most part, stable and static. The last major disturbances were nationwide protests in 1991 against Morocco's participation on the side of Kuwait in the Gulf War. The king, however, permitted these demonstrations, expressed his sympathy for the Iraqi people, and has called for the lifting of sanctions against Iraq. The civil war in neighboring Algeria has further weakened the popularity of militant Islam as most Moroccans fear that the rise of Islamic political groups in their country could lead to the same widespread violence and anarchy. An overwhelming majority of the Moroccans I spoke with are not willing to sacrifice peace and stability for an Islamic revolution. The monarchy continues to benefit from the Sahara issue as the army has consolidated its hold on the Western Sahara and most Moroccans still emphatically support its integration with Morocco.

It appears that political Islam in Morocco is almost entirely the domain of King Hassan II and the government. The *ulama* are highly supportive of the monarchy and, as is the case in the other countries being considered, frequently issue *fatwah* supporting the regime's policies (Munson 1986). The appointment of clerics to mosques is controlled by the Ministry of Religion, all Friday sermons are reviewed by government inspectors, and mosques are closed during the day to prevent them from becoming centers of opposition politics. Finally, the king has taken steps to ensure that the regime is in touch with the "Islamic pulse" of the country by training Ministry of the Interior officials in Islamic law, advising the *ulama* to be up to date on contemporary issues, and creating a council of religious leaders to advise the regime (Entelis 1989). The state-owned television channel also broadcasts a number of programs that provide answers to viewers' questions regarding Islam or that feature *ulama* giving sermons. Finally, leaders of Islamic political groups are co-opted. Many former members now spread the message as teachers in the nation's public schools (Eicklelman 1987).

Contextual Factors

The Moroccan government is plagued with many of the typical problems relating to development and modernization. The country's population has more than doubled since independence, and roughly 40 percent of its inhabitants are under eighteen. Providing jobs for this rapidly growing population is a Herculean task. As mentioned, estimates of Morocco's unemployment rate range from 20 percent to 30 percent. At the same time, a large segment of Morocco's rural poor have moved to the city, creating Casablanca's infamous Bidonvilles. A government's inability to provide for its citizens has been a factor that has been associated with the rise of radical Islam in other countries. In Morocco, this dilemma is particularly severe as it has also suffered from a stagnant economy since independence. Unlike Saudi Arabia, or even Tunisia, there is little reason to support the status quo because most citizens' material needs are not being provided for.

Morocco's relative poverty and large national debt have forced the government to cut back on subsidies and social programs to please the IMF and World Bank. There is almost no government safety net for the poor while a small, wealthy, and privileged class exploits an unlimited supply of cheap labor. Education, at the same time, has rapidly expanded and the country's illiteracy rate, although still over 50 percent, is rapidly falling. In addition, low-cost higher education is producing far more college graduates than the economy can absorb. As in other Middle East and North African countries, Moroccan college campuses are political hotbeds with active Islamic political groups. Consequently, it would appear that the social and economic conditions in Morocco are ripe for Islamic insurgency as the country remains poor, corruption is widespread, a generation of college graduates remain unemployed, and the government appears to serve only the interests of the elite.

These economic and social difficulties are alleviated by several factors. In contrast to Saudi Arabia, Iran, and Algeria, Morocco has never really experienced a period of rapid growth and rising aspirations. Poor Moroccans have never really experienced raised expectations and hopes for significant improvement in their personal fortunes. Most lower- and middle-class Moroccans I spoke with had resigned themselves to their current conditions. Also, some find employment in Europe, as roughly 1 million Moroccans work abroad. However, in recent years, the demand for guest workers in Europe and the Persian Gulf countries has decreased.

Morocco's enduring poverty and the lack of a government safety net have produced a strong self-reliant ethic. Many unemployed Moroccans in their late teens and twenties simply live with their families. I encountered a large number of Moroccan families with single adult children living at home. Many poor Moroccans also earn a living in unofficial sectors such as selling goods on the streets, providing "services" to tourists, and as day laborers. In short, most lower-income males are too busy trying to survive to concern themselves with political matters, which might not be the case if the government had a comprehensive welfare system. Also, begging is not frowned upon as it is in the United States, and many indigent survive on handouts from fellow citizens. Finally, because jobs are so scarce, those that hold them do not want to jeopardize them through association with outlawed political groups.

Illiteracy and isolation, as is the case in Egypt, also help to maintain support for the regime. Again, the half of Morocco's population that has not yet benefited from education is politically inactive as they have not developed a sense that they can influence their futures. Outside of a small elite, the rural sector is also unconcerned with matters relating to politics and national affairs (Entelis 1989). Consequently, it is no surprise that the government, in recent years, has implemented a policy of limiting migration to urban areas. As will be discussed, the Islam practiced in rural areas focuses on saint worship and superstition and does not have an activist political agenda (Gellner 1981). Finally, the spread of modern education has meant that more citizens learn about the benevolence of the monarchy and that the Islam propagated by the government is true Islam.

A final contextual factor, which has limited the influence of radical Islamic groups, is that Morocco does not have an established radical tradition. Morocco's colonial occupation was quite short (fifty years), relatively benevolent (when compared with that of neighboring Algeria or Egypt), and ended without a prolonged struggle. The monarchy, as discussed, remained intact, and the primary opposition party, the Istiqlal, was traditionally oriented and rooted in Islam. In addition:

- Morocco has never experienced a successful coup or change in its form of government that would have raised the expectations of the population.
- In contrast to the other countries under consideration, Morocco (along with Jordan and Saudi Arabia) has not gone through a period of Arab socialism or secular-based government, which did not provide representative government but did offend the sensibilities of the population.

- All of Morocco's radical secular parties have either been disbanded or been co-opted into supporting the monarchy or loyal opposition.
- The thirty-seven–year tenure of Hassan II and the 400-year reign of the Alawi family have led many Moroccans to fear the unknown consequences (such as radical Islam) of change.
- Moroccan political culture is historically conservative, and Moroccans tend to be weary of bold action. In short, there is a strong sense of mutual distrust and fear that antagonizing someone will lead to catastrophic retribution.[15]

Regime Strength

It should now be evident that the regime of King Hassan II is in control of Morocco's political system. To review:

- The king weakened the political parities by causing internal fragmentation and creating a number of small parties that were all beholden to him.
- All opposition figures, who posed a threat to the regime, have either "disappeared" or were co-opted through the granting of positions in the government or the private sector.
- A thirty-seven–year reign has allowed Hassan II to establish an aura of invincibility. Among traditional Moroccans this translates into his rule being blessed by God (*baraka*). Among more educated Moroccans, this translates into a resigned acceptance that the benefits of supporting the system outweigh the costs of falling from favor.
- The royal family owns approximately 40 percent of the private sector, which gives it further control over Moroccan society.
- The Green March, the subsequent war in the Sahara, and the current campaign to gain international support for Morocco's control of the region have deflected attention away from economic stagnation, social malaise, and authoritarian government.
- The king is also given credit for obtaining a high profile for Morocco in international affairs through mediating conflicts in the Arab and Muslim worlds, serving as a bridge between the Islamic world and the West, and playing a role in attempts to resolve the Arab-Israeli conflict.

It is also important to reiterate that the king has been, for the most part, successful in portraying himself as an Islamic ruler who is in tune with the Moroccan "Muslim consensus" (Entelis 1989). The traditionally oriented lower class and uneducated segments of society accept the religiosity of the monarchy. The more Westernized and secularized segments of Moroccan society support the king's propagation of a moderate Islam that is tolerant of the less observant. As many Moroccans informed me, the king appears to have a finger on the pulse of Moroccan society and political culture.[16]

The Moroccan religious establishment is firmly controlled by the monarchy and contributes to legitimizing the religious authenticity of the royal family. Finally, radical and extremist Islam does not appear to jibe with Morocco's political culture.

The military has been the most difficult crucial sector to control. As mentioned, two coups were launched from the air force in 1970 and 1971, and a third was preempted in 1981. Hassan II responded by decentralizing power in the military, by diversifying the composition of the Berber-dominated armed forces, and by calling on the elite families to encourage their sons to choose a career in the military. He also took a stronger role in the affairs of the armed forces and, later, turned control over to the crown prince, Sidi Mohammed. Finally, economic opportunities were provided to officers through land grants and shares of businesses in the private sector (Zartman 1987). Also, the status of the military has risen as it has been increasingly successful in the Western Sahara.

The Islamic Opposition

Neotraditional. Three significant Islamic political groups have operated in Morocco. The first was the loosely organized followers of Sheik al-Zamzani, a Tangier preacher. This group posed the least significant threat to the monarchy as al-Zamzani preached a Neotraditional Islam. This orientation is more concerned with the proper performance of ritual and preventing Western influences from entering Islam than political revolutions. Al-Zamzani (1979) did rail against excessive wealth, corruption, and the neglect of the poor, which could be taken as criticism of the monarchy. However, he was careful not to directly criticize the king and called for the reforming of individuals rather than society. Zamzani was popular with members of the lower middle class, such as shopkeepers and laborers (Munson 1993). Again, this segment of Moroccan society is largely apolitical. Al-Zamzani's censure by leaders of more radical groups and his not being arrested by the regime are telling signs that he was not a threat to the political order. Finally, his influence declined after his death in 1989, despite his sons' efforts to maintain the movement.

Radical. Two radical groups are known to exist in Morocco.[17] The first is the *Jihad al-Islamiyya* (Islamic Revolution) led by Abd al-Karim Muti. Muti's ideology is typical of the radical strain. Morocco was in a state of decline because it had strayed from Islam. The king was to blame because it was he who encouraged Westernization, modernization, and secularization. Islamic Revolution did not become a significant force as Muti was forced to flee the country in 1979. Since then, its membership has been limited because of fragmentation and government repression. Many of its constituents have drifted to legal Islamic study groups and clubs. Some even tried to gain recognition as a political party (Tozy 1989).

The Islamic Justice and Benevolence Society has been Morocco's strongest radical Islamic political group. Its leader, Sheik Yasin (1974), as mentioned, sent the king a ninety-page letter criticizing his abuse of power, luxurious lifestyle, and Western tendencies. Yasin's writings and speeches are also based around the central theme of a society in decline because the country had turned away from Islam. Yasin (1982) wrote that all Western influences must be driven from Morocco, the monarchy should be dissolved, and wealth should be equally distributed. Yasin (1982) also made it clear that he was against democracy, all political parties would be banned, and that government would be in the hands of "men of God" (Yasin 1982). The appeal of the Islamic Justice and Benevolence Society, like Islamic Revolution, has been limited by government repression. Yasin, after being released from a mental institution, has been under house arrest and banned from printing.

Several factors limit the appeal of radical groups in Morocco.

- They are out of tune with Morocco's moderate and tolerant political culture.
- Their violent nature is particularly unattractive, given the events that are unfolding in neighboring Algeria.
- Most Moroccans believe that the current regime is sufficiently Islamic.
- There are legal Islamic revivalist organizations that focus on personal reform and education.
- The Neotraditional Islam of a majority of Moroccans is apolitical. Hence, the government funds societies and festivals that honor local saints.

However, there is a growing class of Moroccans who are frustrated with authoritarianism and economic stagnation. Under these conditions, there is always the potential for radical solutions to win favor.

Supporting Cleavages

The fortunes of Islamic political groups in Morocco have not been supplemented by exploitable ethnic, regional, class, or sectarian cleavages. The primary ethnic cleavage in Morocco is the Arab-Berber division. Although the Alawi family and a majority of the "500 families" are of Arab descent, a significant Berber nationalist movement does not exist. Once of Morocco's important postindependence political parties, the Mouvment Populaire was founded by Berbers. However, it has a socialist orientation and has always supported the monarchy. Four factors limit the appeal of radical Islam in the Berber community.

- Since the arrival of the Arabs in Morocco, there has been significant mixing of the populations. Thus, ethnic-based appeals from Islamic groups have little appeal.

- The Berbers, who left the countryside, have done well in the city as they have come to dominate several economic sectors, such as neighborhood grocery stores.
- Most Islamic radicals look down on the Berber practice of Islam, which has strong elements of saint worship and superstition.
- The king, of course, has co-opted a majority of the Berber notables.

Sect is also not an important factor in Morocco as the Muslim population is almost exclusively Sunni. The country's remaining Jewish population (approximately 4,000) is not large enough to pose a threat to the overwhelming Muslim majority. In fact, most Moroccans are proud of the king's benevolent protection of Morocco's Jews. However, given the residual anti-Semitism that exists in Morocco, this might not have been the case if most of Morocco's Jewish population had not departed for Israel, Europe, and North America. However, their historical presence has strengthened the tolerant nature of Moroccan culture.

Regional favoritism, in spite of the distinct nature of Morocco's localities and enduring regional rivalries, is also not a divisive factor in Moroccan politics. The last outlying area, the Rif, to rebel against central authority was pacified in the early 1950s. The government, in the last ten years, has granted more power to elected local councils and provincial authorities. This decentralizing tendency has opened new channels for political participation and allowed for the expression of regional variation. Consequently, Islamic political groups, in contrast to Syria, Egypt, and Algeria, do not have a strong hold on a particular region.

Class-based anger, as has been true in the other countries being considered, has fueled the forces of radical Islam in Morocco. A majority of the members of Islamic political groups originate in Morocco's urban lower middle class. Again, important grievances of the Islamists include unequal distribution of wealth and the exploitation of the masses by a small elite. The luxurious lifestyle of the royal family in a poor country is also a sore point with many Moroccans.[18] However, discontent by the urban lower middle class does not guarantee the success of radical Islam. If so, Islamic political groups would rule in all of the countries being considered. In addition, many Moroccans feel that the king *should* live better than the rest of society.

THE FUTURE OF ISLAMIC MONARCHIES

Little has changed in Saudi and Moroccan politics. The Saudis survived the Gulf War and, as has been par for the course, made cosmetic changes in response to the calls for reform from Western-oriented elites and religious groups. Two terrorist attacks against American targets in 1996 and 1997 appear to have been planned by forces outside the country and were not a sign of a large-scale insurrection. Hassan II remains firmly in control of Morocco's political system and also makes minor adjustments when change is demanded. In 1990, he created a Ministry of Human Rights in response to both domestic and international criticism of Morocco's human rights record. In 1994–1995, he was involved in negotiations to form a new government and, in the spring of 1995, he shuffled the cabinet and removed the highly unpopular minister of the interior, Driss Basri. The Saudis continue to enforce a rigid, traditional, and puritanical Islam. When the *ulama* and other conservatives agitate, the regime clamps down on women, foreigners, and unislamic behavior. In contrast, official Islam in Morocco remains diverse and tolerant.

The future of Islam and politics remains tied to political culture and important nonreligious variables. Most likely, the day of reckoning in Saudi Arabia will come when declining oil revenues or the depletion of the oil reserves cause a significant lowering of the standard of living. Given Saudi Arabia's history, society, and culture, it is likely that the Saud family would be replaced by another traditional and rigid Islamic-based regime. The open question is whether the new regime would offer any pluralization of the political system. A more imminent concern is the failing health of King Fahd as questions of secession have caused turmoil in the past and have provided an opportunity for opponents of the monarchy to strike.

The event that will play a large role in defining Morocco's future is the end of the reign of King Hassan II. Although he has been grooming the crown prince for the throne, this might be the moment when disgruntled actors take action. The unknown factor in this transition is particularly significant because the last transfer of power was in the early 1960s. Poor performance or the complete abuse of power by Sidi Mohammed could also lead to insurrection. Morocco could go in any of a number of directions ranging from military rule, to Islamic government, to democracy. The 1997 constitutional referendum, which provided for a bicameral legislature with the lower house being selected by popular elections, could be a sign that the king is preparing the country for a more pluralized political system following his death. Given Morocco's relatively well-developed democratic institutions, mixed political culture, and ethic of tolerance, this option is viable.

The cases of Saudi Arabia and Morocco have provided further evidence against the proposition that Islam is incompatible with democracy and that it is the source of abusive government. I have shown that factors relating to history, societal structure, demography, geography, and wealth have led to an authoritarian and puritanical Islamic monarchy in Saudi Arabia. These variables have produced different conditions in Morocco, which facilitate an Islamic monarchy that permits limited democracy, encourages tolerance, and accepts Western influences with little difficulty. Islam does play a strong role in supporting and legitimizing authoritarian ruling families in both countries. However, it will most likely be an Islamic political group in Saudi Arabia that might install a more democratic form of government. In Morocco, an Islamic monarchy co-exists with democratic institutions and, some day, may truly share power with them.

NOTES

1. This was made clear to me on arriving and returning flights from Casablanca to Tunis on Saudia airlines. Outbound, I sat next to a Saudi, who told me that the Moroccans were not true Muslims and that Morocco was controlled by Jews. Returning, I sat next to a Moroccan who informed me that the Saudis are primitive barbarians.

2. For an entertaining collection of tales of the extravagance of the royal family, see Mackey (1987).

3. In addition to the Mutawaeen, several other government agencies, such as the Committee for Preservation of Virtue and Prevention of Vice and the World League of Muslim Youth encourage and enforce Islamic norms. Also, the heads of several ministries, such as health and higher education, are usually clerics.

4. The Shia compose approximately 30 percent of Saudi Arabia's population and are concentrated in the Al-Hasa area near the Persian Gulf. Iran is predominately Shia, and its government adheres to Shia doctrine.

5. Immediately after the war, a group of female professionals drove through Riyadh as a sign of protest against their second-class status. They were all dismissed from their positions and harassed by the religious police even though no laws had been broken.

6. It was widely believed, in the late 1970s and early 1980s, that the Shia were planning an insurgency that would lead to merging Saudi Arabia with Iran.

7. References to personal conversations and observations relate to information obtained from September 1994 to July 1995 during my residency in Morocco.

8. Since French rule in Morocco was a "protectorate," the monarchy, in theory, still reigned. However, Mohammed V, Morocco's first postindependence king, was exiled during the protectorate when he called for Moroccan independence.

9. This "mixed" Moroccan culture is best exemplified in the way many Moroccans naturally switch back and forth between Moroccan Arabic and French in daily conversations.

10. The Moroccan constitution states that is illegal to criticize the person of the king, the form of government, or the Islamic nature of the state. The king appoints the prime minister and the government, has veto power, and may dismiss the parliament. In short, he is the country's true legislative and executive power.

11. The ruling family also dominates the economy as it is estimated to own up to 40 percent of the private sector. At the same time, Hassan II has co-opted what is known as the "500 wealthy" families that dominate the Moroccan economy and government.

12. It is well known that elections are, to varying extents, rigged. Also, until 1997, one-third of the parliament was elected indirectly by local councils, which are, of course, tied to the monarchy. In 1997, the electorate voted to go to a bicameral legislature with the lower house selected completely by popular elections.

13. My lower-class Moroccan acquaintances frequently displayed apathy toward

politics because they felt powerless to change anything. When I asked them their opinions about political matters they usually would politely switch the topic or tell me that Morocco was not like the United States and that a king was appropriate for their country. Most viewed Islam in terms of its religious obligations (prayer, fasting, abstaining from alcohol, etc.) and not as a solution to Morocco's political and economic woes.

14. I spoke to several Moroccans and foreigners who were in Fez during the 1990 riots in which a luxury hotel and several other buildings were burned down. They all told me that the day after the military had restored order, life remarkably returned to normal as if nothing had happened.

15. For an in-depth discussion regarding the historical development of Moroccan political culture, see Waterbury (1970).

16. A Moroccan friend who would like to see a more open democracy put it best. "Although I do not agree with our form of government and everything it [the king] does, he really is one of us. He represents what our culture stands for."

17. There are also a number of small secretive Islamic cells across the country, particularly on university and high school campuses.

18. A good example of this resentment is the $400 million mosque that the king built in Casablanca to commemorate himself.

6

Algeria and Iran

RADICAL ISLAM

The cases of Algeria and Iran seem to provide the strongest evidence of Islam's incompatibility with democracy and its association with turmoil and extremism. The rise of Islamic political groups in Algeria and their victory in local and parliamentary elections threw the country into a catastrophic civil war that still rages. The Iranian Revolution brought an Islamic regime to power that has repressed political discourse and behavior that falls outside of proper "Islamic" parameters, eliminated its opponents, worked to spread radical Islam, and supported terrorism. Algeria and Iran (along with the Sudan) have caused political Islam to be labeled a dangerous and regressive force. An important objective to be achieved in this chapter is to discover how Algeria and Iran differ from the six other countries under consideration according to the variables relating to history, regime strength, regime strategy, economics, demographics, development, supporting cleavages, and the nature of Islamic opposition groups.

Regime strength and strategies for dealing with Islamic opposition, again, will be a central focus. A related task is to investigate the extent to which the FLN in Algeria and the secular-oriented regimes of the Shah of Iran are responsible for their own demise and the radicalization of political Islam. The Algerian civil war was instigated by the military's seizing control of the government, outlawing of the Islamic Salvation Front (FIS), arrest of the FIS's leadership, and nullification of the results of the fair and democratic elections that had brought the FIS to power. The Shah ruthlessly repressed the Iranian clergy and attempted to marginalize Islam's role in Iranian society to an extent that was unacceptable to most Iranians. In short, the victory of radical Islam may be a result of regimes selecting the wrong strategy for dealing with political Islam.

It is important to note that the opening of the Algerian political system in the late 1980s and early 1990s was associated with the rise of political Islam, and that Iran is more democratic today than it was under the Shah. To understand why, it is necessary to discuss the nature of the the FLN regime in Algeria, the Pahlavi regime in Iran, the the rise of political Islam in both countries, and the interplay between government and opposition when the Islamic oppositions challenged secular authoritarianism. In Algeria, I will focus on the period beginning in the late 1980s leading up to the army's intervention in 1992, which resulted in the end of Algeria's experiment with democracy. I will also discuss what transpired during the brief period when the FIS controlled a majority of Algeria's local and regional governments and its role in the ongoing civil war. The key interval in Iran was the 1970s up to the Iranian revolution and the subsequent return of the Ayatollah Khomeini. Finally, it will also be important to consider changes in the nature of political Islam in Iran after the death of the Ayatollah, the end of the war with Iraq, and the maturing of the revolution.

ALGERIA

The Disruptive Influence of French Occupation

The ambivalent relationship between Islam and politics in contemporary Algeria has its roots in the 130-year French occupation. Unlike the French protectorate in Morocco, which left Moroccan culture and society largely intact, the French occupation of Algeria was total and devastating. The attempted integration of Algeria with the motherland necessitated a policy of transforming it into a Westernized Francophone society. Also, the indigenous population became second-class citizens to the hundreds of thousands of French who settled in Algeria. A result of French rule was that traditional cohesive units—such as family, local community, Islam, tribe, and ethnic group—were weakened or eradicated (Vatin 1983). Also, French replaced Arabic as the country's official language and the language of business, government, and the elite, which served to cut off several generations of Algerians from their cultural heritage. The imposition of a foreign language and culture also alienated many Algerians from France and the West. Other important disruptions were:

- The French fought the influence of rural Islam as its focus on saint worship and superstition inhibited the Frenchifying of the population, which furthered the sense of anomie among traditional Algerians.

- A large portion of fertile agricultural land was expropriated for the French settlers, which forced native Algerians to migrate to the city. The native population, in general, was moved about to serve the economic needs of the French. It is estimated that one-third of the population was relocated during the colonial period.

- Associations, such as political parties, labor unions, and other organizations that threatened French interests, were banned.

- The French played on regional rivalries and the Arab/Berber divide and mixed competing tribes and ethnic groups in political units to pacify the country. These fractures continue to affect Algerian politics and society today.

- The eight-year war of liberation against the French served to radicalize Algerian politics, raise expectations for postindependence Algeria, and sharpen the divide between Arab/Muslim culture and Western/secular culture.

An important consequence of France's anti-Arab and anti-Muslim policies was to intertwine these two identities with Algerian nationalism (Reudy 1994). One of the first groups to organize in opposition to French occupation was the Association of Algerian Ulama, which stressed cultural authenticity as a means of fighting the French. The major nationalist movement, the FLN (National Liberation Front), also played on Islamic themes and used Islamic terminology to rally opposition to the French. Because of the overriding objectives of driving out the French and gaining independence, the FLN served as an umbrella organization (primarily military in nature), which included factions spanning the ideological spectrum from Marxism to Islamism (Jackson 1977). However, after these goals were achieved, the FLN became the country's sole legal political party, and it adopted a secular-based Arab socialist/Arab nationalist orientation.

Independence

The first twenty years of Algeria's existence was a period of state and national identity building. The second president, Houari Boumidienne, implemented socialist, state-centered policies, such as the collectivizing of agriculture and the development of heavy industry. Under Boumidienne's charismatic leadership, Algeria served as a model of a progressive, developing nonaligned country. At the same time, Islam was brought under the control of the state authorities and, as in Egypt, efforts were made to convince the population that socialism and Islam were compatible (Entelis 1986). Algeria, unlike Egypt, did not have a reputable institution such as Al-Azhar or a cadre of trained clergy. At one point, the government even brought in a notable Egyptian *alim* to lead the newly founded Islamic seminary and to serve as a spokesman for the government (Vatin 1982). In short, the government's Islamic legitimacy and credibility have always been questionable.

Boumidienne's regime remained largely unchallenged from external sources as the novelty of independence, the process of state building, the country's prominent role in the nonaligned and Arab socialist movements, and the president's personal popularity served to maintain support for the government (Jackson 1977). Also, the country's economy enjoyed a period of growth as the world's hydrocarbon market was in a boom period. However, after Boumidienne died in 1978, the weakness of the government and fractures in Algerian society became evident.

- The military remained the true power in politics as both Boumidienne and his successor, Chadli Bendjedid, were career army men. At the same time, opposition outside the FLN was repressed, independent associations such as trade unions were banned, and the press was censored heavily.

- Both the agricultural collectives and the heavy industry developed under Boumidienne failed as the country began to import food during the 1980s, and the industries produced goods that could not compete internationally and were of little use domestically.

- The FLN remained ideologically vacuous and factional infighting prevented effective governance. Corruption was also widespread, and personal interests took precedence over public policy.

- The government's Arabization policy led to a sharp cleavage between those who spoke French and those who did not. Despite all official documents being in Arabic, French remained the elite language. Those who were educated after independence spoke only Arabic and were served by a terrible public school system. Soon, this language cleavage transformed into a class division with lower-class, Arabic-speaking, traditionally oriented Algerians on one side and upper-class, French-speaking, secular-oriented Algerians on the other.

- The government began to falter in providing key services such as water, health care, employment, and housing.

Political Islam Rises to Fill the Void

Most Algerians, given the preceding, were skeptical and cynical about their government and political system in the years following Chadli Bendjedid's rise to power. As has been the case in the other countries being considered, Islam became an appealing solution to the country's growing malaise. During the late 1970s and early 1980s, signs of the growing strength of political Islam were manifest in increased mosque attendance, the building of new mosques without government permission, and demonstrations by Islamic students on college campuses (Vatin 1982). The government attempted to tap into the growing Islamic sentiment and to co-opt it as more Quranic schools were opened, religious education was introduced into the *lycees*, Friday replaced Sunday as the day of rest, and a return to a more traditionally oriented personal status code was considered (Vatin 1982). It is important to note that unlike Egypt and Jordan (and similar to Syria and Tunisia), Islamic groups were not formed with the consent or assistance of the government but in opposition to it. The importance of this factor will be considered later.

Algeria's economic situation worsened throughout the 1980s as the price of hydrocarbons continued to plummet. It also became clear that the state-controlled economy was inefficient and riddled with corruption. Consequently, Bendjedid put the country on a course of economic liberalization and privatization that resulted in rising prices, increased unemployment, a growing disparity between the haves and the have-nots, and resentment from mangers and technocrats, who previously had been guaranteed employment. The Islamists were quick to capitalize on the growing despair and blamed the government for the mess, because it had turned from Islam and toward the Western values of consumerism, individualism, and secularism (Entelis 1986). At the same time, Islamic groups, with funding from Saudi Arabia, began to step in and provide welfare, health care, and other social services.

The disenchantment of a growing segment of the Algerian population was exhibited in frequent riots and demonstrations. Tensions also arose between Berbers and the Islamists. Algerian Berbers are secular oriented and saw the Islamic groups as attempting to enforce an Arabic/Islamic hegemony over the country (Duran 1992). Bendjedid, like Mubarak, King Hussein, and Ben Ali saw opening the political system as a way to relieve the pressure that was coming from below and as a way of consolidating control over the unruly FLN (Entelis 1992b). As would be expected, the party's old guard, the bureaucracy, and the military disapproved of economic liberalization because it weakened their own power.[1] Within three years, Algeria was to go from a one-party authoritarian state to an open multiparty democracy. An Islamic political group, the Islamic Salvation Front (FIS), was to be a key player in this transformation.

The Transition to Democracy

The process of major reform began in 1988 following major rioting in Algiers and other cities against unemployment and a corrupt and repressive political system. The Islamists played an important role in the demonstrations, and many of their activists were among the 500 dead and 300 arrested (Entelis 1992). It was then that Bendjedid decided to take a conciliatory stand, met with several opposition preachers, and promised to move the state toward an Islamic moral foundation. On November 8, 1988, voters approved an amendment to the constitution separating the government from the FLN, and, in the ensuing months, the cabinet was reshuffled to include many reformers. In 1989, additional amendments were passed creating a multiparty system and protecting freedom of the press, freedom of speech, and freedom of organization.

The FIS and several other Islamic parties were formed in 1989 to compete in the 1990 municipal elections. Although formed in opposition to the government, the FIS adhered to a policy of nonviolence and the achievement of an Islamic state through democracy. Many of its followers were protesting economic decline and the corruption of the FLN, but a majority supported the return to Islamic values and the implementation of *Sharia*. The meteoric growth of the FIS was a result of its networks of neighborhood mosques, which were outside the control of the Ministry of Religion. Their preachers railed against the government, and, as mentioned, they also provided social services and welfare when the government became incapable of doing so (Roberts 1992). Consequently, the 1990 elections for local and regional council took shape as a contest between the FLN and the FIS.[2]

The elections resulted in a stunning victory for the FIS as it gained 53 percent of the vote and control of over half of the councils, including the major cities of Algiers, Oran, and Constatine. The FIS's record as the party in power was mixed as it focused on problem solving and quality of life issues in some areas but also attempted to enact strict Islamic behavior codes in others (Entelis 1992b, 1994). Bendjedid then announced that two-stage national legislative elections would be held in the summer of 1991. Riots, however, followed as the FIS protested the electoral laws that favored the rural areas where the FLN support was strongest. They also called for Bendjedid's resignation as well as presidential elections. After a state of emergency was declared for the army to restore order, the elections were held. The FIS won another overwhelming victory in the first round, gaining 188 out of 430 seats, and it would have gained a majority in the second round.[3]

The army, after Bendjedid had entered into talks with the FIS regarding power sharing, forced the president to resign and nullified the results of the elections. A High Security Council was set up, and a leader of the provisional government during the war of independence, Mohammed Boudiaf, was brought back to serve as president after twenty-eight years in exile in Morocco. The military then turned on the FIS and arrested its leaders, Dr. Abassi al-Madani and Ali Belhaj, and 500 other activists. The suspension of the constitution was followed by violent rioting. Since 1992, the country has been engaged in a catastrophic civil war pitting the Islamic militias against the army. The FIS has been involved in the war but, at the same time, has offered to negotiate an end to the violence and called for a truce in September 1997. An extremist splinter faction, the Armed Islamic Group (GIA), has vowed to fight until the government falls, and it has assassinated government officials, civilians, foreigners, entertainers, journalists, and other purveyors of secular culture (Waltz 1994).

It is important to emphasize that it was not the FIS or other Islamic groups that terminated the democratic process but, rather, the military. The FIS had been an eager participant in the democratic process from the start and did not turn to insurrection until after it was outlawed, and the military canceled the second round of elections. Islamic groups had demonstrated and protested in 1991, but this was in response to unfair election rules that favored the FLN. The FIS also stated that it did not want to compel people to practice Islam by law and that individual observance was a personal decision. Its leader, Abassi al-Madani called for moderation and told Algerians that the rights of all citizens would be respected under an FIS-led government (Entelis 1992b). Therefore, it is difficult to blame the termination of Algeria's brief democratic interlude on the FIS. My analysis of the relationship between Islam and politics in contemporary Algeria will focus on two questions. (1) What factors led Bendjedid to open Algeria's political system and seek accommodation with the FIS and (2) Why did this experiment end in failure?

Contextual Factors

Problems related to the economy and modernization had a strong influence on Bendjedid's decision to open the political system, because the widespread discontent in Algerian society during the 1980s was partly due to the country's declining economy. As mentioned, the agricultural sector had been disrupted by French colonization and Boumidienne's collectives. Consequently, the government was forced to spend revenues importing food. Shortages, however, still existed. In addition, the cost of Algerian food products was inflated by the high salaries paid in the agricultural sector, which were intended to stop migration to the cities. Algeria, like Morocco, has a 20 to 30 percent unemployment rate, which was rising because of privatization (Reudy 1994). Rapid population growth led to overcrowded cities. Urban areas, despite the attempt to keep people in the countryside, have large concentrations of unemployed young males, many of whom have become members of the FIS and other Islamic groups (Labat 1994).

Bendjedid was also left to deal with the failed heavy industries of the Boumidienne era. Closing the factories deepened the unemployment problem and alienated the FLN cadres who managed them. The factories, however, were an economic drain that the state could no longer support. The decrease of hydrocarbon prices from $40 per barrel to $10 per barrel also cut into government revenues. The FIS boosted its credibility when it stepped in to provide food, services, and welfare when the government could not (Roberts 1992). Bendjedid's solution—privatization—to Algeria's economic woes isolated him from his party and strengthened the FIS.

As mentioned, the old guard of the FLN, the bloated bureaucracy, and the mangers in the state industry all benefited from statism and socialism and, consequently, resisted reform.

Bendjedid, given the party's reluctance to accept economic change, was forced to weaken the FLN's grip on power. Hence, he decided to go to a multiparty system that would make him the powerbroker over the competing parties. The disunity and infighting resulting from Bendjedid's policies, however, hurt the FLN's ability to mount effective campaigns in the 1990 and 1991 elections (Entelis 1992b, 1994). Although Bendjedid, ironically, was trying to transform Algeria into a competitive market economy, he, as a result of his association with the FLN, was blamed for its past failures and the growing pains of change (Entelis 1992b, 1994). The FIS also supported economic liberalization, which influenced Bendjedid's desire to bring it into legitimate politics. At the same time, the increasing gap between rich and poor, which was partly caused by privatization, was political hay for the FIS. It claimed that this gap was a result of government corruption, favoritism, and inefficiency. Naturally, a party based on Islamic morals and values would not fall subject to these practices (Entelis 1992b, 1994).

Bendjedid may have erred in opening the political system at a time when the economy was in decline and economic change was already shaking the foundations of Algerian society. The current politics of Russia and other Eastern European countries are further evidence that it is difficult for a fledgling democracy to support the change from socialism to capitalism. In Russia the "fundamentalist" solution is to go back to hard-line Soviet communism; in Algeria it is to return to Islam. It is important to emphasize the influence that the French occupation and the War of Independence had on Algeria. The French, as mentioned, destroyed or weakened most of the traditional structures, such as Islam, family, and tribe, which provided comfort (and still exist in Morocco) during periods of rapid change. Their exacerbation of tribal and ethnic cleavages also helped prevent the development of national identity and unity. Finally, the long, arduous, and costly revolution raised hopes and aspirations for postindependence Algeria (Entelis 1986). The FLN's failure to deliver fostered cynicism, skepticism, and contempt, which led many voters to the FIS. This ambivalence also explains why there was little surprise or opposition when the army ended democracy.

Regime Strength

The move to multiparty democracy, as was the case in Egypt, Jordan, and Tunisia, was a result of a weakened political order. In addition to the problems related to economic decline and modernization, Bendjedid also had to deal with a historically fractured and ineffective party, the FLN.

- The FLN's monopoly on Algerian politics meant that it was an umbrella for a wide range of ideological orientations. Hence, it never presented a clear and coherent plan of governance to the Algerian people.

- These factions were constantly in conflict, which led to clandestine power plays and personal interests taking precedence over public policy.

- Because the FLN was tied to the military, the bureaucracy and other government institutions, favoritism, corruption, and other abuses of power were widespread as there was no check on authority.

- The intertwining of the FLN with the army has translated into the military being the real powerbroker in Algerian politics. Two Algerian presidents have been removed through soft glove coups.

The power of the Algerian presidency, in short, lies in the individual rather than institutions (Waltz 1994). Boumidienne was a strong president because of his charismatic personality, the continued spirit of independence, a booming economy, and his leadership of the state-building process. Bendjedid took office in a period of economic decline and had to deal with the failed statist policies that he inherited from Boumidienne. Later, Bendjedid became the victim of the public's realization that the promises of development and equality born in the revolution had not been kept. At the same time, Algeria's status in world affairs declined with the demise of the Arab socialist and nonaligned movements. At odds with his own party, a weak Bendjedid had to bring newcomers into the political system in order to shore up his regime. He, however, was not strong enough to maintain control of the new system.

Bendjedid had no choice but to seek an accommodation with the FIS and other Islamic groups because there was no viable secular opposition. Although the FIS agreed with Bendjedid's economic policies, used primarily nonviolent methods, and supported democracy, the president was taking a risk. In contrast to Egypt and Jordan, the Islamic groups were not co-opted by the regime, nor were they dependent on it for their continued existence. Consequently, there was no mutual understanding or regime-defined "rules of the game," while in Egypt and Jordan, clear parameters were set for the Muslim Brotherhood to enter legitimate politics. Consequently, the FIS would have been free to change the rules, because it was in no way beholden to the man who brought it into the political system.[4] The prospect of the FIS in control of the country was a risk that the military could not chance and a frightening prospect to many Algerians.

Bendjedid also made the mistake of miscalculating his own strength as he thought that the FLN would prevail in multiparty elections. Given the lack of viable secular opposition parties, Bendjedid believed that most Algerians would pick the old standby (FLN) out of fear of an FIS-dominated government (Entelis 1992b, 1994). Consequently, his main election strategy was to warn Algerians that extremism would result from an FIS victory. His own party, however, did not offer a competing moral vision for the country and was in a state of disunity. Of greatest importance, Bendjedid did not realize the contempt and disdain that a majority of Algerians felt toward the FLN (Entelis 1992b, 1994). Hence, the overwhelming FIS victory and the army's decision to intervene.

The rapid transition to democracy was also problematic. Algeria, as mentioned, went from a one-party authoritarian regime to a multiparty democracy in less than two years. The military, the FLN, the FIS, and other groups were not given sufficient time to adjust to the new arrangements, and there was no trust or confidence-building period where elites develop a mutual interest in building democracy. The lack of a unifying institution, such as the monarchy in Jordan, to oversee the transition left the country facing a complete unknown after the 1991 elections. Algeria also did not have the cohesive society and the strong national identity that are necessary to alleviate the tensions caused by political competition. Consequently, the military resumed its role as the ultimate arbitrator of the country's political system when democracy steered the country toward an unknown path. In summary, Bendjedid was too weak to rule by himself but not strong enough to share power with a group that was not controlled or trusted by the army.

The Islamic Opposition

The strength and ideology of the primary Islamic political group in Algeria, the FIS, helps explain both Algeria's move toward democracy and the subsequent military takeover. Two other Islamic parties, Hammas and Al-Nahda also participated in the 1991 elections but were largely unsuccessful.[5] The FIS resembles the FLN as it is a front composed of groups representing diverse ideological orientations.[6] One faction sought to inject Islam into the current government, while others saw the system as unreformable, and a third faction called for a focus on reforming individuals (Labat 1994). The broad scope of the FIS is symbolized by its two leaders, Ali Belhaj and Abassi al-Madani. Belhaj (1988) is of a more radical bent and has stated that if the FIS was victorious, it would not maintain a Western-style democracy and would implement strict Islamic law. He has also justified the use of violence to achieve Islamic government. Al-Madani (1989), a Modernist, preaches moderation, a slow transition to Islamic government, continuation of democracy, and spreading Islamic values through proselytizing rather than coercion.

The behavior of the FIS also reflected its simultaneous use of hard-line and soft-line approaches. It did organize as a political party and supported the democratic process. However, the creation of the FIS resulted from the 1988 riots, and it took to the streets in 1991 and confronted the military when it wanted a change in the electoral laws. The FIS's record when it controlled a majority of the country's local and regional power was also mixed. Hence, the military and the rest of the country really did not know what to expect when the FIS was on the verge of controlling the National Assembly. The contradictory ways of the FIS continued after the state of emergency was declared, and the civil war began as it had been engaged in the violence. However, the Islamists claim that they were only defending themselves and have called for a negotiated end to the conflict. The FIS's reputation has also been tarnished by the assassination of citizens, government officials, and foreigners by splinter extremist groups, such as the GIA.

It is likely that Bendjedid would have preferred a more reliable opposition. However, the strength and size of the FIS forced the former president to include it in legitimate politics, despite a constitutional ban on religious parties. The FIS's core constituency was the lower middle class that was falling behind as a result of the opening of the economy. The young men had received a poor education in the country's substandard schools and found advancement to better jobs difficult because they did not speak French (Labat 1994). The antigovernment, anti-Western, and antisecular tirades of Belhaj struck a resonant cord with this group. University students, who faced uncertain futures and saw a corrupt government controlling channels for advancement, were also well represented in the FIS. Many voters, however, simply chose the FIS as a protest against the FLN. In all, the FIS's constituency was large enough to ensure its inclusion in legitimate politics (Labat 1994).

The meteoric rise of the FIS was facilitated by the government's weak Islamic credentials. Islam's importance to the FLN was as a cultural heritage more than as a spiritual force, it and certainly was not a guide for governance (Jackson 1977). The FLN was also tarnished by its socialist past, and it did not have any deeply rooted Islamic institutions such as the Saudi and Moroccan monarchies or Al-Azhar to rest upon. In short, the mantle of the defender of Islam was up for grabs. Because religion was not a crucial legitimating factor for the Bendjedid regime (unlike the monarchies in Jordan, Saudi Arabia, and Morocco), an independent religious force was tolerable. It was also hoped that the inclusion of the FIS in the government—as a junior partner—would make democracy acceptable to religious Algerians. Banning the FIS would have led to widespread violence (as it eventually did) and would have delegitimatized the elections. Bendjedid, therefore, had to chance it with the ideologically and tactically two-headed FIS.

Supporting Cleavages

The initial rise and subsequent collapse of democracy in Algeria was also influenced by societal divisions that deepened the religious/secular divide.

Although Algeria is almost exclusively Sunni Muslim, ethnic, class, and linguistic cleavages have exacerbated tensions between the FIS, the government, and the Berber population.

Ethnic. The Arab/Berber cleavage falls along the fault line between religious and secular.[7] Ironically, the Berbers and the Islamists were among the first to protest for more representative government. The Berbers practice a less rigid Islam and view the FIS as trying to enforce an Arab/Muslim cultural identity upon them. They also resent the government's Arabization program and feel that their culture is subject to official persecution. The Islamists, in turn, see the Berbers as untrue Muslims. As a result, there have been several riots on university campuses between Berber and Islamic groups (Vatin 1982). This cleavage also has a regional dimension as the Berbers are concentrated in the Qabliyah region. The Berbers voted overwhelmingly for the socialist parties, and there was talk of secession in these areas if the FIS was allowed to lead the government. The Berbers viewed the military intervention as being preferable to a Bendjedid/FIS–dominated government.

Class/Linguistic. The significance of language in Algerian politics should now be clear. As mentioned, a divide developed between those who spoke French and those who only spoke Arabic. This gap also separated the well educated from the poorly educated and, to some extent, the rich from the poor. The Arabic-speaking, Algerian-educated lower classes viewed the upper-class French speakers as serving the interests of the West and exploiting the poor. Although the government had sponsored Arabization, the FIS was able to direct this anger at the FLN. The FIS, in general, was able to portray itself as the vanguard of Arab/Muslim/Algerian culture. In other words, the Islamists now embodied the values of the revolution. In contrast, the FLN had become corrupt, too Westernized, and represented only the elite. This societal fracture pushed many of Algeria's downtrodden and unemployed to demonstrate and support the FIS.

IRAN

A Case of Poor Leadership

Iran is the case that appears to refute best my argument that Islam does not hinder democracy or facilitate brutal and repressive political systems. However, after I outline the events that led to the Iranian Revolution of 1977–1979 and consider the factors that led to the transformation to an Islamic government, it should be clear that it was a combination of influences—declining regime strength, economic malaise, rapid modernization, a charismatic opposition leader, the mobilization of the lower classes—that facilitated the excesses of the regime of the ayatollahs. Some of these conditions did not exist in the other countries discussed while others were more severe in Iran. The key, however, to understanding the ascendancy of extremism in Iran are the Shah's poor record in governing, the many mistakes he made while in power, and his failure to establish legitimacy.

The weakness of the Pahlavi "dynasty" and the Mohammed Shah regime can be traced to their establishments.[8] Reza Shah, a former military officer, took power through a gradual coup that resulted in the abrogation of the 1906 constitution and the termination of democracy. Reza Shah then began the process of modernizing Iran's infrastructure and administration. As an adherent of Ataturk, Reza Shah also set out to weaken the influence of Islam and the independent power of the clergy. He, however, was forced to abdicate in favor of his son, Mohammed, by occupying British and Soviet forces when he began to court Nazi Germany. Following World War II, the nationalist prime minister, Mohammed Mossadeq, asserted himself at the expense of the young Shah and nationalized the British-owned oil industry in 1951. This action led to a military coup, which was orchestrated by the CIA, that removed Mossadeq and put Mohammed Shah in full control of the government. Hence, both the Pahlavi dynasty and the Mohammed Shah regime came to power without the support of the population and at the expense of more representative government.

The Shah's dependence on outside forces for his ascension to the throne and the removal of the popular Mossadeq tarnished his legitimacy from the beginning (Arjomand 1988). This contrasts with Ibn Saud, who unified Saudi Arabia by leading military campaigns and forming an alliance with the Wahhabi. Also, the Shah's (from this point, unless noted, I will be referring to Mohammed) rise to power when the dynasty was still in its infancy meant that his reign was not ingrained in the country's psyche, as was the case with Hassan II in Morocco. Finally, because Iran had not been occupied by a European power or the Ottomans, the Pahlavis were faced with the task of building a modern nation-state. They, however, erred in mounting a frontal attack on both Iran's religious establishment and its Islamic-based political culture.

The continued existence of monarchies in Jordan, Saudi Arabia, and Morocco is dependent on their ruling families' utilization of Islam as a legitimating factor. The Pahlavis, in contrast, decided that Shia Islam was a regressive force that was hindering the development of a modern society. Consequently, they chose to emphasize an Iranian nationalism that connected to pre-Islamic Persia and ignored 1,000 years of Iranian history (Ahkavi 1980). This was an offense to most Iranians who saw Shia Islam as the cornerstone of their culture and national identity.[9] Ironically, the Iranian clergy supported the coup against Mossadeq because they were concerned about his socialist leanings. However, after the Shah felt that he was firmly established in power, he resumed his father's campaign of rapid modernization and concurrent secularization.

The first major clash between the Shah and the *ulama* resulted from his

"White Revolution," a modernization campaign that was to help Iran catch up with countries, such as Japan, by the turn of the century. The *ulama* strongly objected to provisions that gave voting rights to women and minorities and that instituted a massive land reform program. The former flew in the face of Islamic tradition, and the latter directly hurt the clergy, as Iranian religious leaders held large tracts of land that they used to support their religious institutions and seminary students (Tabari 1983). It is important to note that the clergy in Iranian Shia Islam (in contrast to Sunni *ulama*) have traditionally resisted control by the state. Rather, they tend to operate as an opposition force and pressure the government against policies that hurt their interests or are against Islam.[10] Eventually, after adamant opposition by the Ayatollah Khomeini and a period of demonstrations, the Shah proceeded with the entire White Revolution, including the provisions opposed by the *ulama*. From that point, the Shah waged a battle against the influence of Islam and the clergy, which included expelling Khomeini to Iraq, where he continued to vehemently oppose the regime and lead the call for revolution.

Land reform was intended to break the power of the rural aristocracy and the *ulama* and to gain support among the peasants. However, collectivization and the failure of many peasants to make a living forced them to sell their land and move to the cities (Green 1982). The disheartened urban poor eventually became the backbone of the revolution. Many other seeds of discontent were also planted during the 1960s.

- The regime developed a dependency on the United States as vast amounts were spent on American armaments and goods. Americans also flooded to Iran to work in the oil industry, manage industries, and supervise the modernization process. American influence furthered the image of the Shah as being a tool of American interests and replacing Iranian culture with Western culture.

- The government wasted large sums of money on unnecessary projects, such as the development of heavy industries, the construction of a subway system in Tehran, and high-tech weaponry.

- Multiparty democracy was terminated, and the Shah created "majority" and "loyal opposition" parties. At the same time, dissent was repressed, civil liberties were violated, and human rights abuses became common.

- The Shah attempted to modernize Islam by creating a "Religious Corps" and a Department of Religious Propaganda, which preached loyalty to the regime and the wisdom of the Shah's policies. At the same time, the government took control of the religious endowments (the *Vaqf*) from the clergy. The Shah frequently railed against the backwardness of the *ulama* and their hindrance of progress.

- The Shah's pro-Israel stance and Iran's diplomatic relations with the Jewish state also alienated many Iranians, particularly Khomeini.

Social and Political Mobilization

An important consequence of the Shah's modernization campaign was the social and, subsequent, political mobilization of a large segment of the population (Green 1982). Increased access to education and the media, along with opportunities to travel and study abroad, helped many Iranians see the shortcomings of the Pahlavi regime. Two "Islamic Marxist" groups, the *Fedayeen* and the *Mujahadeen* launched various bombings, assassinations, and other acts of insurgency. The secret police, SAVAK, however, was successful in infiltrating and weakening these groups. Iranian groups abroad also began to organize and launched anti-Shah propaganda campaigns in the West. Several intellectuals, most notably Ali Shariati (1979, 1980), Ait Ahmad (1961), Mehdi Barzagan (1976), and Abol Hassan Bani-Sadr (1979), published works criticizing the Shah and called for a remaking of society based on Iranian culture, Islam, egalitarianism, and social justice.[11]

The push of the intellectuals and the middle class for political reform intensified during the 1970s. The Shah called for reform but resisted real change as the large and well-equipped Iranian army and the wealth produced by the oil boom of the early 1970s created the false impression that the regime was on stable ground (Green 1982). The period from 1973 to 1975 was a time of amazing economic growth as the GNP rose by 32 percent, government expenditures nearly tripled, and oil revenues quadrupled from $4 billion to $16 billion. This growth actually hurt the regime as:

- The Shah's refusal to control oil production gave the appearance that he was willing to sell off Iran's most important natural resource at a bargain price to please America and the West.

- The waste of resources during the 1960s on grandiose projects and the glorification of the Shah became even more distasteful as the inadequacy of basic infrastructure, such as water and electric systems, became apparent; given Iran's new wealth, this was intolerable to many Iranians.[12]

- The rapid growth of the economy also caused 41 percent inflation, which, of course, had the most adverse affect on the lower and lower middle classes.

- The incoming wealth, for the most part, ended up in the hands of the wealthy and government officials as the gap widened between the rich and the poor.

The Shah's problems worsened in 1975 when the oil boom ended, and the Iranian economy fell into a rapid decline. By this time, the population of major cities had tripled and a large class of unemployed young men, who had recently emmigrated from rural areas (partly because of the failed land reform scheme) began to show signs of disgruntlement. The intellectuals, the clergy, and a large segment of the middle class had already positioned themselves against the regime. These groups would have been satisfied with a return to the 1906 constitution, which called for a division of power between the monarchy and the parliament, democracy, respect for Islam's role in society, and civil liberties (Arjomand 1988). It was at this point that the Shah's blundering proved to be fatal as the disheartened and disgruntled class did what it has yet to do in the other countries that have been considered—it became politicized and gave its active support to the opposition.

The Fall of the Shah and the Rise of Khomeini

The Shah, following the economic downturn of 1975, committed a number of major errors. The first was his failure to appreciate the widespread discontent in his country. Up to 1977, he continued to attribute the growing unrest and turbulence to the previously mentioned "Islamic Marxist" organizations (Arjomand, 1988). In fact, these groups were relatively small and were largely controlled by the secret police. This led to his second error, the failure to begin the process of opening the political system and initiating real reform. As has been seen in Egypt, Jordan, Morocco, and (to a lesser extent) Tunisia, a move toward pluralization can strengthen an authoritarian regime. Instead, the Shah disbanded the puppet loyal and opposition parties and created a single party, the *Rastakhiz* (Resurgence). The Rastakhiz, however, was not a forum for free political expression and participation, but, rather, it was an organization for propaganda and for mobilizing support for the regime (Salehi 1988).

The intellectuals, the middle class, and, increasingly, state employees easily saw through the scheme and became convinced that the Shah was unreformable.[13] A third mistake was the use of the Rastakhiz, in 1975, for a campaign against corruption and greed, which was mostly aimed at the shopkeepers and merchants of the Bazaar. The Bazaari merchants are traditionally oriented and have provided financial support to the *ulama*. Consequently, many saw the antiprice gouging campaign as an attack on a group that opposed the Shah and an attempt to deflect the blame for Iran's economic woes (Milani 1988). This sense of incompetence and scapegoating was furthered by the constant replacing of the prime minister and the cabinet from 1975 through 1977. A fourth mistake was the Shah's continued dependence on the United States as, by this time, the Shah was consulting with the U.S. government before making major decisions (Bill 1988). However, the unquestioned support given in the Nixon Doctrine was taken away by Carter, as the Shah was becoming a liability.

Another costly error was the continued attack on the religious establishment, particularly the Ayatollah Khomeini. Some of the more revered religious leaders, such as Barzagan and Shariat'madari, maintained a moderate course and called for called for the Shah to institute reform (Bahireyeh 1984). However, their position was weakened as the regime outlawed polygamy, raised the age of consent for marriage, gave women the right to sue for divorce, and switched from the Islamic calendar to the ancient Zoastrian calender. Furthermore, the government newspaper published a blistering and slanderous attack on Khomeini that enhanced his status as leader of the opposition. Khomeini, since his exile, had remained steadfast in his campaign against the Shah, while others had sought accommodation. Also, the mysterious death of Khomeini's son was also blamed on the Shah. Finally, the Shah erred in requesting that Iraq expel Khomeini in 1978, because the Ayatollah went to Paris where he received the attention of the world media (Milani 1988).

I do not have the space to detail the specific events that led to the fall of the Shah in 1978–1979. In short, after a year of demonstrations, strikes, protests, civil disobedience, and sporadic acts of violence, the Shah got on a plane and left. For my purposes, the important aspect of the Iranian Revolution was the mobilization of the urban lower classes and an overwhelming majority of the Iranian population. As has been discussed, this process, for varying reasons, failed to take place in the other countries being considered, with the possible exception of Algeria. The rapid disintegration of the seemingly invincible Pahlavi regime, which Jimmy Carter had called "an island of stability" one year before the Shah's departure, is a reminder of the importance of regime strength and decisionmaking. The fall of the Shah and the rise of Khomeini is also an important lesson in what happens when a leader attempts to separate a political system from its political culture.

Khomeini's eventual consolidation of power following the departure of the Shah was inevitable. He had emerged as the leader of the opposition while in Paris and was the only one who could mobilize the lower classes. In contrast, the liberals, the "Islamic Marxists," and the socialist groups appealed to limited segments of the population. First, the prime minister appointed by the Shah, Shapour Bakhtiar, was forced into hiding. The provisional government eventually fell under Khomeini's control, which was solidified by the war with Iraq in 1980 (Bakash 1986). Soon after, *Sharia* became the law of the land, minorities were persecuted, and rigid Islamic social codes were enforced. That, however, is not the end of the story as Iran began to transform itself and move toward a more participatory form of government after Khomeini's death.

Contextual Factors/Regime Strength

Modernization and the Economy. It is impossible to separate the influence of contextual factors and regime strength because so many of the

Shah's policies related to modernization and the economy helped to cause his own downfall. As mentioned, the White Revolution planted the seeds of discontent in Iran. The land reform program led to massive migration to the cities and the expansion of the disinherited and disheartened class. This group had difficulty finding employment and was alienated by the Western values and culture that were taking hold in Iran's cities. The mobilization of this class was crucial in bringing down the Shah and facilitating Khomeini's rise to power. Modernization and development in Iran also resulted in the wasting of revenue and resources on unnecessary projects, which made the Shah appear to be out of touch and interested only in self-aggrandizement. At the same time, the regime could not deliver electricity and water, which tarnished its credibility with an already skeptical public.

Increased access to education, both in Iran and abroad, led to social mobilization and the subsequent demand for political participation. The university students in Iran and Iranians abroad were among the first to organize in opposition to the Shah and call for reform. Ironically, many of these Iranians, who were educated in order to fill the ranks of the bureaucracy and run Iran's modern industries, instead, turned on the regime and supported the opposition (Green 1982). At the same time, many of the imported modern consumer goods, such as tape recorders and photocopy machines, were used by the opposition to stimulate countermobilization against the regime. In short, the Shah wrongly believed that modernization and economic development could take place without allowing citizens the opportunity for real political participation. Schemes such as the Rastakhiz further alienated the middle class and intellectuals.

The intertwining of modernization and Westernization was another policy that backfired, as Iranians felt that the Shah was subverting Iranian culture and identity to that of the West. The banning of the veil in universities and the switch from the Islamic calendar were offensive to the sensibilities of many Iranians. Emphasizing the symbols of ancient Zoastria and Persia failed to weaken the bond that most Iranians maintained with Islam. The feeling of cultural alienation was exacerbated by Iran's close ties with the United States and the presence of a large number of Americans in the country. Of greatest importance, these anti-Islamic policies and the regime's constant attacks on the *ulama* mobilized the clergy and their allies against the regime. The *ulama*, in turn, preached against the Shah in the mosques and seminaries. It is easy to see the contrast between the Shah and the kings of Morocco, Jordan, and Saudi Arabia who, while modernizing, have emphasized Islamic values.

The Shah's mishandling of the oil boom and the economy, particularly his failure to put the brakes on the rapidly expanding economy, also contributed to his downfall because of the resulting high inflation and unemployment, which had the most severe impact on the lower classes. The dependence on oil hurt the regime when the boom ended in 1975; the government was forced to cut back on spending, and the unemployment problem grew worse. At the same time, many Iranians believed that Iran's oil production was secretly being controlled by the United States (Milani 1988). Finally, a small group (members of the royal family, the military, international businessmen, and foreigners) led extravagant lifestyles while the average Iranian was struggling. Again, an Islamist, the Ayatollah Khomeini, offered the turning away from religion as the source of this corruption, abuse, and an unequal distribution of wealth. The religiously oriented disinherited class was receptive to Islam as the solution.

Legitimacy and Support. The Shah had little leeway in dealing with the strains caused by modernization, the economy, and his own bungling of these matters, because the Pahlavis had never established legitimacy or developed a solid base of support. The Shah, as mentioned, was brought to power by the British and Soviets and kept there by the CIA in 1953. The suspicion that the ruling family was beholden to outside forces and its lack of populist appeal is said to have made the Shah insecure and disdainful of his own people (Saikal 1980). This would explain his dependence on the United States for aid and council, which was sufficient when American support was absolute. However, when the United States began to call for reform and its support for the Shah wavered, the opposition intensified its campaign because it believed that it had U.S. tacit support. At the same time, the Shah vacillated and felt abandoned by his old friends (Bill 1988).

It was the Pahlavi's search for legitimacy and support that led both Reza and Mohammed to modernize and secularize. Both leaders, through modernization, hoped to weaken antagonistic groups, such as the clergy, the merchants of the Bazaar, and the rural landholders, and create new cadres of supporters. As mentioned, Mohammed's land reform program was intended to win over the peasantry. The modernization strategy backfired as the only group that still supported the Shah at the end of his regime was the military. The Bazaaris and the clergy maintained their traditional alliance, with the former providing the financial support for the latter's campaign against the Shah. Ultimately, most of the peasants moved to the city and turned on the regime. Three important "modern" groups—the new middle class, the intellectuals, and the state employees—also defected to the opposition when it became clear that the Shah was not going to initiate serious reform. Ironically, these less religious groups threw their lots in with Khomeini figuring that they would wind up as winners after the revolution (Bakash 1986). They, too, made a fatal strategic error.

The military also abandoned the Shah as soldiers, who were trained to fight foreign armies, refused to fire on fellow citizens and defected in large numbers (Arjomand 1988). If the Shah had acknowledged the new elites and permitted autonomous institutions, such as parties, unions, and private businesses, to develop, he might have cultivated a group with a vested interest in the system. If he had been more cautious in trampling on Islamic sentiments and reached out to moderate clergy, such as Shariat'madari, he might have isolated the more extremist Khomeini. As discussed, King Hassan II and King Hussein, who seem to have learned from the Shah's downfall, provide good contrasts. Iran's Islamic revolution was more a result of one man's poor political judgment and another man's character than a mass desire for a rigid, orthodox Islamic government. This will become clear after the discussion of the Islamic opposition.

The Islamic Opposition

The structure of the Islamic opposition in Iran differed from those in the other countries under consideration because of the independent nature of the clergy in *Shia* Islam. In Iran, the *ulama* remained outside of government control and received most of their funding from private sources. As a result, they have served as an independent pressure group on Iranian regimes (Tabari 1983). Following the announcement of the White Revolution, the subsequent raid on the Ayatollah Khomeini's seminary in Qom, and the Shah's attacks on Islam and the clergy, the *ulama* felt that their interests were seriously threatened and organized to defend them. Although there is a hierarchy in the Iranian religious establishment, variations exist in the political leanings of the highest ranking *ulama*. In addition, there were intellectuals outside of the clergy, such as Shariati, who were also offering Islamic-based ideologies to mobilize opposition to the Shah. However, outside of the "Islamic Marxist" groups, there were no large, organized opposition movements like the Muslim Brotherhood. Hence, I will focus on the ideas and followers of key personalities.

Islamic Marxists. This group is best represented by the previously mentioned Fedayeen and Mujahadeen. These organizations were composed of students and other intellectuals who sought to synthesize Islam and socialism. This type of thought is best represented in the works of Ali Shariati who studied in Paris and was well versed in Marxist thought. Shariati (1979) emphasized the egalitarian ethic in Islam (the community of believers) and Shia Islam's historical role in fighting tyranny. Given that Shariati and his followers called for a synthesis of Marxism and Islam, the two forces that the Shah detested the most, accommodation was neither possible or necessary, as the power of the Fedayeen and Mujahadeen was limited by their small numbers and SAVAK's success in infiltrating these groups. Shariati was, however, quite influential in intellectual circles and taught his ideas at an educational institution, Hosseini-ye Ershad, which was eventually closed by the government. The writings and ideas of Shariati, along with Ahmad (1961), Barzagan (1976), and Bani-Sadr (1979), are credited with stimulating opposition to the Shah in the early 1970s and winning support for the institution of Islamic government. Eventually, these groups, which supported Khomeini during the revolution, fell out of favor when they criticized the increasingly absolute nature of his rule.

Moderates. There were moderate elements in the Iranian religious hierarchy. Most notable among this group was the Ayatollah Shariat'madari. Like Khomeini, he was a *marj'a taqlid*, one of the six highest ranking clergy in Iran. Although he frequently spoke out against the authoritarian and abusive nature of the monarchy, he also called for support of the 1906 constitution. Unlike Khomeini, he did not think that the clergy should run the political system, but, rather, they should pressure from the outside for adherence to *Sharia* and government by Islamic principles (Ahkavi 1980). During the unrest and revolution, he frequently spoke to the Western media and hinted that an Islamic Iran would not necessarily be hostile to the West. However, he and his supporters never gained significant public support because of the Shah's hostility to all religious forces. The cultivation of Shariat'madari and his followers, early on, could have given the regime religious credibility. However, the Shah's unyielding opposition to Islam drove most Iranians to support the more extremist Khomeini.

Khomeini. I have already discussed the genesis of Khomeini's opposition to the Shah in the White Revolution and the attack on his seminary in Qom. At first, he demanded that the Shah institute *Sharia* and Islamic government. However, following his expulsion, he called for a government led by a religious scholar (*viliyat al Faqih*) and the toppling of the regime. In his writings, the theme of cultural treason is quite prevalent as the Shah is constantly portrayed as being a tool of the Americans and the Israelis (Khomeini 1981). The Shah, as a result, had instituted policies that were detrimental to the bulk of the Iranian people and that were destroying the country's moral and social fabric (Khomeini 1981). Khomeini's writings and speeches came back to Iran with his followers, who visited him in Iraq and, later, Paris. Ironically, his expulsion gave him the freedom to openly and vehemently criticize the regime without fear of retribution, which enhanced his credibility and brought him attention. As mentioned, the alleged murder of his son by SAVAK and his refusal to compromise his principles also won him respect.

Khomeini (1981), although explicit in his writing on most matters, was elusive in his proclamations about his plans for Iran after the Shah was gone. At some point, he hinted that he favored democracy and rights for women. However, he was intentionally vague so that he would not frighten the liberals and secular-oriented opposition. The crucial factor that led to his rise to the symbolic leadership of the revolution was his ability to mobilize the lower class through his supporters among the clergy in Iran. Many young lower-class men were not particularly observant, but they were still deferent to the *ulama* and strongly believed in the righteousness of Islam. In the Ayatollah, they saw a principled man who was willing to make sacrifices for the nation (Mattadeh 1985). Eventually, all groups involved in the revolution acknowledged Khomeini's leadership in order to expedite the departure of the Shah. However, the secular-oriented groups, which had instigated the call for reform in the early 1970s, were outflanked after the Shah finally left. After suffering the abuses of the monarchy, they proceeded to suffer the abuses of the ayatollahs.

Supporting Cleavages

The outstanding feature of the Iranian Revolution was the opposition of almost all segments of society to the regime. The groups that had originally opposed the Shah—the clergy, the Bazaari merchants, the intellectuals, and the liberals—were eventually joined by the urban lower class, the middle class, and even government employees. The Shah failed to establish a connection with any segment of Iranian society, with the exception of the rural peasantry (a rapidly shrinking group). It is also important to note that the country's major minority ethnic groups, the Kurds and the Azarbijanis, also supported the revolution. Even the Sunni and Arab minorities threw their lots in with the Shia-dominated revolution. In short, all class, ethnic, regional, and sectarian cleavages became secondary to the cleavage between the Shah and the rest of the country. The Shah also suffered from the perception that he favored Iran's minuscule Bahai and Jewish minorities.

THE REALIGNMENT AND DEALIGNMENT OF POLITICAL CULTURE

Algeria and Iran continue to serves as examples of the necessity of force in keeping countries out of alignment with their political cultures. The Algerian civil war still rages on as of March 1999 with both the army and the Islamic militias engaging in frequent acts of violence against each other and civilians. There are frequent reports of massacres in locations throughout the country with the government and the Islamists laying the blame at each other's feet. The extremist GIA has targeted journalists, foreigners, entertainers, and government officials for assassination, while the military branch of the FIS has called for a truce and negotiations. Neither side appears to be close to obtaining victory, despite the army's claims to the contrary. A National Dialogue Conference in 1994 was boycotted by most opposition parties because the FIS was not invited. Presidential elections, however, took place in November 1995 with two of the four candidates representing Islamic parties. The elections are reported to have been fair, although the FIS was, again, banned from participating. The winner, Liamine Zeroual, who had been serving since being appointed by the military in 1994, stated that he was committed to democracy and parliamentary elections. It is doubtful, however, that Algeria's problems will be solved without the inclusion of the FIS in the process of reconciliation, but only progovernment parties were permitted to run in local and parliamentary elections in 1996 and 1997.

Iran, in the last fifteen years, has moved toward a more open political system, if not a more liberal society. Parliamentary and presidential elections have taken place on a regular basis since 1980, and political parties are permitted if they "do not violate the independence, sovereignty, unity and principles of the Islamic Republic." However, candidates have yet to be allowed to declare partisan affiliation, and no opposition parties have been sanctioned.[14] Significant debate does occur in the Iranian parliament, which usually pits the reformers, supported by President Khatami, against a collection of hardliners. With the country's economy in shambles and a growing number of Iranians chaffing under strict Islamic law, newspaper articles critical of the government have begun to appear and citizens are increasingly free to speak their minds. In sum, Iran is a more democratic country today than it was under the Shah. The likelihood of future change in Iran is signified by the overwhelming victory of the more liberal candidate, Khatami, in the 1997 presidential elections. In May 1998, thousands of Iranians demonstrated in support of the president and his attempts provide a more free and open society.

Algeria and Iran do not support the notion that Islam is conducive to arbitrary government and cannot support democracy. An Islamic group, the FIS, in Algeria led the call for democracy, participated in two sets of elections, and appeared to accept democratic norms. The current civil war is a product of a turbulent history, a military that is used to controlling the political system, a troubled economy, a miscalculation by Chadli Bendjedid, and a divided society. Despite the military's annulment of the 1991 election results and the persecution of the FIS, the Islamists are still prepared to negotiate with the government. Democracy brought Algeria's political system closer to its political culture. If Algeria's government would have become more religious based than is acceptable to most Algerians, elections could have, again, restored the balance. However, many were concerned that the Islamists would terminate the democratic system that brought them to power.

Iran's political system also was taken, by force, away from its political culture. This situation might been resolved without a resort to extremism if it were not for the blundering of the Shah. His refusal to adapt Iran's political system to meet the needs of a rapidly modernizing society led many Iranians to the person who had the greatest potential to bring down the monarchy. The regime that took power after the Shah's departure was characterized by the zeal and extremism that often follow a costly revolution. In this case, the zeal and extremism were of an Islamic nature. In recent years, democracy has begun to take root and more pragmatic policies are being implemented. Algeria and Iran both have long roads to travel before they can be considered democracies. At this point, it should be clear that Islam will not be the force that prevents these two troubled nations, along with the six other countries that have been considered, from developing free and open political systems. The next task is to test this assertion across a large number of cases.

NOTES

1. High ranking officers in the Algerian military often moved into important political positions.

2. Secular opposition parties were slow to form as most key secular opposition leaders had been "eliminated" or fled the country. The now legal socialist party, the Socialist Forces Front, boycotted the elections.

3. The FLN won only fifteen seats, and the Berber-dominated FFS won twenty-five. The second round was for runoffs in districts where no candidate had achieved a majority.

4. The FIS, most likely, would have had the two-thirds majority necessary to change the constitution if the second round of elections had taken place as scheduled.

5. Both of these parties are moderate and remain legal. Hammas has no ties to its Palestinian namesake.

6. For an in-depth analysis of the primary ideological groupings in the FIS, see Labat (1994).

7. Again, religious and secular are relative terms as most Berbers remain believing Muslims.

8. Although the 2,500-year anniversary of the Iranian monarchy was lavishly celebrated by the Shah in 1971, the Pahlavi dynasty dated back only to 1926 and includes only Mohammed and Reza Shah.

9. Iran is the largest Shia majority country, and its adherence to Shia Islam, along with the Persian language and ethnic identity, have separated it from its Sunni Arab neighbors.

10. The Shia contend that the Twelfth *Imam* disappeared from the earthly realm and is in hiding. Until his return from hiding, no government can be deemed truly Islamic. Hence, they have accepted secular rule as long as Islamic principles and *Sharia* are followed. This contrasts to the Sunni *ulama*, who generally tended to sanction whoever was in power and were part of the state apparatus. Also, the resistance of the Caliph, Hussein, and his followers against the majority in a dispute over Caliphal secession created a tradition of Shia martyrdom and opposition to unjust rule. For an in-depth discussions of Shia Islam see Enayat (1982), Guillaume (1954), and Keddie (1983).

11. Hence the term "Islamic Marxists."

12. The Shah's claim that Iran would soon overtake Sweden seemed ridiculous as Tehran was subject to regular blackouts in the early 1970s.

13. It is interesting to note that the Rastakhiz idea came from American-educated political scientists who were familiar with the works of conservative development theorists, such as Huntington and Apter (Green 1982).

14. The government party, the Islamic Republican party, was disbanded in 1987.

7

Islam and Democracy: Cross-National Analysis

RESULTS OF THE CASE STUDIES

The evidence provided in the previous four chapters strongly suggests that Islam does not hinder democracy or facilitate harsh, authoritarian government. Given the ambiguous and amorphous nature of the discussion of government and economics in the basic sources of Islam and in the works of contemporary Islamic political theorists, this conclusion should come as no surprise. Now it is time to examine Islam's influence on political systems and government policies across a broad sample of predominantly Muslim countries and to compare these Muslim countries with developing non-Muslim countries. In the following chapters, I will systematically investigate the relationship of Islam with democracy and human rights, while controlling for the affect of other influences. In this chapter, I will first summarize the factors identified in the case studies that were determined to have significant influences on political systems. The next task will be the operationalization of those influences that can be quantified reliably. I will then develop hypotheses relating to the relationship between Islam and democracy. Finally, I will outline the research design and statistical methods to be used here and in chapter 8 and discuss the results of my hypothesis testing.

The factors that were found to influence the relationship between Islam and democracy in contemporary nation-states can be divided into seven general categories:

1. Historical influences, such as experience with colonial rule, a period of government enforced secularization, and the results of an involvement in international conflict

2. The strength of regimes in terms of their grip on the political system and society as a whole

3. The regime's strategy for dealing with political Islam

4. The strength and ideological orientation of Islamic political groups

5. Contextual factors relating to modernization, economics, and demographics

6. The existence of politicized sectarian, ethnic, linguistic, or class cleavages, which further the divide between secular-oriented and religious-oriented groups

7. The presence of a minority religious group

The first four of these categories cannot be quantified reliably because they deal with relatively abstract concepts, data are not readily available, or they cannot be on placed on a numerical scale.[1] Consequently, I will briefly discuss the hypothesized influence of each of these unquantifiable factors and then discuss and operationalize variables from the last three categories, which can be quantified reliably.

History

Colonialism. Radical Islam appears to be stronger in countries such as Algeria, Syria, and Egypt, which were subject to long, complete, and disruptive periods of colonial rule. In contrast, political Islam takes less of a defensive and extreme form in countries like Morocco and Tunisia, where colonial rule was comparatively short, mild, and left society intact. This difference in colonial experience manifests itself in three ways.

1. There is a stronger lingering hostility toward ideas attributed to the West (liberalism and democracy) and Westernized classes because of their association with the former colonial overlords.

2. This hostility was exacerbated because the systematic attack of the colonial rulers on Islam and tradition was more severe (in countries like Algeria) and more complete.

3. Higher expectations, which were rarely met, were placed on postindependence governments because more suffering and repression took place under colonial rule. As a result, extremist solutions to political, economic, and social woes are more appealing.

The lack of a period of colonial domination can also affect the contemporary relationship between Islam and politics. This was seen in the discussion of Saudi Arabia, where the ascension to power of the Nejdi tribes, which had remained largely isolated from the outside world, over the more worldly Hijazis led to the enforcement of a more rigid and puritanical Islam. The absence of a period of colonial domination also meant that the Sauds, like the Pahlavis in Iran, had to complete most of the process of modernization. In both cases, the modernizing monarchs met with opposition from the *ulama* and Islamic political groups. This conflict over modernization and, concurrently, the integration of ideas and technology from the West also led to a radicalization of opposition religious political groups.

International Conflict. Defeats in wars and other humiliations in the international arena have also served to stimulate and radicalize political Islam. The resurgence of political Islam in Egypt (and much of the Arab world) was partly a result of that country's humiliating defeat in the Six Day War. One of the major complaints of the Islamic Action Front was Syria's siding with the Christians in Lebanon and its refusal to oppose Israeli forces in the 1978 and 1982 wars. Finally, Islamic opposition groups in Saudi Arabia pointed to the military's poor performance in the Gulf War as proof of the ruling family's corruption and incompetence. On the other hand, military success can help in neutralizing Islamic opposition. A prime example of this tendency was Hassan II's use of the Green March and the subsequent occupation of the Western Sahara to rally support for the regime. Also, Sadat's "Islamification" of the "victory" over Israel in 1973 won him temporary favor with Islamic groups in Egypt.

Enforced Secularization. A period of government-enforced secularization also serves to radicalize Islamic groups and to weaken the possibility of accommodation. This was the case, to varying extents, in Iran, Syria, Algeria, Egypt, and Tunisia, where government secularization campaigns led to the formation of Islamic political groups. In contrast, radical Islamic groups are weaker in Jordan and Morocco, where the monarchies and the political systems have remained firmly rooted in Islam. The conflict between uncompromising secular-based regimes, such as the Shah's, and Islamic opposition groups rapidly becomes a zero sum game, which rules out the possibility of the regime opening the system to Islamic groups. Consequently, the opposition becomes more extreme and resorts to violence. In contrast, some Islamic groups and *ulama* in Morocco, Jordan, and Saudi Arabia have determined that utility may be gained from working within a system that is already somewhat Islamic. These actors are not fighting for a complete overhaul of government but, rather, reform. The same process was also beginning to unfold in Egypt, Algeria, and Tunisia, where Islamic groups attempted to enter legitimate politics when leaders, who appeared to be mindful of Islam, replaced secularists.

Table 7.1
Regime Strategies and Their Consequences

Country	Strategy	Result
Egypt	Accommodation/Repression	Minor Democratization
Jordan	Accommodation	Moderate Democratization
Syria	Violent Repression	Secular Authoritarianism
Tunisia	Accommodation/Repression	Minor Democratization
Saudi Arabia	Repression	Islamic Authoritarianism
Morocco	Co-optation/Repression	Moderate Democracy
Iran	Repression	Islamic Revolution/Moderate Democracy
Algeria	Accommodation/Repression	Democracy/Anarchy

Regime Strength

A second factor that shapes Islam's influence on political systems is a decline in the ability of authoritarian regimes to control their respective political systems and societies. Each regime considered in the cases studies faced, or is facing, a crisis of authoritarianism, which was caused by a number of factors:

- economic malaise
- defeat in war
- failure to provide basic services
- denial of civil liberties
- rapid modernization
- unemployment
- dependence on the United States
- corrupt and inefficient bureaucracy

The classes and segments of society that suffered the most from these problems and saw the greatest threat to their way of living usually participated in the formation of Islamic political groups. The weakened regimes were then faced with the dilemma of neutralizing the Islamic opposition.

Regime Strategy

A crucial variable in explaining the relationship between Islam and political systems is the strategies that regimes utilized in dealing with the rise of political Islam and Islamic political groups. I have summarized the strategies used by the regimes and their consequences in Table 7.1. It is obvious that accommodation is usually associated with a move toward increased democracy while repression leads to authoritarianism or violence. If permitting Islamic political groups to enter legitimate politics often leads to accommodation, why did some leaders chose to repress their Islamic oppositions?

- Some regimes, such as those in Syria and Tunisia, were still powerful enough to resist successfully the pressure of the Islamic opposition.
- Leaders, such as the Shah of Iran, overestimated their own strength and undervalued the power of the Islamic movement.
- Radical secularists, such as the Shah and Bourghiba, and Arab socialists, such as Nasser and Assad, viewed Islam as incompatible with their political programs.

The preceding strongly suggests that political Islam is not a dark cloud that overwhelms society and that it is not the force that is repressing democracy in Muslim nations. Islamic political groups are a response to specific sets of social, economic, and political conditions. Most Islamists want access to the political system and are receptive to offers of accommodation by regimes. Ironically, in Tunisia, Syria, and Algeria, Islamic political groups called for greater democracy and were repressed by secular-oriented regimes.

Islamic Political Groups

The nature of the Islamic political groups, of course, plays a role in influencing regime strategy. The moderate/modernist nature of the Muslim Brotherhood in Egypt and Jordan supplied Anwar Sadat and King Hussein with loyal Islamic oppositions, which were brought into the political system to support the regime and to provide outlets for dissent. Also, regimes in Egypt, Morocco, and Jordan helped in organizing and funding moderate Islamic groups. In Egypt, there was also a union of interests in supporting a market economy and countering the influence of radical groups. In Algeria, the FIS's acceptance of democratic norms and its desire for a market economy led Chadli Bendjedid to attempt to bring the Islamists into legitimate politics. The army, however, was unwilling to see if the FIS would, indeed, play by the rules.

I also determined that it was not the radical or extremist nature of the Islamic groups in Syria, Tunisia, and Iran that led political leaders in those countries to adopt a policy of confrontation. The case of Al-Nahda in Tunisia is particularly telling, as that group called for democracy and agreed to work for the implementation of Islamic law through teaching and propagation rather than violence. The Islamic Action Front in Syria also supported democracy and stated that the practice of Islam would be left to individual discretion and would not be enforced by the government. The problematic aspect of the platforms of the IAF, the radical Islamic groups in Morocco, and the Ayatollah Khomeini was their insistence on deposing the existing leadership. Most of these groups, however, moved to these extreme positions only after they became convinced that the regimes in power were unreformable. Most radical groups, which call for the immediate implementation of *Sharia* and which use violence, have usually been marginal.

The last three groups of variables, contextual factors, cleavages, and minority religious groups, which affect Islam's influence on political systems, are quantifiable. Consequently, I will discuss their hypothesized influence and operationalize them in the next sections. By now, it should be clear that the case studies have shown that Islam can be compatible with democracy and does not automatically facilitate harsh, authoritarian government. In order to test this assertion, I have developed an index of Islamic political culture, which will be used to rank the extent to which Islamic political culture influences political systems in twenty-three predominantly Muslim countries. If Islamic political culture does affect political systems, its varying influence on governments in predominantly Muslim countries should explain the variance in levels of democracy and the protection of the individual. In order to provide further evidence that will disconfirm the "Islam Is Everything" explanation, I will control for other factors that influence the establishment of democracy.

HYPOTHESES

Islam

A significant body of evidence has been presented that suggests that Islam does not prevent democracy. At the same time, it cannot be assumed that Islam is conducive to democracy as none of the countries in the cases studies with regimes that are highly influenced by Islamic political culture are democratic. Many political systems throughout the Muslim world, such as Saudi Arabia's, are clearly Islamic based and authoritarian. I have shown that, in some countries, the rise of political Islam was associated with the growth of democracy. Consequently, it is expected that Islamic political culture will not have a significant relationship with levels of democracy.

H₁—Islamic political culture does not affect levels of democracy in predominantly Muslim countries.

Cleavages

Various cleavages, which exacerbate the divide between governments and Islamic opposition groups, were found to play a significant role in preventing accommodation and pluralization in several of the countries in the case studies. For example, sectarian, regional, and class cleavages all intensified the animosity between the Assad regime and the Islamic Action Front in Syria. It is likely that one of the causes of the turbulence in Algeria and the tranquillity in Morocco is the differing levels of ethnic-based politicization among the Berbers. In Algeria, the Berbers are politicized as an ethnic group, but, in Morocco they, for the most part, are not. The importance of ethnicity's influence on democracy, in general, has been recognized in the growing body of literature on this topic.[2] The presence of ethnic, sectarian, and linguistic cleavages is expected to have a negative relationship with democracy.

H_2—If a country has a politicized sectarian, ethnic, or linguistic cleavage, its political system will be less democratic.

Minority Religious Groups

It was also found that the presence of a minority religion tends to radicalize political Islam. These minority religious groups are often seen as being agents of the West (as they were often favored by the colonial powers) against Islam. The granting of equal civil and political rights to these groups can stimulate anger because Jews and Christians, legally and politically, are considered second-class citizens (dhimminis) in Islamic law, while other religions are not recognized. Also, leaders of regimes and opposition groups often use minority religious groups as scapegoats for their countries' social and economic problems. This was seen in the cases of the substantial Coptic population in Egypt and Jewish and Bahai populations in Iran. In contrast, the minuscule Jewish communities in Morocco and Tunisia do not stimulate the same fear and animosity. Hence, the existence of a minority religious group is also a factor that should repress democracy.

H_3—If a minority religious group exists in a country, then its political system will be less democratic.

Economic Conditions

The relationship between wealth and democracy was established in Lipset's (1959) seminal piece on the social and economic foundations of democracy and was discussed in chapter 1. In short, economic development is viewed as a prerequisite for the growth of democracy. Consequently, it might be that poverty, rather than Islam, is the reason for authoritarian rule in predominantly Muslim countries because many are developing nations and most are poor as well. Following the logic of Lipset and others, wealth should be associated with democracy. However, in this sample, it might be that extreme wealth and poverty will hinder the development of representative government. It is important to remember that, in the case studies, I argued that Saudi Arabia's extreme wealth helps facilitate the tolerance of authoritarian rule. The same is true of other oil rich nations, such as Kuwait, the United Arab Emirates, and Bahrain.

The dislocation caused by rapid economic change, on the other hand, should act against the growth of democratic institutions. In most of the countries considered in the case studies, rapid economic growth and decline were associated with the rise of political Islam. The boom and bust of the Iranian economy and the subsequent revolution and the failure of Algeria's democratic experiment following the same economic trend are excellent examples of this pattern. Rapid growth and decline is often associated with inflation, a widening unequal distribution of wealth, unemployment, and dislocation. Of course these conditions, coupled with an authoritarian political system, are conducive to extremist politics in all countries.

H_4—The greater a country's wealth, the more democratic it will be.

H_5—If a country is extremely wealthy, it will not be democratic.

H_6—If a country experiences rapid economic change, it will be less democratic.

Modernization and Democracy

The first generation of development theorists (Lerner 1958; Rostow 1960; Inkeles 1974; Deutsch 1961) predicted that modernization would lead to social mobilization, political mobilization, and, ultimately, democracy. The case studies, however, illustrated a modernization process that causes disruption, turmoil, and controversy. It is logical, on the one hand, to expect that education, communication, travel, and other benefits of modern society would cause individuals to become politically active and to demand a role in the running of society. However, the rapid change and dislocation, which often result from modernization, have also led people to look to religion for comfort. Very often they are drawn to a form of political Islam that supports authoritarianism. At the same time, some Islamic groups have led the recently socially and politically mobilized in the call for democracy. In short, modernization seems to both support and attack the establishment of democracy. Therefore, I have derived two hypotheses relating to modernization. The first deals with the effect of social mobilization and the second considers the influence of societal disruption.

H_7—The greater the percentage of a country's population that is socially mobilized, the more democratic it will be.

H_8—The greater the disruption caused by the modernization process, the less democratic a country will be.

OPERATIONALIZATION OF VARIABLES

Developing a Measure of Islamic Political Culture

My primary objective in developing an indicator of Islamic political culture is to capture the most important dimensions of contemporary Islamic political ideology. Many typologies that classify Islamic ideologies have been produced in recent years.[3] As mentioned, I will expand on William Shepard's typology (1986), which classifies Islamic ideologies according to two characteristics—*comprehensiveness* and *authenticity*. The independent variable representing the extent to which a political system is influenced by Islamic political culture will combine these two dimensions. It is important to note that this measure deals only with a country's political culture and not with the extent of its religiosity or adherence to Islam.

Comprehensiveness. (Shepard labels this dimension "totalism.") This first dimension relates to the extent to which Islamic law is followed. The implementation of *Sharia*, simply put, is a cornerstone of Islamic government. Included in this dimension is not only Islamic jurisprudence, but also the use of the *Quran, Sunna,* and *Hadith* as the guiding principles of governance. The importance of *Sharia* to Islamic government is best exemplified in the writings and speeches of the theorists and ideologues who were considered for this book. All agreed that Muslims can only reach their potential in a society guided by Islamic law. Adherence to *Sharia* is what separates Islamic governments from other governments. The coding of the *comprehensiveness* dimension is based on the extent to which *Sharia* is used in the following legal spheres:

- Issues of personal status such as marriage and divorce
- The regulation of economic matters such as banking and business practices
- Prescribed religious practice such as restrictions on women's clothing, alcohol, and other practices that are considered against Islam
- The use of Islamic criminal law and punishment
- The use of Islam as a guide for governance

Islamic law, in these areas, varies from Western secular-based legal codes. Consequently, it is expected that the implementation of *Sharia* should produce political systems and public policies that differ from those of non-Muslim countries. By looking at the constitutions of the countries in the sample and various texts, which discuss their political systems, I will determine the extent to which Islamic law is used in each of the previously mentioned five legal spheres above. I will use a 0, 1, 2, 3 scale for each dimension, where zero means that Islamic law is not used and 3 means that it is used exclusively. A nation's scores from each of the five spheres will be totaled (producing a range from 0 to 15) and combined with its score from the second dimension, authenticity.

Authenticity. (Shepard labels this dimension, "acceptance of Western ideas and sciences.") This dimension captures the extent to which, and how, a regime and its leaders are willing to accept ideas, institutions, and technologies that originate outside of the Muslim world. This factor is also an important aspect of contemporary Islamic political culture, because political Islam is often viewed as a movement that seeks to return to traditional and indigenous doctrines and practices (Shepard 1986). Consequently, the way in which a regime accepts, rejects, or accommodates ideas, institutional frameworks, and technologies that are associated with the West must also be included in a measure of contemporary Islamic political culture. This dimension, however, is a more difficult concept to measure, but based on Shepard's description of authenticity, my classification will utilize the following designations, which also proceed on a scale from 0 to 15.

- 0–2. Nonauthentic ideas, institutions, and technologies are accepted without reference to Islam.
- 3–5. Nonauthentic ideas, institutions, and technologies are utilized but are claimed to be compatible with Islam.
- 6–8. Nonauthentic ideas, institutions, and technologies are utilized but are claimed to be improved by Islam's spiritual components.
- 9–11. Nonauthentic ideas, institutions, and technologies are utilized, but efforts are made to trace their roots in Islam.
- 12–15. A complete (or near complete) rejection of nonauthentic ideas, technologies, and institutions.

In contrast to the first dimension (comprehensiveness), this is not an additive scale where scores from each subunit are added to produce a total score. Rather, a nation is placed into one of the five categories and then given score. The inclusion of three possible scores within each grouping is intended to account for the variance among countries placed in a specific category. Also, ideologies and political cultures do not fit perfectly into the groupings. Regimes, such as Turkey's (during the period being considered), which almost completely accepts nonauthentic ideas, institutions, and technologies would receive a 1. In contrast, Senegal's government, which accepts some non-Islamic institutions and technologies without reference to Islam but which also claims that Islam is compatible with Western ideologies, would receive a 3 or a 4. Scoring is based on statements by the government leaders, texts on the political systems, constitutions, and media reports.[4] In coding both dimensions, I also consulted with embassies and personal contacts from the various countries included in the sample. Finally, I sent a survey to members of the Middle East Studies Association in order to see if my scoring would be replicated by others. For an in-depth discussion of how I tested the reliability of the coding process, see appendix I.

Cleavages

An ethnic, sectarian, or linguistic cleavage will exist when more than fifteen percent of a country's population are members of a minority ethnic (Arab/Berber), sectarian (Sunni/Shia), or linguistic group. In addition, this cleavage must be politicized and separate the regime from the minority group in question. A simple 1/0 (presence of a cleavage/absence of cleavage) dummy variable will be utilized.[5]

Religious Minority

I will use 5 percent of a country's population (not including expatriates) as the minimum size for a religious minority. Once again a 1/0 (religious minority/no religious minority) dummy variable will be used. I use a lower cutoff for the religious minority variable because a minority ethnic group or sect must be large enough to threaten the regime. In contrast, a minority religious group is expected to have an affect simply by being a noticeable presence.

Contextual Factors Relating to the Economy

Wealth. I will use GNP per capita as a measure of wealth, because I am concerned with the fortunes of individuals. Supposedly, increasing personal wealth translates into individuals having the time and means to take an interest in politics. In addition, I will test a model omitting the GNP per capita variable and substitute dummy variables separating the wealthier countries (those whose GNP per capita is $8,000 a year or greater) and poorer countries (those with a GNP per capita below $500 per year). As mentioned, the authoritarian regimes of some of the countries in the sample, which are highly influenced by Islamic political culture, are supported by oil wealth.[6]

Economic Growth and Decline. I will also include a variable measuring changes in rates of economic growth as an indicator of the disruption caused by a volatile economy. To capture changes in growth, I will use the annual rate of growth/decline in GNP for the ten-year periods preceding 1980 and 1990. All GNP data have been taken from the World Bank's *World Development Reports* and *Social Indicators of Development*.

Contextual Factors Related to Modernization

The measuring of development is a source of debate and controversy. For my purposes, I am looking for indicators that will capture both the social mobilization and the dislocation that result from development. It is important to note that modernization has had the same disruptive affect on all developing nations, not just Islamic ones. The religious resurgence of the 1980s was felt worldwide as rapid change took place in all societies (Keppel 1994). Hence, it cannot be claimed that antimodernization is unique or inherent to Islamic political culture. In other words, antimodernization—a separate concept from anti-Westernism—is not covered in the indicator of Islamic political culture. Hence, it is important to include variables that capture elements of the modernization process to see if they, independently, are affecting levels of democracy.

Social Mobilization. Literacy captures both the ability to absorb ideas and the potential to be mobilized socially. People who cannot read or write remain isolated from the rest of their society and the world around them. The large illiterate classes in Morocco and other countries support authoritarianism simply by being ambivalent to politics. Literacy enables an individual to realize that there are alternatives to authoritarianism and that he or she has the ability to have a say in determining his or her future.

Societal Displacement. A second indicator, the average annual growth rate of urban areas over a decade, will represent the disruptive elements of modernization. As mentioned, it was migration from the countryside, the rapid growth of cities, and the creation of the urban dispossessed and disheartened class that helped fuel the growth of Islamic political groups. Data for both indicators are taken from the previously noted World Bank publications.

Democracy

Freedom House's seven-point scale (seven represents the most democratic governments) for political rights will be used as the indicator for democracy. Their coding is based on 10 criteria that are common to democracies.[7] I have chosen Freedom House's measurement because it separates civil and political rights. Including civil rights in a definition of democracy adds a "liberal bias." In short, I do not feel that liberalism and democracy are one and the same. It is possible that there may be such a thing as Islamic democracy but not Islamic liberalism. Furthermore, the relationship between Islam and civil liberties will be evaluated in chapter 8. See Table 7.2 for a summary of all variables and indicators.

SAMPLE AND METHODS

The sample includes twenty-three countries with a significant Muslim majority (80 percent of the population), excluding the newly independent

Table 7.2
Summary of Variables and Indicators

Variable	Indicator	Source
Democracy	Political Rights	Freedom House
Islamic Political Culture	Comprehensiveness + Authenticity	developed by author based on Shepard's typology
Cleavages	Dummy Variable: cleavage = at least 15% of pop. and politicized	*World Almanac*, author's determination
Religious minority	Dummy Variable: religious minority = at least 5% of pop.	*World Almanac*
Wealth	1. GNP per capita 2. Dummy Variables for wealthiest/poorest nations	World Bank
Economic Growth/Decline	Change in GNP PC over 10-year period	World Bank
Social mobilization	Literacy rate	World Bank
Displacement	Change in urban % of population	World Bank

republics of the former Soviet Union. A list of countries is included in appendix II. The regression analysis uses observations for each of the twenty-three countries for the years 1980 and 1990, which will provide forty-six units of analysis.[8] The first set of tests are bivariate regressions using only the Islamic political culture variable. I then complete mutivariate regressions, which includes the other independent variables, in order to demonstrate the importance of controlling for other influences when evaluating the relationship between Islam and democracy. I then run a series of bivariate and multivariate regressions, which include a set of twenty-three non-Muslim developing nations. This control group was randomly selected from the World Bank's list of developing nations. The Islamic political culture score for these countries will, obviously, be 0.

FINDINGS

Alignment of Cases

The findings show that Islamic political culture does not have a significant affect on democracy. This insignificant relationship can be seen clearly in Figure 7.1, which shows a relatively random distribution of levels of democracy across the predominantly Muslim nations.[9] The most striking aspect of the alignment of the cases is the overall low levels of democracy among the predominantly Muslim countries, as most of the democracy scores are clustered between one and four. It is also interesting to note that, although four of the five most democratic political systems are predominantly secular, the Islamic political culture scores for most of the least democratic countries range between 0 and 3. This pattern supports my assertion

Figure 7.1
Islam and Democracy

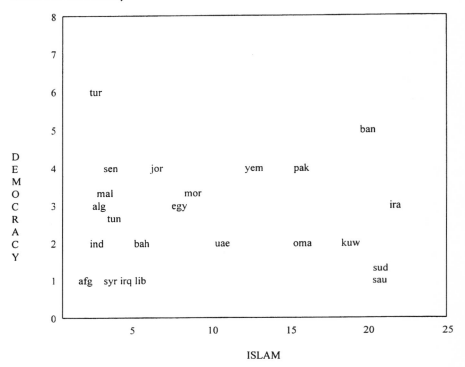

ISLAM

that Islam must be allowed to play a role in government and politics if predominantly Muslim countries are to be democratic. However, the "moderate" countries with Islamic political culture scores between 6 and 15 also appear to be randomly distributed, which contradicts the notion of competition between more religious groups and less religious groups leading to pluralization. Rather, as was the case in Morocco, it is likely that this "moderation" is propagated and enforced by governments. On the other hand, the presence of three of the six countries with the highest Islamic political culture scores at or above the mean democracy score (3) is evidence that Islam might facilitate democracy (see Figure 7.1).

Bivariate Regressions

The regression results presented in Tables 7.3 and 7.4 also provide evidence of the insignificant relationship between Islam and democracy. Table 7.3 includes the results of the bivariate regressions, which includes only the Islamic political culture variable and does not control for the influence of

Table 7.3
Bivariate Regression Results (Islam and Democracy)

Predominantly Muslim Countries (N=46)

Variable	B	Standard Error	Significance	Adjusted R^2
Islamic Political Culture	-.07	.04	no	
Equation			no	.05

Entire Sample (N=92)

Islamic Political Culture	-.06	.03	.02	
Equation			.02	.05

other factors. The Islamic political culture variable is insignificant at the .05 level in the sample of predominantly Muslim countries. Therefore, even when other factors are not considered, Islamic political culture does not explain variations in levels of democracy among Muslim countries. However, when the matching sample of non-Muslim developing nations is added, the Islamic political culture variable becomes significant at the .02 level. This difference between Islamic and non-Islamic developing countries suggests the Islamic political culture is, indeed, an important influence on levels of democracy. However, the low R^2 statistic, .05, tells us that Islamic political culture only tells a very small part of the story of democracy in developing nations. This point will become clear in the multivariate regressions, where control variables representing other factors that influence levels of democracy are added.

Multivariate Regressions

The addition of variables representing ethnic cleavages, minority religions, wealthy nations, poor nations, percentage change in GNP, literacy rates, and percentage change in urban population in Table 7.4 caused the Islamic political culture variable to be insignificant both in the sample of predominantly Muslim countries and the full sample. This finding supports the argument that I have been emphasizing throughout this book. The low levels of democracy in the Islamic world are a result of factors that are not related to Islam. The fact that the variable representing Islamic political culture was insignificant across the full sample demonstrates that, in general, Islamic countries are not significantly less democratic than other developing countries. This finding was substantiated by replacing the continuous Islamic political culture variable with a dummy variable separating the Islamic countries from the rest of the countries in the sample, which was also insignificant.

I also tested to see if there was a significant correlation between changes

Table 7.4

Multivariate Regression Results (Islam and Democracy)

Predominantly Muslim Countries Only (N=46)

Variable	B	Standard Error	Significance	Adjusted R²
Islamic PC	-.02	.04	no	
Ethnic Cleavage	-.72	.55	no	
Minority Religion	-.75	.63	no	
Wealthiest nations	-1.56	.85	.07	
Poorest Nations	-.73	.73	no	
% Change in GNP	-.02	.01	.03	
Literacy	-.03	.02	no	
% Change urban pop	-.10	.13	no	
Equation			.001	.30

Entire Sample (N=92)

Islamic PC	-.04	.03	no	
Ethnic Cleavage	-.60	.38	no	
Minority Religion	-.25	.40	no	
Wealthiest Nations	-.84	.58	no	
Poorest Nations	-.86	.44	.06	
% Change in GNP	-.02	.01	.01	
Literacy	-.01	.03	no	
% change urban pop	-.02	.02	no	
Equation			.001	.23

in the influence of Islamic political culture on political systems and changes in levels of democracy between 1980 and 1990. The correlation coefficient, although negative (-.24), was insignificant.[10] The question now becomes what factors do influence levels of democracy in developing Muslim countries? The low R^2 statistics for both the full sample and the predominantly Muslim sample show that most of the factors that explain the slow emergence of democracy in Islamic countries are extraneous to the model. This finding is not surprising given the importance of the influences related to history, regime strength, regime strategy, and Islamic groups, which were discussed in the case studies but could not reliably be quantified and are not included in the statistical analysis.

A noteworthy finding is the negative association of the "% Change in GNP" variable with democracy. In fact, this was the only variable that was significant at the .05 level in both the full sample and the group of predominantly Muslim countries. This finding was expected as almost all Muslim countries have developing economies and societies. The difficulty of sustaining democracy during periods of rapid economic change was illustrated in the discussion of the rapid growth that preceded the revolution in Iran and in the discussion of the current anarchy in Algeria, which went to a free market economy and then immediately opened its political system. Another interesting finding relates to wealth.[11] The variable representing the most wealthy countries was significant in the predominantly Muslim sample but not in the full sample. This, of course, is a result of the oil rich countries, which are all nondemocratic and comprise about one-fifth of the countries in the sample of predominantly Muslim countries. The influence of extreme wealth is weakened in the full sample with the addition of nonoil–producing wealthy counties, which are often more democratic.

A surprising finding was the *negative* (but insignificant) relationship of literacy, which is often thought of as a prerequisite for participation in politics, with democracy. It is important to remember that Pakistan and Bangladesh, which have low literacy rates and that are somewhat democratic, contradict this assertion. This finding also supports elite theories of democracy, which contend that democracy begins with a consensus among elites and eventually spreads to the rest of the population. Under such conditions, mass literacy is not necessary for the expansion of opportunities for real political participation. At the same time, many leaders, such as the Shah and Bourghiba, encouraged social mobilization, but also saw it as a threat and tried to channel political participation into regime-supporting activities rather than into the development of representative government.

The variable representing displacement, "% Change in Urban Population," was also insignificant (although negative). This was also unexpected, because I hypothesized that urbanization represents the disruption in people's lives that results from modernization. Consequently, this group would be expected to bring about political change or further government repression by causing turmoil. However, the large urban poor class, except in Iran and Algeria, has remained largely ambivalent to politics and has not been mobilized politically. It is also important to note that it was the leadership of educated elites that stimulated this class to action in those two countries rather than a spontaneous desire for political participation. The insignificance of the variables representing minority religions and supporting cleavages was also unexpected, given the importance of these factors in the case studies. It might be that those countries would not be democratic, even if they had homogenous populations. However, it could be that ethnic cleavages and minority religions influence human rights practices, the subject of the next chapter.

CONCLUSION

The results of the statistical analysis in this chapter provide the final piece of evidence in support of my contention that Islam is not the cause of the lack of democracy in predominantly Muslim countries.

- The influence of Islamic political culture on political systems in Muslim nations does not have a significant relationship with levels of democracy.
- Predominantly Muslim nations are not significantly less democratic than other developing nations.
- The appearance that Islamic countries are less democratic than other countries is more a result of the failure to consider the influence of factors relating to history, regime strength, regime strategy, economics, modernization, and the nature of Islamic political groups.
- Oil wealth and rapid economic change have been particularly potent influences on preventing democracy in the Islamic world.

These findings are, of course, tentative. Much has happened in the Islamic world since 1990. Another round of fair elections took place in Jordan, which saw the removal of the Islamic Brotherhood from power. Free elections took place in Yemen, which were followed by a civil war. Democracy remains tenuous in Asian Islamic countries, such as Malaysia, Pakistan, Bangladesh, and Indonesia. Of greatest interest, post–Khomeini Iran has moved toward a more pluralized political system. In short, the Islamic world, despite several setbacks, appears to be inching toward representative government. At the same time, evidence is also accumulating to support the notion that democracy helps to moderate Islamic political groups. This certainly has been true in Jordan, Malaysia, Indonesia, and Turkey and might have been the case if Islamic groups had not been forced from legitimate politics in Egypt, Algeria, and Tunisia. Given the preceding findings, we should spend less time thinking about whether Islam is compatible with democracy and focus on how to create conditions in Islamic countries that facilitate democracy.

The answer to the question of Islam and democracy, however, remains unsettled because an important scenario—Islamic political groups gaining complete control of a government through democratic means—has yet to unfold. Will the Islamists then proceed to destroy the democratic institutions that facilitate their rise to power? Will they limit legitimate political participation to Muslims or to groups and individuals that support an Islamic state? What will happen to the rights of women and non-Muslims? This situation could result in the irony of Islamic political groups destroying the democracies that they have helped to create. Unfortunately, the Algerian army prevented the answering of these questions by nullifying the results of the 1991 elections and outlawing the FIS. The Muslim Brotherhood in Jordan demonstrated relative tolerance when it controlled the Jordanian parliament. Of greatest importance, it accepted its defeat in 1991 elections. However, it is important to remember that the Brotherhood's actions were constrained by King Hussein's dominance of the political system. In summary, I can only conclude that Islam does not hinder democracy, but its ability to facilitate representative government is still in question.

The negative reputation of political Islam is not solely based on the notion that it is antidemocratic. The irrational dark cloud view of political Islam also paints a picture of harsh and abusive government. Consequently, an investigation as to whether Islamic political culture influences how governments treat their citizens is necessary. It might be that, although Islam does not have a significant affect on political systems, it may influence government policies. A discussion of Islam and human rights is pertinent because this relationship is also being debated at the theoretical level and on an ad hoc basis. Once again, cross-national comparison, which controls for the influence of other factors and compares the human rights practices of predominantly Muslim countries with those of other developing countries, is needed. That will be the focus of the next chapter.

NOTES

1. It, for example, would be hard to come up with a scale to score how disruptive colonialism was in a particular country or to judge reliably the extent to which a regime is in control of a political system.

2. Interesting examples of works in the ethnicity and democracy literature are Lijphart (1977), Gurr (1994), and Horowitz (1985).

3. For a discussion of these typologies, see Shepard (1986). In short, Shepard finds that most of the other typologies focus on the same dimensions as his.

4. My primary media sources were Western as I relied heavily on Foreign Broadcast Information Service (FBIS). I also consulted a variety of newspapers, news magazines, and journals from both the West and the countries being considered.

5. Dummy variables place units of analysis (in this case, countries) into two groups. For example, countries with a politicized cleavage will be placed into one group and be given a score of 1 (presence of the variable). Countries without a politicized cleavage will be placed into a second group and will be given a score of 0 (absence of the variable).

6. The continuos GNP per capita variable and the dummy variables representing the poorest and wealthiest countries cannot be tested in the same statistical model, because there is a strong relationship between the continuous GNP variable and the dummy GNP variables. This relationship would alter seriously the results of the statistical tests.

7. These criteria include: election of the chief executive and legislators, fair election laws, all groups in the electorate have a voice in policy formation, existence of more than one legal political party, shifts in power through elections, significant opposition vote, government free of military control, all adults must be eligible to participate in politics, decentralized power, and opposition parties have a role in government.

8. Regression is a statistical test that estimates how much change in a dependent variable is produced by one unit of change in an independent variable. For example, a B statistic of .07, where the independent variable is Islamic political culture and the dependent variable is democracy, would mean that each 1 unit increase in a

country's Islamic political culture score would result in a .07 increase in its democracy score. The t statistic tells whether this relationship is significant and at what level. Generally, a relationship is significant at the .05 level and highly significant at the .01 level. The F statistic tells if the entire regression equation, including all the independent variables, is significant. Finally, the R^2 statistic estimates how much of the variance in the dependent variable is explained by the regression equation. This statistic ranges from 1.0 (a perfect relationship) to 0 (no relationship). For example, an R^2 of .40 would mean that the model captures 40 percent of the factors that influence levels of democracy in the countries in the sample.

Bivariate regression tests the influence of one independent variable on a dependent variable. Multiple regression tests the influence of any number (greater than one) of independent variables on a dependent variable. This is important because multiple regression allows me to examine the relationship between Islam and democracy, while accounting for the influence of other factors that affect levels of democracy.

9. For a list of abbreviations and country names see appendix II.

10. A negative coefficient means that an increase in the influence of Islamic political culture was associated with a decline in levels of democracy.

11. I have only included the results of the regression models using the dummy variables representing the wealthiest and poorest countries in the samples. The continuous GNP per capita variable was insignificant in the tests using both the full sample and the tests using only the predominantly Muslim countries. As mentioned, this, most likely, was caused by the oil rich countries in the sample, which are not democratic.

8

Islam and Individual Rights

ANOTHER CASE OF DECEPTIVE FIRST APPEARANCES?

The debate regarding Islam's influence on human rights policies is reaching rapidly the same intensity as the debate on Islam's influence on democracy. Scholars are examining the *Quran, Sunna, Hadith,* and *Sharia* to determine whether Islam can facilitate the protection of fundamental human rights. At the same time, they are reading the works of modern Islamic political theorists and the various human rights documents, which have been produced in the Islamic world, to see if they are compatible with international human rights declarations. Finally, they are looking at the human rights practices of various Islamic countries on an ad hoc basis. As was the case with democracy, the prognosis for Islam and human rights appears to be grim. The *Quran,* again, is amorphous and can be interpreted to support a variety of positions. The *Sharia* is troublesome, particularly in the areas of rights for women and non-Muslims. Islam, in general, has been interpreted in ways that stress people's obligations to society rather than their rights against government.

It still cannot be concluded that Islam influences human rights policies in predominantly Muslim countries, because that would mean that culture has a significant affect on government policies. If Islam has a limited affect on political systems, as was demonstrated in the previous five chapters, why would it affect public polices? It is also important to remember that it appeared, at face value, that Islam cannot facilitate democracy. However, after rigorous analysis, which controlled for other factors, of the Islam/

democracy question across a large sample of Islamic countries and other developing countries, face values were shown to be deceiving. In this chapter, I will investigate the relationship between Islam and human rights using the same methodology that was employed in the last chapter. Once again, I will take a debate regarding political Islam from the theoretical and ad hoc levels to the empirical level. First, I will look at the general role of culture in human rights. Second, I will briefly discuss arguments regarding Islam's compatibility with human rights. Third, I will test this relationship across a large sample of Islamic and non-Islamic developing countries.

CULTURE AND HUMAN RIGHTS

Cultural Relativism

The role of culture is an important issue for both practitioners and scholars in the field of human rights. Practitioners are faced with the problem of accounting for local cultures when drafting universal human rights documents. Saudi Arabia's refusal to sign the *Universal Declaration of Human Rights* in 1948 was based on the claim that the document violated Islamic law, which already guarantees human rights. Since then, there has been an ongoing debate as to whether there are such things as universal human rights (Donnelly 1989). For example, many Muslims claim that Islam emphasizes economic, social, and collective rights while the West emphasizes political, civil, and individual rights (an-Naim 1995). Consequently, several human rights schemes have been drafted in the Islamic world that vary significantly from international human rights documents. Two particular areas—women's rights and religious freedom—where there is disagreement between Islamic conceptions of human rights and those of the West, will be discussed later.

Another source of controversy regarding culture and human rights is the contention that universal human rights schemes are simply a ploy to strengthen the Western Christian world's dominance of the developing non-Christian countries (Tabandeh 1970). This position has often been advocated by Iran, when its human rights record has been criticized (Mayer 1991). Along the same lines, it is claimed that Western nations have committed a variety of human rights violations, which are usually swept under the rug, while Muslim countries are publicly lambasted. Finally, Western criticism of human rights practices is attributed to long-standing Western hostility to Islam (an-Naim 1995). Adherents to this argument point to the West's condemnation of Saddam Hussein's human rights violations, while it ignores those of Israel in the occupied territories. Furthermore, the West often ignores violations of the rights of Muslims under the control of non-Muslims in Bosnia and various countries in Western Europe. Cultural variations, in short, make it difficult to define human rights and to claim to study them objectively.

The Systematic Study of Human Rights

The dilemmas caused by the defining of universal human rights and cultural relativism help to explain the omission of culture from most cross-national studies of human rights, because the inclusion of variables representing various cultures exposes researchers to two types of criticism.

1. Singling out specific cultures or religions is a sign of bias against the culture(s) in question.
2. A finding that a particular culture or religion is abusive of human rights can be dismissed by the claim that that culture has a different conception of human rights.

A more significant obstacle to including culture in cross-national studies of human rights is defining and operationalizing culture. One needs only to look at Samuel Huntington's (1993) controversial "The Clash of the Civilizations" article in which he divided the world into seven culturally based civilizations. One of the dominant themes in criticisms of Huntington's argument was the artificial nature of Huntington's demarcation of cultures (Ajami 1993). Consequently, culture has not been included in most quantitative studies of human rights.

It is important to note that the scientific study of human rights has only been undertaken in the last fifteen years.[1] Therefore, it is unreasonable to expect that a reliable indicator of culture would be developed in this short period of time, as researchers have yet to agree on a standard measure of human rights. There have, however, been a small number of studies that have accounted for culture. Mitchell and McCormick (1988) included a variable representing countries that experienced British colonial rule, as it was expected that the British would have transmitted Western human rights values to the cultures that they dominated. This variable, however, was found to be insignificant. Park (1987) used the percentage of a country's population that is Christian as an indicator of culture, but this variable was also found to be insignificant.

Both of these indicators of culture stand on shaky theoretical ground. British colonial rule is not a measure of a country's native political culture, but, rather, it is an indicator of the extent to which it is influenced by an external culture. The size of a country's Christian population tells us little about the extent to which its government is influenced by Christian political culture. One needs only to consider Poland and the United States, both of which are overwhelmingly Christian, to see this weakness. This chapter will help to fill the "cultural void" in cross-national studies of human rights through the inclusion of a variable that reliably measures the extent to which a political system is influenced by a political culture. Islamic political culture provides a good case to test culture's influence on human rights, because it is widely believed that Islam facilitates abusive government. Also, Muslims and non-Muslims alike argue that Islam has a unique conception of human rights. In the next section, I will briefly outline how human rights are dealt with in Islam's fundamental texts, *Sharia*, and contemporary Islamic human rights schemes.

ISLAM AND HUMAN RIGHTS

The Basic Sources

The *Quran, Hadith*, and *Sunna* do not contain many discussions that deal, specifically, with human rights. As was the case with democracy, various *sura* (verses) of the *Quran* can be interpreted to support a variety of positions. Verse 13 of chapter 44, for example, calls for mutual understanding and cooperation between people and states that a person's worth is based on one's moral conduct toward others. This type of language appears to be very supportive of respect for individual rights. However, the same verse also mentions that this is especially true of those in the sight of God. As a result, this verse can be interpreted to apply to Muslims only (al-Naim 1995). The fact that the *Quran* is addressed to "mankind" and "The Children of Adam," not the clergy or other interpreters, also emphasizes the primacy of the individual. It is this respect for the individual and Islam's moral principles that have led many contemporary Muslims to claim that Islam, 1,400 years ago, presented the first program of human rights (Mawdudi 1980). However, Islamic law and tradition have developed over the ensuing 1,400-year period in a manner that facilitates the restriction of human rights.

Islamic Law and Tradition

The three primary forces, *Sharia*, the closing of the gates of *ijtihad* (an individual's right to make his or her own interpretation of Islam when there is no clear precedent in the basic sources), and the precedence of duties over rights, work against the protection of human rights and are as much a result of historical development as they are a product of Islam's basic sources. Following the development of Islam's four schools of jurisprudence, Islamic law and the practice of Islam have remained fixed up to the present day. Also, Islamic jurists and scholars have maintained almost complete control over the interpretation of *Sharia* and Islamic tradition (Traer 1991). Finally, several facets of the *Sharia* appear to place sharp restrictions on human rights. With the closing of the gates of *ijtihad*, Muslims have been compelled to follow the rulings and interpretations of the *ulama* on a body of law that has not changed in this millennium (Piscatori 1986). Given that individuals are denied the right to interpret Islam for themselves and the primacy of following the *Sharia* in Islamic political culture, individual autonomy is severely restricted.

It is also important to remember that Islamic law developed in response to the social conditions of 1,000 years ago. The *ulama's* refusal to reevaluate *Sharia* has led to an Islamic legal system that is based on the conditions of a patriarchal, authoritarian, and traditional society. Two areas, the status of women and the rights of non-Muslims are of particular concern. Mayer's (1991) in-depth study of Islamic law and international law regarding human rights concludes that *Sharia*, in these areas, is incompatible with most international human rights agreements.[2] Restrictions on women can be traced to several verses in the *Quran* and the *Sharia*, which discuss women's intellectual, emotional, and physical inferiority to men. The status of women, however, harkens back to the earlier discussion of cultural relativity as Islamic women, by Western standards, are most definitely second-class citizens.

The views of Muslim women regarding their role in society is another question. Some Muslim women are vocal in their criticism of the status of women in contemporary Muslim societies (see Mernissi 1987, 1988; Sadawi 1982). At the same time, a majority of the women I talked to in Morocco vehemently defended the position of women in Islamic society. Some went as far as claiming that they have it better than Western women, who are expected to work and raise a family. Given the preceding, I am going to sidestep the whole issue of the rights of women in Islamic countries. This, of course, is an important topic, which should be researched and debated. However, I do not have the space to give it due consideration in this chapter. Consequently, women's rights are not covered in the indicators of human rights and civil rights that will be used in the hypothesis testing.

A second area of concern for Mayer (1991) is the rights of religious minorities. According to the *Sharia*, non-Muslims are second-class citizens in Islamic political systems. Jews and Christians (people of the book) are given status as *dhimminis*. They are allowed to practice their religion and to regulate their own internal affairs if they pay a tributary tax (*jizya*). They are not entitled to hold political office, serve in the military, or to convert Muslims. Also, their testimony in court proceedings is not of equal value to that of a Muslim. Although Jews and Christians have fared better in Muslim countries than Muslims and Jews have in the Christian world, there has been a historical pattern of discrimination (Lewis 1993). Finally, according to *Sharia*, pantheists, pagans, and nonbelievers have no rights.

In short, they have the options of conversion or death. This concern regarding the treatment of nonbelievers is supported by the persecution of the Bahai in Iran and guest workers in Saudi Arabia.

Rights versus Obligations and Order

A general area of divergence between Islamic conceptions of human rights and those that are represented in international human rights treaties is whether the needs of the individual or the society take precedence. Liberalism's overwhelming concern is protecting the rights of individuals. Consequently, the primary purpose of human rights schemes developed in the West is to demarcate individual rights that cannot be violated by governments. The Bill of Rights in the United States Constitution is the most noteworthy example of the setting aside of rights for citizens, which shield them from arbitrary use of the power of the state. A reading of the major post–World War II human rights conventions, such as the *Universal Declaration of Human Rights* (1948), *The International Covenant on Economic Social and Cultural Rights* (1966), and *The International Covenant on Civil and Political Rights* (1966) finds the same overriding objective of protecting individual liberties from the whims of government.

Mayer's (1991) analysis of the *Universal Islamic Declaration of Human Rights* (1981) and the *Draft of the Islamic Constitution* (1979) published by the Islamic Research Academy of Al-Azhar University concludes that human rights in these documents are really obligations.[3] This conclusion is not surprising given the strong communitarian ethic in Islam. Muslims do not face God as individuals, but rather as a community (the *umma*) and, a Muslim can best lead a truly Islamic life only in a state governed by *Sharia*. Consequently, the government that enforces *Sharia* is to be obeyed, because it is facilitating the society that will lead to the perfection of mankind. It is therefore an individual's obligation to obey the government and to do well unto others so that the *umma* will remain in God's favor. In short, individuals will benefit from obeying the government and following the law more than from having certain rights against the government protected by the law (Mayer 1991).

Another trend in Islamic societies, which has developed over the past 1,000 years and which could act against the protection of human rights, is an emphasis on order. This stressing of the importance of political order is found in the writing of the famed Muslim sociologist Ibn Khaldun (1958). Khaldun wrote that one of the most important duties of political leaders is to maintain order so that commerce can thrive. This philosophy, for the most part, has been sanctioned by the *ulama* up to modern times, because it was thought that even order based on harsh government was preferable to chaos (Esposito 1991). As a result, the abusive treatment of citizens by governments became acceptable in many Islamic societies. This practice, of course, had no precedence in the *Quran* or the life of the prophet. Today, Islam, as well as being used as a legitimizing tool of authoritarian regimes, is the ideological force that often motivates opposition to abusive government and the *ulama* who support corrupt regimes.

Islam and Human Rights: The Current Record

This perception that Islamic political culture is not conducive to the protection of human rights is supported by the records of countries such as Iran, Sudan, Saudi Arabia, and Pakistan, which have claimed to have governments that are based on *Sharia*. Once again, a second look sheds doubt on this assertion. Iran and Sudan had abusive governments before Islamic-oriented regimes rose to power. Pakistan's human rights record has improved as that country moved toward democracy following General Zia's death. Although the Saudi government is Islamic based, both Islamic and secular-oriented opposition groups have taken it to task for its abuse of human rights. It was found in the case studies that Islamic opposition groups in Syria, Tunisia, Morocco, and Iran frequently listed the failure to protect human rights as one of their major grievances against their respective regimes. Also, secular-based regimes in predominantly Muslim countries, such as Syria and Iraq, are among the worst violators of human rights.

Another important consideration in evaluating the relationship between Islamic political culture and human rights is the record of Islamic countries in signing international human rights treaties. I mentioned that Saudi Arabia refused to sign the *Universal Declaration of Human Rights*. Pakistan, however, not only signed the declaration, but also their UN representative criticized the Saudi contention that the treaty violated Islamic law and principle. Both Donnelly (1989) and Mayer (1991) have found that a majority of Islamic countries have signed the major human rights declarations, and neither could discern a distinct pattern of Islamic countries not signing important human rights agreements. In fact, some have better records in this matter than the United States. Thus, it appears that most Islamic countries have accepted the legitimacy of accepted international norms of human rights protection. The presence of human rights issues in the debate between government and opposition groups is a sign that abusive government is not an accepted aspect of contemporary Islamic political culture.

Another piece of ad hoc evidence against the argument that Islamic political culture is associated with harsh government is the existence of human rights organizations in several Islamic countries. Susan Waltz (1994) documented the development of human rights groups in Morocco, Tunisia, and Algeria. Despite various forms of government repression, these groups have been active in challenging abuses committed by the regimes in their respective countries. Morocco, as a result, created a Minister for Human Rights.[4] It is of interest to note the Islamic groups in Algeria and Tunisia were quite happy to receive the assistance of human rights groups, which have secular-oriented leadership. This suggests that the poor human rights records of many Islamic countries are a result of authoritarian government rather than Islamic political culture. I have already demonstrated that Islam is not the primary cause of authoritarian government in predominately Muslim countries. It is now time to take the examination of the relationship between Islam and human rights from the theoretical and ad hoc level to the level of rigorous cross-national analysis. The sample and methods used will be the same as in chapter 7. Bivariate regressions will be completed for both the sample of Islamic countries and then the full sample with the control group of non-Muslim developing countries. Then, the control variables will be added and multiple regression models will be tested.

HYPOTHESES

Islam, Human Rights, and Civil Rights

It is expected that Islamic political culture will not have a significant influence on human rights protection, as it is difficult to find justification for torture or government-sponsored random acts of violence against individuals in Islamic texts, law, or traditions. Although some Islamic-based regimes have poor human rights records, many have signed various international human rights conventions. On the other hand, given the second-class status of non-Muslims and restrictions on individual behavior in Islamic law, it is probable that Islamic political culture will have a negative influence on levels of civil liberties.

H_{1A}—Islamic political culture will not have a significant influence on human rights protection in predominantly Muslim countries.

H_{1B}—The greater the influence of Islamic political culture on a government, the less it will protect civil liberties.

Cleavages, Human Rights, and Civil Liberties

Ethnic, sectarian, and linguistic cleavages will all have a negative influence on the protection of both human rights and civil liberties. Some of the worst atrocities in recent history have been committed by ethnic groups in control of the state against their rivals. Bosnia, Rwanda, Lebanon, Iraq, and Guatemala are all examples of cases where politicized primordial cleavages have been associated with government-sponsored brutality. The treatment of the Shia in predominately Sunni nations is particularly relevant to Islamic countries. As was seen in the case studies, this abuse has included both arbitrary imprisonment, discrimination, and restrictions on religious practice.

H_2—If a country has a politicized ethnic cleavage, then its government will have a poor record in protecting human rights and civil liberties.

Religious Minorities, Human Rights, and Civil Liberties

The same negative affect is expected when a country contains a religious minority. This relationship should be particularly significant, given the second-class status accorded to Christians and Jews and the rejection of nonbelievers and monotheists in Islamic law.

H_3—If a country contains a significant religious minority, then its government will have a poor record of protecting human rights and civil liberties.

Economic Conditions, Human Rights, and Civil Liberties

Following the logic of the liberal modernization theorists, it is expected that wealth should have a positive relationship with human rights and civil liberties. However, in this sample, it might be that extreme wealth will be associated with the abuse of human rights and civil rights, just as it was associated with authoritarian government, because of the oil-producing countries of the Arabian Peninsula. The dislocation caused by rapid economic change should facilitate harsh government and repression because the dispossessed classes tend to take to violence on a periodic basis. Also, regimes use the importance of fostering economic growth as a rational for denying civil liberties and using force to eliminate dissent.

H_4—If a country is extremely wealthy, then it will have a poor record in protecting human rights and civil liberties.

H_5—If a country is extremely poor, then it will have a poor record in protecting human rights and civil liberties.

H_6—If a country experiences rapid economic change, it will have a poor record of protecting human rights and civil liberties.

Modernization, Human Rights, and Civil Liberties

The social mobilization aspect of modernization should facilitate the protection of human rights and civil liberties. An increased awareness by the citizenry of the activities of government and a push for greater participation will lead the government to be wary of violating human rights and to grant more liberties for the population. At the same time, the process of development disrupts people's lives and society as a whole, which pushes people toward extremist politics and causes turbulence. Governments, in these situations, often respond with martial law, repression, and counter-violence.

H_7—The greater the percentage of a country's population that is socially mobilized, the better its government will protect human rights and civil liberties.

H_8—The greater the disruption caused by the modernization process, the more a government will abuse human rights and civil liberties.

Democracy, Human Rights, and Civil Liberties

There is an obvious expected relationship between democratic government and the protection of human rights and civil liberties. It is highly unlikely that Islamic despots treat their citizens worse than other despots treat their citizens. Most cross-national studies have, indeed, found that democracy is the most significant factor in explaining human rights practices (Cingranelli 1992; Poe and Tate 1994).

H_9—The more democratic a country's political system, the better it will protect human rights and civil liberties.

OPERATIONALIZATION OF VARIABLES

Individual Rights

I have decided to utilize two indicators of individual rights, one for human rights and one for civil liberties. The aspects of *Sharia* and Islamic political culture that appear to act against the protection of individual rights are related to civil liberties rather than human rights. It is very difficult to interpret any aspect of Islamic political culture, be it the basic sources, Islamic law, or traditions, that would sanction the violations of the most fundamental human rights, freedom from torture, freedom from imprisonment, and respect for the sanctity of one's home. However, the emphasis on obligations over duties and the second-class status of non-Muslims may, indeed, lead to violations of civil liberties, such as freedom of speech and freedom of religion. Consequently, I will use variables representing both human rights and civil liberties in the regression analysis.

Human Rights. I will utilize the coding scheme developed by David Cingranelli and the Binghamton University human rights data set project.[5] Scores, which range from 0 to 6, are based on three equally weighted subscores (ranging from 0 to 2) representing the frequency of the use of torture by the government in question, the frequency of disappearances (which are attributed to the government), and the number of political prisoners being held. Zero will represent the lowest level of human rights protection and 6 will represent the highest.

Civil Liberties. Scores for this indicator will, again, range from 0 to 6 with 0 representing the lowest level of civil liberties given to citizens and 6 representing the highest. The civil liberties indicator will be based on three equally weighted subscores (again, ranging from 0 to 2) representing government censorship of the media, restrictions on religious practice, and restrictions on the freedom of assembly. Information for the coding of both the human rights and civil liberties variables is taken from Amnesty International and the State Department annual reports on human rights practices in the world.

Independent Variables

The independent variables to be used in this chapter were discussed in chapter 7 (see Table 7.2).

These variables represent factors such as political culture, ethnic cleavages, religious minorities, wealth, economic growth and decline, social mobilization, and development, which have been included in many quantitative studies of human rights practices. It is important to note that the Freedom House indicator of political rights, which represents democracy, is now a control variable, because democracy has been shown to be an important predictor of human rights practices in previous studies of human rights practices.[6]

FINDINGS

Islam and Human Rights

Alignment of Cases. Figure 8.1 illustrates the insignificant relationship between Islamic political culture and human rights practices, as many of the countries with the worst human rights records, Syria, Iraq, Libya, and Afghanistan (when the Soviet-installed regime was still in power) have had secular-oriented regimes. A closer look at the distribution of cases finds what appears to be a curvilinear relationship between Islamic political culture and human rights as both highly secular and highly Islamic governments, for the most part, have the worst human rights records. In contrast, countries with moderate or mixed political cultures, such as Jordan, Egypt, and the United Arab Emirates, have higher human rights scores. This finding seems logical as extremist governments must repress opposition groups at the opposite ideological pole as well as moderate opposition. It is important to note the tenuous nature of this relationship because of the small

Figure 8.1
Islam and Human Rights

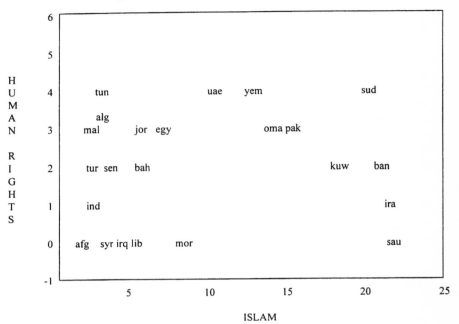

ISLAM

variance across the sample. Eighteen of the twenty-three predominantly Muslim countries have human rights scores at 3 or lower and the highest score in the sample is 4. This tells us that something is repressing human rights in these Islamic nations.

Bivariate Regression. Further disconfirmation that Islamic political culture facilitates the human rights abuse argument can be seen in the results of the bivariate regression in Table 8.1. Although the Islamic political culture variable does have a slightly negative coefficient in both the sample of predominantly Muslim countries and the full sample, the t statistic is insignificant. The R^2 statistics of zero in both samples means that Islamic political culture has almost no measurable influence on human rights practices. This finding supports my assertion that it would be difficult to use religion as a justification for government-sponsored torture and murder. Consequently, it is necessary to evaluate the results of the multiple regressions to see what is repressing human rights in predominantly Muslim countries.

Multiple Regressions. Authoritarian government, as expected, is the factor that is negatively influencing human rights practices in predominantly Muslim countries. The results in Table 8.2 show that democracy is clearly associated with the protection of human rights in both the full sample and

Table 8.1
Bivariate Regression Results: Islam and Human Rights

Predominantly Muslim Countries (N=46)

Variable	B	Standard Error	Significance	Adjusted R²
Islamic Political Culture	-.01	.03	no	
Equation			no	0

Entire Sample (N=92)

Islamic Political Culture	-.4	.41	no	
Equation			no	0

the sample of Islamic countries. Since strong evidence has already been produced that shows that Islam is not repressing democracy in predominantly Muslim countries and that Muslim developing countries are no less democratic than other developing countries, it can also be concluded that Islamic despots are no worse than non-Islamic despots (or secular-oriented despots in predominantly Muslim countries). Wealth, surprisingly, was also positively associated with the protection of human rights in both samples.[7] This could mean that citizens of more affluent societies have the time, means, and ability to monitor government abuses. At the same time, the power and autonomy of groups such as the middle class, which are valuable to the state, have expanded to the point where repression no longer benefits the regime because its economic interests might suffer.

Another interesting finding is the variance in the results between the test using the full sample and the test using the sample of predominantly Muslim countries. First, the F statistic for the regression equation for the predominantly Muslim sample is insignificant while the F statistic for the entire sample is significant at the .01 level. Second, the R^2 statistic (.07) for the sample of Islamic nations is half that (.14) of the full equation. This variance could be a result of the smaller number of cases in the sample of Islamic countries lowering the explanatory power of the model. Another cause of the difference between the two models is the variable relating to social mobilization, literacy. This variable has a positive relationship with human rights protection in both samples, but this relationship is significant in the full sample but not in the sample of Islamic countries. This difference suggests that modernization is leading to social and, perhaps, political mobilization in non-Muslim developing countries but not in the predominantly Muslim developing countries. Here, I am following the logic that modernization leads individuals to believe that they can control their own destiny and, subsequently, to take an interest in what their government is doing. Discovering the cause of this variance is a task for future research.

Table 8.2
Multivariate Regression Results: Islam and Human Rights

Predominantly Muslim Countries Only (N=46)

Variable	B	Standard Error	Significance	Adjusted R^2
Islamic PC	-.01	.04	no	
Ethnic Cleavage	-.24	.51	no	
Minority Religion	-.59	.52	no	
Democracy	.33	.14	.02	
GNP per capita	.02	.01	.06	
% Change in GNP	-.01	.01	no	
Literacy	.02	.02	no	
% Change urban pop	.02	.12	no	
Equation			no	.07

Entire Sample (N=92)

Islamic PC	-.03	.03	no	
Ethnic Cleavage	-.30	.39	no	
Minority Religion	-.26	.40	no	
Democracy	.35	.11	.01	
GNP per capita	.01	.01	.03	
% Change in GNP	-.01	.01	no	
Literacy	.04	.02	no	
% Change urban pop	-.02	.02	no	
Equation			.01	.14

A final finding of note is the overall low explanatory power of both models. This is not surprising, as I stated at the beginning of the chapter that it is unlikely that political culture would have an influence on human rights practices and that it is hard to find justification for torture and abuse in Islamic texts and tradition. It also seems logical that human rights practices are highly subject to random events and that they fluctuate from year to year. Sudan, for example, has an overall record of poor human rights protection but had a comparatively high score of 4 in 1990. Years when nations experience rebellion and turmoil are more likely to have more human rights violations than relatively calm years. It is unlikely that the model picked up trends in countries' human rights practices because observations are included only for 1980 and 1990. Democracy, on the other hand, is less susceptible to yearly fluctuations resulting from random events, which increases the probability that two observations for each country accurately capture its form of government. In short, human rights practices are highly influenced by current events while political systems are more enduring.

Figure 8.2
Islam and Civil Liberties

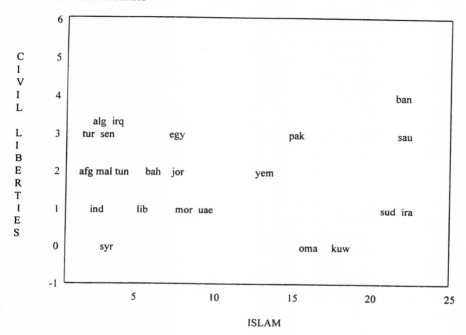

Islam and Civil Liberties

Alignment of Cases. A look at Figure 8.2 shows that, contrary to theo-retical expectations, there is an insignificant relationship between Islamic political culture and civil liberties protection as, once again, there is a ran-dom distribution of cases. As was true with human rights, levels of civil rights protection in predominantly Muslim countries are low. Only Bang-ladesh (with a score of 4) has a civil rights score that is higher than 3. It is doubtful, however, that the influence of Islamic political culture is the factor that is causing these low scores. It should now be apparent that it is authoritarian government, as will be seen in the multiple regressions, that is the primary cause of this trend. Here, there is no hint of a curvilinear relationship as countries with Islamic political culture scores between 6 and 13 are also randomly distributed.

Bivariate Regression. The bivariate regression results, however, tell a dif-ferent story. The Islamic political culture variable has a significant, negative influence on the protection of civil liberties in both the full sample and the sample of predominantly Muslin countries. It is of interest to note that the R^2 statistic is higher for the sample of predominantly Muslim nations (.15) than it is for the full sample (.07). In contrast to what would be expected,

Table 8.3
Bivariate Regression Results: Islam and Civil Liberties

Predominantly Muslim Countries (N=46)

Variable	B	Standard Error	Significance	Adjusted R^2
Islamic Political Culture	-.09	.03	.01	
Equation			.01	.15

Entire Sample (N=92)

Islamic Political Culture	-.06	.02	.01	
Equation			.01	.07

the addition of the control group weakened, very slightly, the influence of Islamic political culture, which further supports my argument that Islamic political culture is not responsible for the repression of individual rights in Muslim nations. At any rate, it is unlikely that the significant relationship between Islamic political culture and the repressing of civil liberties will endure the adding of control variables in the multiple regressions, where we will discover the real cause of poor civil liberties practices in Islamic countries (see Table 8.3).

Multiple Regression. The importance of controlling for other factors is evident, once again, as the addition of the independent variables representing ethnic cleavages, minority religions, democracy, wealth, economic growth and decline, literacy, and displacement caused the Islamic political culture variable to be insignificant in both the full sample and the sample of predominantly Muslim countries. A look at the results in Table 8.4 shows that, as expected, democracy is the most important determinant of levels of civil rights protection in both predominantly Muslim and non-Muslim developing countries. In fact, democracy was the only significant variable in the full sample and one of two (the other being presence of a minority religion) significant variables in the sample of predominantly Muslim countries. The comparatively high adjusted R^2 statistics (.38 for the sample of Muslim countries and .30 for the full sample) attest to the extreme importance of democracy. Logically, it only makes sense that countries with open political systems, would provide their citizens with freedom of expression and assembly, while authoritarian regimes would fear that these rights would lead to demands for political change.

The only other finding of interest is the significant relationship between the presence of a minority religious group and the protection of civil liberties in the sample of predominantly Muslim countries. This comes as a surprise because Islamic law relegates Jews and Christians to second-class

Table 8.4
Multivariate Regression Results: Islam and Civil Liberties

Predominantly Muslim Countries Only (N=46)

Variable	B	Standard Error	Significance	Adjusted R²
Islamic PC	-.03	.03	no	
Ethnic Cleavage	-.33	.42	no	
Minority Religion	.88	.43	.05	
Democracy	.42	.12	.01	
GNP per capita	-.01	.01	no	
% Change in GNP	.08	.07	no	
Literacy	-.01	.01	no	
% Change urban pop	-.03	.09	no	
Equation			.01	.38

Entire Sample (N=92)

Islamic PC	-.03	.02	no	
Ethnic Cleavage	.03	.30	no	
Minority Religion	.35	.31	no	
Democracy	.48	.89	.01	
GNP per capita	-.01	.01	no	
% Change in GNP	.01	.01	no	
Literacy	.01	.01	no	
% Change urban pop	.01	.01	no	
Equation			.01	.30

citizens and denies rights to nonbelievers and polytheists. Consequently, it was expected that the presence of a minority religion in a predominantly Muslim country would lead to restriction of their civil rights. It is important to note that expatriates are not included in the counting of religious minorities so countries such as Saudi Arabia, Kuwait, and the UAE were coded as not having a religious minority. Also, the religious minority variable was not significant in the full sample, which means that minority religious groups in Islamic countries are probably treated no better or worse than those in other developing nations.

CONCLUSIONS

This chapter has provided the final piece of evidence supporting my argument that Islamic political culture does not facilitate abusive or authoritarian government. I found that Islamic political culture does not have a significant relationship with human rights practices or the protection of civil liberties. In the case of human rights, Islamic political culture was found to be insignificant even before control variables were added to the model. The testing of the relationship between Islamic political culture and civil liberties demonstrated, once again, the importance of considering alternative explanations when examining the relationship between Islam and politics. The Islamic political culture variable was significant in the bivariate regressions but was insignificant when the control variables were added in the multiple regressions. The only factor that was consistently found to influence human rights practices and civil liberties was democracy, which replicates the findings of most other cross-national analyses of human rights and civil liberties practices.

The findings in this chapter provide evidence that culture is not a significant determinant of human rights practices. Despite all of the doctrinal and theoretical differences between Islamic law and international law regarding human rights, Islamic countries still uphold roughly the same standards (or lack of standards) as other developing countries. Again, it is very hard to use *Sharia* or Islamic political culture as a justification for torture or government-sponsored violence against individuals. Regimes often do use Islam as a justification for censorship, persecution of religious minorities, and other violations of civil liberties. However, the findings in this chapter show that they do this because they are despots, not because they are following the dictates of Islam. Secular authoritarian regimes in Muslim countries have also not been generous in granting civil liberties to citizens. It is likely that the spread of democracy, not the secularization of politics, will sharply reduce these practices.

NOTES

1. A standard-bearing article in the field is Poe and Tate (1994), which also contains a comprehensive review of the literature in the cross-national study of human rights.

2. Mayer is in no way alone in reaching this conclusion. Scholars and practitioners, both Muslim and non-Muslim, point to the divergence between Islamic law and Western international law in these areas.

3. Human rights scholar Jack Donnelly (1989) makes the same conclusion regarding human rights in Islam really being obligations.

4. The domestic press, political parties, and labor unions frequently take the Moroccan government to task for its human rights record. Many editorials in Moroccan newspapers have argued that human rights abuse is intolerable, because it violates the principles and spirit of Islam.

5. I am grateful to Dr. Cingranelli for sharing this data and for providing me with instructions for coding countries that were not included in the data set.

6. I did not use Freedom House's civil rights score for my civil liberties dependent variable, because some of the factors considered in Freedom House's coding are accounted for in my human rights dependent variable.

7. In this chapter, I used the GNP per capita variable and omitted the dummy variables representing the wealthiest and the poorest nations. The latter were insignificant, meaning that oil wealth does not have a significant relationship with poor human rights practice.

9

Does Culture Matter?

POLITICAL ISLAM: A DARK CLOUD OR PARTLY CLOUDY

The case of political Islam, if commonly accepted notions regarding the relationship between Islam and politics are true, should have provided evidence in support of a relationship between shared values and attitudes and political systems. If Islam, as has been claimed, is a dark cloud that overwhelms societies and causes harsh and authoritarian government, Islamic political culture should repress democracy and facilitate the abuse of human rights and civil liberties. The evidence produced in the case studies and the statistical analysis in this book has disconfirmed this hypothesis. At the same time, I did not find Islamic political culture to be associated with high levels of democracy and the protection of individual rights. Thus, I have provided evidence in support of the argument that Islam is not a monolithic political force that is the primary cause of political outcomes in predominantly Muslim countries. In this final chapter, I will summarize the results that produced these general conclusions, consider why discovering the connection between political culture and politics is so elusive, and suggest ways in which beliefs and values do influence politics.

Statistical Analysis

Three important conclusions were drawn from the statistical tests of the relationship between Islam and democracy and Islam and individual rights.

1. It is important to consider and control for the influence of other factors when examining the relationship between Islam and politics. This was seen in the tests of the relationships between Islam and democracy and Islam and civil rights. The Islamic political culture variable, by itself, had a negative and statistically significant relationship with both democracy and civil liberties. However, this relationship became insignificant after control variables were added. In short, political Islam can adequately explain the politics of Muslim countries only when the analyst ignores everything else.

2. The use of cross-national analysis is necessary in the study of Islam and politics. A focus on individual countries, once again, leads to the conclusion that "Islam Is Everything," because Islamic political resurgence is usually the most visible and attention-grabbing political process in predominantly Muslim countries. However, the comparison of causal factors and processes across a number of countries facilitates the identification of other important variables and the discovery of patterns. Cross-national analysis also destroys the image of political Islam as a monolithic force and leads to the discovery of great variance among the ideologies of Islamic political forces.

3. It is also essential to compare Muslim nations with other developing nations. Yes, most political systems in the Islamic world are authoritarian and have poor human rights records. These problems can be attributed easily to Islam when a researcher focuses exclusively on Muslim nations. However, when other developing nations are added to the analysis, it becomes clear that the countries in the Islamic world are experiencing the same problems as other countries that gained independence from colonial rule after World War II.

It is important to note the limitations of the statistical analysis in chapters 7 and 8. A first concern is that the analysis ends with the year 1990. Many important changes, which have affected levels of democracy and human rights in the Islamic world, have taken place since that time. Democracy is tenuous or is struggling to survive in Indonesia, Pakistan, Malaysia, and Bangladesh, while Kuwait, Iran, and Jordan continue to show signs of becoming more democratic. There have, however, also been setbacks for democracy in Egypt and Algeria. In the area of individual rights, there has been a growing movement in several Muslim countries calling for governments to improve their human rights practices. Another shortcoming of the research design is that it is limited to two observations, 1980 and 1990, for each country. As mentioned in the previous chapter, this is cause for caution in making generalizations about the relationship between Islam and the protection of human rights and civil liberties, because government practices in these areas are highly dependent on random events, which cause policies to fluctuate from year to year.

A final caution regarding the strength of the results is the validity of the measurement tools. Of greatest concern is the coding of the Islamic political culture variable for the predominantly Muslim countries. Although I have consulted with experts and taken surveys to insure that the coding was accurate, there will always be variation, based on information and personal opinion, on how individuals view a phenomenon. In addition, I have spent more than a week in only one of the predominantly Muslim nations. As a result, the possibility always exists that the scores for the Islamic political culture variable simply do not represent reality. My coding, however, were largely replicated in the surveys sent to over 500 scholars of Islam and Islamic countries. A discussion of the coding process and the survey results is presented in appendix I. The Freedom House political rights scores have also been criticized for representing that organization's conservative bias (Bollen 1993). Their democracy scores, however, were the most comprehensive and the most readily available when I began the project in 1992.

Case Studies

The case studies detailed a number of factors that influence the nature of political Islam in specific countries. Once again, evidence was presented contradicting the notion of political Islam as a "dark cloud" and the "Islam Is Everything" explanation of the politics of Muslim countries. Political Islam was shown to be highly dependent on conditions that are unique to specific countries.

- Regimes were shown to play a crucial role in determining what form political Islam takes in their respective nations.
- Islamic political groups represent a variety of ideologies. Often these groups have led the call for representative and humane government. Most have entered legitimate politics when the opportunity has been presented to them.
- The major dilemmas facing predominantly Muslim nations are rapid economic change, dislocation caused by modernization, and colonial rule or dependency on the West—not political Islam.

The case studies also demonstrated the importance of selecting countries that represent a variety of relationships between Islam and politics. Many studies have only included countries or Islamic groups that represent radical or extremist political Islam (Wright 1986; Hiro 1989). Consequently, it is not surprising that other authors have concluded that political Islam is an extremist force that threatens the West and liberal democracy. The addition of cases representing secular-authoritarian regimes and moderate Islamic regimes in this study led to a very different conclusion. An important project for the future is to complete rigorous case study analysis using Muslim countries outside of the Middle East and North Africa. As mentioned, most of the emerging Islamic democracies are located outside of that region. This phenomenon might be related to cultural and historical backgrounds, which are associated with different geographical regions. Hence, it is necessary to end the Middle East/North Africa bias in the study of political Islam.[1]

THE ENDURING QUESTION OF CULTURE AND POLITICS

Political Islam

It is necessary to go back to the discussion of Islam's basic sources and contemporary Islamic political thought in chapter 2 to understand why political Islam is not a dark cloud and why it is difficult to produce substantial evidence supporting the argument that culture influences politics. The primary conclusion of chapter 2 was that Islamic doctrine is very amorphous and vague on matters relating to government and politics. Consequently, a number of political and economic programs have been offered over the years that are claimed to be Islamic. The diversity in these programs was illustrated in the works of Shariati, Qutb, Mawdudi, and Iqbal. In short, it is difficult for Islamic political culture to influence politics and government when so many political programs can be deemed Islamic. In addition, there are important divides within Islam that are not directly related to politics but which may influence political outcomes.

- Sect (Sunni, Shia, and other Islamic sects)
- The four legal traditions within Sunni Islam
- Styles of practice such as the scriptural Islam of the *ulama* and the *Sufi* mystic Islam
- Region (Middle East, North Africa, Asia, Sub-Saharan Africa)

Israeli Judaism

Islamic political culture is not alone in being vague and subject to interpretation, as will be seen in a brief look at Israeli/Jewish and American political cultures. Israeli political culture is an interesting point for comparison because Islam and Judaism are so similar.[2]

- Both religions are legal based and the following of religious law is essential to the development of the community of believers.
- Judaism also shares Islam's emphasis on the community over the individual.
- Religion and politics have also historically been intertwined in Jewish doctrine and tradition.

- Judaism, like Islam, requires a political entity for the achievement of its ultimate destiny.

It is no surprise that one sees the same diversity in Judaism and Israeli/Jewish political culture as has been seen in Islam and Islamic political culture. Again, this is the result of amorphous basic texts with vague principles that leave ample room for interpretation. Consequently, Israeli political culture includes:

- Traditionalists, who have recreated a nineteenth-century Jewish community in modern Israel
- Messianic Nationalists, who hope to bring back the Messiah through territorial acquisition
- Secularists, who call for the complete separation of religion and politics
- Modernists, who emphasize the humanist aspect of Judaism

All (even the secularists) find justification for their positions in the Torah, *Halachah* (Jewish Law), and other Jewish sources. Each of these groups has participated in politics, influences the political system, and shapes Israel's political culture. Consequently, it is difficult to argue that the current Israeli democratic political system is a product of Israeli/Jewish political culture. Israel's political system at the present time happens to be based on a political culture, which includes some Judaic content, that facilitates democracy. To find out why, one must look at the needs of political actors and the factors that were considered in the case studies in chapters 3 through 6.

American Liberalism

An analyst would have the same trouble in attributing America's political and economic systems to its political culture. According to Weber (1958), the Protestant ethic of the Puritans facilitated the development of modern capitalism in the United States. Critics have argued that this development was due to factors relating to geography, natural resources, freedom from international conflict, and a growing population (see the essays in Eisenstadt 1968). In addition, Michael Walzer (1973) writes that the same Puritan ethic actually facilitated the authoritarian streak in American politics. Anthony King (1973) connects the late development and small scale of social programs in the United States to a unique American political culture. This, however, leads one to ask what caused the ideas that make up this political culture to take root in America? Concurrently, one sees variance across time in the extent to which the ideas are held to be true and how they are interpreted. What caused American liberalism to shift from the extreme individualism of the nineteenth century to the welfare state of the twentieth century? It, most likely, was changing economic and social structures in combination with the needs of politicians running for office.

The endurance of the question of the relationship between political culture and major political outcomes, given the preceding, is no accident. A political culture, be it liberalism, Islam, or Judaism, is based on a vague set of ideas and principles, which are subject to interpretation. American political culture has supported both the Republicans and the Democrats.[3] Iranian political culture supported both Khomeini and Shariat'madari. Israeli political cultures supports both Peace Now and those that use Judaism to justify expelling Israel's Arab population. The popularity of the opposing interpretations of each of these country's political cultures is based on social and economic conditions, historical circumstances, and the needs of political actors. Political cultures, in short, can facilitate a variety of political systems and public policies. That is why it is impossible to label political Islam a dark cloud that overwhelms societies. It also explains why the relationship between political culture and politics always appears to be partly cloudy.

OF WHAT IMPORTANCE IS POLITICAL CULTURE?

Political Mobilization

The confirmation of the notion that Islamic political culture does not have a significant affect on political systems and how governments treat their citizens does not mean that political culture does not have an important influence on politics. The case studies suggested that Islamic political culture plays a key role in several political processes. It was shown that Islam plays a crucial part in political mobilization, as Islam is the most potent tool for organizing opposition to harsh, corrupt, ineffective, and authoritarian government in Muslim countries. At the same time, many regimes also use Islam as a means of mobilizing the citizenry on their behalf. The use of the symbols and language of religion as a means of political mobilization is common to all societies. The Catholic church played a key role in liberation movements in Latin American and the Solidarity movement in Poland. Politicians attempting to demonstrate that they are in tune with shared beliefs and values is a universally important aspect of political competition. This point is particularly relevant to American elections, when campaigns center around issues such as flag burning.

Discourse and Political Competition

Political culture is also a crucial element in political discourse and debate. Religion, most certainly, is the primary political language in the Islamic world (Lewis 1988). Earlier, I demonstrated that even secular leaders must make references to Islam and frame calls to action in an Islamic context. Debate on important political, social, and economic issues in Islamic countries almost always has a religious dimension, which can be seen in matters ranging from banking to relations with non-Muslim countries. If Islam plays such an important role in political discourse and debate, it should have some affect on government policies. Although it was found that Islamic political culture does not affect human rights and civil liberties practices, it is important to remember that these are only two of the many spheres in which governments make and implement policy. It could be that Islam affects more mundane matters such as how governments allocate their resources and social policy. The connection between political culture and public policy is a topic for future research.

Public Policies

Two areas where political culture most definitely influences government polices are personal status and social conduct. Most matters relating to personal status, such as marriage, divorce, family law, and inheritance are determined according to religious law in many Islamic countries, which contrasts with America and the West, where these matters are predominantly regulated by secular civil law. As illustrated in the introduction, the regulation of social behavior is also influenced by political culture. Even in a moderate Muslim nation, such as Morocco, it is illegal for unmarried men and women to be seen together in public after dark. The major difference between Islamic and American conceptions of the role of women in society was considered in chapter 8. It appears that political culture, indeed, sets parameters for some government policies and for regimes. This harkens back to the discussion of Morocco in chapter 5, where I concluded that the remarkable staying power of King Hassan II is partly a result of his ability to keep his regime in tune with his country's political culture.

Setting Parameters

The notion of political culture as setting parameters on policies and political systems is logical because political culture is beliefs, attitudes, and values regarding politics that are shared by most members of a society. Elites and government officials are usually not representative of a country's entire population. The average member of the U.S. Senate or House of Representatives is wealthier, better educated, and more interested in public affairs than the average American. This divergence in the values of politicians and the values of citizens ensures that policies will not always correspond to the shared attitudes of the people. Regular elections in the United States and other democracies guarantee that this gap remains narrow. The absence of elections and opportunities for citizens to express their preferences in authoritarian governments means that regimes may take policies further away from the parameters of political culture, which suggests that political culture has a greater influence on political systems in democracies. The fact that few of the countries included in this study are democracies may explain why political culture had little affect on the form of government and policies. Exploring whether political culture has a greater influence on politics and policies in democracies is another project for the future.

Political culture's importance is further validated by the fact that it is something that politicians, even in authoritarian political systems, cannot ignore, as was made evident in the discussion of the Shah. In democracies, governments that fail to pay heed to widely held core values and ideals or that offer policies that contradict these values and ideals are voted out of office. Leaders of authoritarian regimes often pay for this mistake with their careers, or worse yet, their lives. It is important to note that force and repression, as was the case in Iran, Algeria, and Nasser's Egypt, were necessary to dealign political systems from their political cultures. The ultimate failure of the governments, in all of these countries, to repress political Islam is further evidence of the resiliency and enduring value of local political cultures. Also, authoritarian rulers, such as the monarchs in Jordan, Morocco, and Saudi Arabia, who are in tune with their county's political cultures, have enjoyed much better staying power.

Political Systems

The importance of political systems being in synch with political cultures can also be seen in variance in the political structures, institutional arrangements, and legal systems among democracies. One needs to look no further than our unique highly individualist political culture and federalist and decentralized political system for proof. It is, therefore, reasonable to expect that if democracy emerges in the Islamic world, it will take a different form than it does in the West and elsewhere. An Islamic democracy might have a state religion or place more restrictions on civil liberties than Western democracies. Here, it is important to separate liberalism, a political philosophy, from democracy, a form of government. This is not a problem in Asian countries, such as Japan, which do not maintain liberal-based political cultures but which do have democratic governments. As stated in chapter 1, if the ideological foundations of societies vary, so should their political systems.

Types of Political Culture

It is also a mistake to say that some political cultures, such as Islam, cannot support democracy because they are "traditional." As has been seen, Islam can facilitate a variety of ideologies and political programs, which range from modern to traditional, and contemporary Muslim societies also span this traditional/modern spectrum. Consequently, tradition and modernity must have a stronger relationship with social development, economic modernization, and connection to the outside world than they do with religion. This study is of value because it has considered some of the specific factors that influence whether Muslim nations are oriented toward traditional or modern interpretations of Islamic political culture. The foundations (*Sunna, Hadith,* and *Sharia*), principles, and values of Islamic political culture are, for the most part, fixed. Tradition and modernity, however, are not permanent. It is likely that a modern and democratic political Islam will gain strength after the Muslim world recovers from the disruption of rapid change and deals with the West on more even terms.

The Role of the United States

A final consideration is what the United States can do to help facilitate the emergence of a moderate and democratic political Islam. A first step would be to stop portraying political Islam as the next great threat to our security. Yes, various Muslim nations, such as Iran, have threatened American interests. However, we have cordial relations with a much larger number of countries in the Islamic world. Our publicly stated opposition to "Islamic fundamentalism" has caused many moderate Muslims to feel that the United States is "against Islam." At the same time, the emphasizing of religion focuses attention on the historic conflict between Christianity and Islam that goes back to the Crusades. This obsession with political Islam, taken in the context of the decline of Islamic civilization at the expense of Europe, colonialism, and U.S. cultural domination, gives Muslims reasons to believe that America is now the leader of a long-standing Western campaign against their religion.

A second step would be to increase contacts with moderate Islamic political groups. This would weaken the perception that the West is against all forms of political Islam and serve notice that there are tangible benefits for moderation. It would also counter the perception that we favor democracy except in Muslim countries. We should also encourage our Islamic allies to consider opening their political systems, as did King Hussein, to Islamic groups that accept democracy and pluralism. Again, the way to weaken radical Islam appears to be to give moderate Islam an independent political voice. However, after the Algerian tragedy, it is clear that the transition to democracy must be deliberate and guided. We should, however, be adamant in expressing our disapproval of human rights violations by friendly regimes in Islamic countries. As was discussed, many of these violations are committed against the members of Islamic political groups. Standing against such practices would, again, show that we do not make exceptions for authoritarianism when it comes Muslim countries.

A final but important policy area is economic development. Given that the ranks of radical Islamic political groups are usually filled with members of the disheartened and dispossessed classes, we need to encourage economic policies that minimize unemployment and underemployment. It is interesting that we panic when the unemployment rate in this country approaches 8 percent yet we expect developing countries (Muslim and non-Muslim) to accept unemployment rates of 25 percent. The situation in the former Soviet Union, where the high levels of unemployment that have resulted from the transition to a market economy has left the Communist party as a threat to regain control of the government, is relevant. In short, a balance must be struck between economic growth and providing for the basic needs of citizens. If not, radical Islamic groups are ready and willing to fill the void.

NOTES

1. One study that includes two non–Middle Eastern countries is Esposito and Voll's *Islam and Democracy* (1996).

2. For an in-depth comparison of Islam and Judaism, see Rosenthal (1962).

3. This point is more relevant prior to the current era in U.S. politics, when there were significant differences between the two major political parties.

APPENDIX I

The Islamic Political Culture Variable

The purpose of this discussion is to detail the process utilized in determining the reliability of the "Islamic political culture" scores assigned to the predominantly Muslim countries. A discussion of the variable, how I went about assigning scores, and the sources consulted can be found in chapter 7. After I completed my coding, I completed two steps to ensure that the scores assigned were representative of reality.

1. Direct consultation and discussion with embassy citizens, government personnel, and experts from the twenty-three predominantly Muslim countries.
2. A survey of scholars of Islam and politics to see if my coding would be replicated by others.

DIRECT CONSULTATION

Embassies

My objective here was to gain the input of people who are experts or who are residents of the countries in the sample. The first sources I consulted were the embassies of each country. This proved to be fruitful in terms of obtaining information (e.g., constitutions and statements of leaders) but of little help, for several reasons, in gaining assistance in evaluating the reliability of my coding because:

- There was no one at the embassy qualified or permitted to comment on such matters
- The person contacted did not think that a concept such as Islamic political culture could be quantified
- The information provided was obviously biased in a direction that favored the country in question
- The person contacted did not comprehend my definition of Islamic political culture or the dimensions of Islamic political culture being considered

Citizens

The second group of sources consulted were citizens of the countries included in the sample. Here, I was successful in gaining the insights of citizens of twenty of the twenty-three predominantly Muslim countries.[1] These conversations were of tremendous value and led to the fine-tuning of many scores. A particularly important discovery, which resulted from these discussions, was that constitutions and stated government policies do not always represent the extent to which *Sharia* is utilized and enforced. Citizens told me that, in many cases, Islamic law regarding religious practice and personal status was enforced by government officials in the absence of national laws. Without the means to visit each of the twenty-three nations, the input of people who are familiar with daily life in these countries proved to be invaluable.

Experts

I also sought the insights of a third group—experts. This was done through conversations at conferences and other academic meetings, as well as contact by telephone and e-mail. In total, I was able to talk to at least one person who claimed to have an in-depth knowledge of each of the predominately Muslim countries. Once again, a great deal of useful input, which resulted in the modification of scores, was gained. Many experts, however, refused to participate because of their opposition to the quantification of Islamic political culture. It is important to note that I did not ask either the citizens or the experts to provide me with numerical scores for the countries, as I wanted the final coding to be my complete responsibility. As stated, the input and comments of the experts and the citizens were used to fine-tune the coding that I had already completed.

SURVEY

The second method of improving the reliability of the coding was the construction and administration of a survey to determine the extent to

Table A.1
Breakdown of Survey Participation

Response Type	Number	Percent
Completed	49	22
Refusal	21	10
Returned Unfilled	13	06
No Response	135	62
Total	**218**	**100**

which my scoring was replicated by others. I sent out 218 surveys to members of the Middle East Studies Association who listed Islamic studies, political science, or one of the countries in the survey as one of their specialties. Names and addresses were taken from the *1993 MESA Directory*, and the surveys were sent out during April 1994.[2] A breakdown of the responses is presented in Table A.1.

An interesting result of the survey was that twenty-one people took the time to explain why they were opposed to the construction of a quantitative indicator of Islamic political culture. In addition, seven of the scholars who completed the survey expressed reservations regarding my methodology. One scholar was outraged to the point where he called me a "fraud" and labeled my work as "garbage." Most simply expressed doubts regarding the reliability of the coding and as to whether an abstract concept such as Islamic political culture can be measured. The latter issue has been discussed in the body of this book, and none of the dissenters responded to my challenge to label other dimensions of Islamic political culture, which should have been included in the indicator or to suggest alternative coding schemes. The former issue, reliability, was shown not to be a problem by the results of the survey.

The first statistical procedure was to determine the extent to which my coding was replicated by the other scholars. I used Spearman's Rho, which provides a rho statistic representing rank-order correlation. In other words, the extent to which my ranking of countries from the one most influenced by Islamic political culture to the one least influenced by Islamic political culture corresponded to the rankings of the survey respondents. The results of these tests, which compared my rankings against those of each of the survey respondents, are presented in Table A.2. The results show high rank order correlation between my coding and those of the respondents, as all of the relationships are statistically significant, and forty-one out of forty-nine have correlations above .7. In short, there is agreement as to the general extent to which the countries in the sample are influenced by Islamic political culture.

A second set of tests was necessary to see if there was agreement on the Islamic political culture scores of the individual countries in the sample.

Table A.2
Rank Order Correlations

rho statistic between	Number	Percent
.9 and 1.0	02	03
.8 and .9	23	46
.7 and .8	16	33
.6 and .7	08	18
Total	**49**	**100**

Table A.3
Comparison of Mean Survey Country Scores with Coded Scores

Difference Between Mean Survey Score and Coded Score	Number of Cases	Percent of Total Cases
0-.9	25	54
1-1.9	13	29
2-2.9	5	11
3-3.9	1	02
4 and up	2	04
Total	46	100

Here, I tabulated the mean score for each of the countries from the survey responses and compared it to my score for each country. For most countries (thirty-eight of forty-six), the difference between the mean score of the survey respondents and my score was less than two, the major exceptions being Algeria and Afghanistan in 1990. Once again, there was a high level of agreement between my coding and those of the scholars who completed the survey. A comparison of the mean survey scores and my scores is presented in Table A.3.

NOTES

1. I was unable to consult with anyone from Afghanistan, Senegal, or Bahrain.

2. Graduate student members were not surveyed because of high probability that their addresses were not reliable. I want to express my gratitude to the political science department at Binghamton University for funding the survey.

APPENDIX II

Country Abbreviations and Islamic Political Culture Scores

Appendix II
Country Abbreviations and Islamic Political Culture Scores

Country/ Year	Abbreviation	Comprehensive	Authenticity	ISLAMIC PC
Afghanistan 90	afg	0	1	1
Afghanistan 80	afg	0	0	0
Algeria 90	alg	1	2	3
Algeria 80	alg	1	1	2
Bahrain 90	bah	3	3	6
Bahrain 80	bah	3	3	6
Bangladesh 90	ban	13	9	22
Bangladesh 80	ban	9	9	18
Egypt 90	egy	4	4	8
Egypt 80	egy	3	3	6
Indonesia 90	ind	1	1	2
Indonesia 80	ind	1	1	2
Iran 90	ira	12	11	23
Iran 80	ira	13	12	25
Iraq 90	irq	2	2	4
Iraq 80	irq	2	1	3
Jordan 90	jor	3	4	7
Jordan 80	jor	2	4	6
Kuwait 90	kuw	12	7	19
Kuwait 80	kuw	11	8	19
Libya 90	lib	2	4	6
Libya 80	lib	3	4	7
Malaysia 90	mal	1	1	2
Malaysia 80	mal	1	1	2
Morocco 90	mor	4	5	9
Morocco 80	mor	4	6	10
Oman 90	oma	10	6	16
Oman 80	oma	10	6	16
Pakistan 90	pak	8	8	16
Pakistan 80	pak	9	10	19
Saudi Arabia 90	sau	13	10	23
Saudi Arabia 80	sau	12	10	22
Senegal 90	sen	1	2	3
Senegal 80	sen	1	2	3
Sudan 90	sud	13	10	23
Sudan 80	sud	9	6	15
Syria 90	syr	1	2	3
Syria 90	syr	1	2	3
Tunisia 90	tun	1	2	3
Tunisia 90	tun	1	1	2
Turkey 90	tur	1	1	2
Turkey 80	tur	1	1	2
Unit. Ar. Em. 90	uae	5	5	10
Unit. Ar. Em. 80	uae	5	5	10
Yemen (So) 90	yem	6	7	13
Yemen (So) 80	yem	6	8	14

APPENDIX III

Islamic Ideologies

The following is a brief summary of the types of Islamic political ideologies, which are based on the classification scheme developed by William Shepard (1986), that are used in the case studies in chapters 3 through 6.

SECULARISM

Secularist ideologies calls for the following of ideas other than those of Islam in most areas of society. Therefore, religion and state are separate and government is based on "Western" concepts and institutions. Of course, modern science and technology are considered essential to society's development. Religion is relegated to the area of personal observance and the state dominates and regulates religious institutions.

MODERNISM

Modernism occupies an intermediate position between radicalism and secularism in both "authenticity" and "comprehensiveness." Modernists claim that Islam was intended to be flexible and is often congruous to modern Western ideologies. They call for the opening of the gates of *ijtihad* and go to great lengths to show that the original sources, the *Quran* and *Sunna*, are capable of being adapted to modern conditions. However, modernists claim that Islam goes a step further by adding a moral and spiritual dimension that is missing in Godless secular ideologies. Finally, modernist explanations are liberal in controversial areas such as when the use of *jihad* is appropriate, the feasibility of polygamy, and the implementation of religious punishments.

RADICALISM

Radicalism is centered around the fusion of religion and state, and religious doctrine and law serve as guides of action in all areas of both public and private life. However, there is some room for flexibility if no established text can be used as an authority. Science and technology from the West are utilized, although they are separated from their Western sources or traced to Islamic roots. Radicals do not compromise on the complete implementation of *Sharia* or feel the need to demonstrate its similarities with Western legal systems. Shepard (1986) writes that radicals do not see themselves as attempting to turn back the clock but, rather, are moving toward a new golden age. Radicalism differs from modernism in its complete adherence to Islamic law and ambivalence to Western ideas, technology, and institutions.

NEOTRADITIONALISM

The neotraditional orientation stresses gradual change. Modern technology is carefully accepted but is not given any symbolic value, as it is in modernism and radicalism. The neotraditionalist does not favor the rapid transition to Islamic law that radicals do because it may result in mistaken practice or interpretation. Neotraditionalism does call for complete and traditional adherence to Islamic practice in some areas rather than moving toward a modernist interpretation in all areas. Followers of this strain of ideology also hold to local tradition and respect "the value, past depth, and complexity of the Islamic world as represented by the learning of the *ulama*" (Shepard 1986). Neotraditionalists may act violently when they feel the secular world is infringing on their adherence to the traditional lifestyle.

TRADITIONALISM

Traditionalism "embodies an attitude that has not yet internalized the impact Western penetration has had on their society" (Shepard 1986). Traditionalists attempt to shut out all things foreign and hold to tradition and superstition. Colonial rulers and secular rulers are tolerated because their presence is a reprimand from God. However, in the end, God will also punish the forces of evil. As is the case with neotraditionalists, traditionalists would oppose the full implementation of *Sharia* if it entailed any alterations of tradition. Therefore, traditionalism ranks lowest of the ideologies on the modernity scale and at the midpoint, in terms of totalism. None of the political groups or regimes that are discussed in this study fall into the traditional category.

Glossary

Alawi. Splinter Islamic sect of President Assad of Syria. They are not viewed as true Muslims by the Sunni.

Alim. A learned man, Islamic scholar.

Ba'ath. An Arab Socialist political party founded by Michel Aflaq (ruling party in Syria and Iraq).

baraka. Blessing, the notion that a political leader's reign has been blessed by God.

dhimmini. Non-Muslim or non-Muslim religion with protected status; generally, Christians and Jews.

fatwah. An official ruling on a point of Islamic law; the application of Islamic law to a novel situation.

Fedayeen. Freedom fighters.

hadith. The recorded tradition of the words and deeds of Mohammed and his followers.

haj. The pilgrimage to Mecca that every Muslim should make in his or her lifetime.

hijra. The flight of Mohammed from Mecca to Medina in A.D. 622 marks the starting point of the Islamic calendar.

Ihkwan. Brotherhood; the Bedouin who adopted Wahhabi Islam and fought for Ibn Saud during his conquest of Arabia.

ijma. Consensus of the Islamic community; policies in Islamic nations should be based on consensus.

ijtihad. To exert one's self; the right to interpret tradition on an individual basis.

imam. The prayer leader in a mosque; a spiritual leader in Islam.

infitah. The open door, free market economic policy instituted in Egypt by Anwar Sadat.

jahiliyah. Period of ignorance prior to the appearance of Islam; sometimes used to refer to those who do not accept Islam.

jihad. A struggle or campaign waged for God.

jinn. Evil spirits.

jizya. A tax levied on dhimminis.

Marj'a Taqlid. Source of emulation; supreme authority on Islamic law (Iran).

Mujahadeen. Soldiers for God and Islam.

Mutawaeen. Saudi religious police.

Quran. The word of God as revealed to Mohammed; the holy book of Islam.

Rastakhiz. A political party created by the Shah of Iran to support his government.

ribah. Usury; interest.

Sharia. Islamic law.

Shia. The group of sects of Islam that accept Ali (Mohammed's son-in-law) as the prophet's successor. There are doctrinal differences between the minority Shia and the Sunni Muslims.

shorfa. Direct lineage to the prophet, Mohammed.

shura. Consultation between an Islamic ruler and the people.

Sunna. A practice of the Islamic community, based on the life of the prophet, Mohammed.

Sunni. Mainstream or orthodox Islam.

sura. Verses from the Quran.

ulama. Religious scholars and leaders (plural of alim).

umma. The Islamic community.

Vaqf. The religious endowments (property) in Iran.

Viliyat al-Faqih. Government by religious authority (Iran).

Waqf. The religious endowments (property) in the Arab world.

zakat. Tax to benefit the poor.

Bibliography

Abd al-Kadr, Ali Hassan. (1983). *Study on Islamic Economy and Contemporary Transactions.* Jeddah: Dar el Maal al-Islaamiya.

Abduh, Mohammed. (1966). *Theology of Unity.* London: Allen and Unwin.

Abir, Mordechai. (1993). *Saudi Arabia: Government, Society, and the Gulf War.* New York: Routledge.

―――. (1985). *Saudi Arabia in the Oil Era: Regime and Elites.* Boulder: Westview Press.

Aburish, Said. (1994). *The Rise and Coming Fall of the House of Saud.* London: Bloomsbury.

Afghani, Jamal al-. (1969). *The Writings of Jamal al-Afghani.* Cairo: Dar Hara (Arabic).

Afkhami, Gholam. (1985). *The Iranian Revolution: Phanatos on a National Level.* Washington, DC: Middle East Institute.

Agernon, Charles. (1991). *A History of Modern Algeria.* Trenton, NJ: Africa World Press.

Ahkavi, M. (1980). *Religion and Politics in Contemporary Iran.* Albany: SUNY Press.

Ahmad, Ait. (1961). *Westoxification.* Tehran: Unpublished.

Ajami, Fuad. (1993). "The Summoning." *Foreign Affairs* 72: 2–9.

―――. (1982). *The Arab Predicament.* Cambridge: Cambridge University Press.

Almond, Gabriel, and G. Bingham Powell. (1966). *Comparative Politics: A Developmental Approach.* Boston: Little and Brown.

Almond, Gabriel, and Sydney Verba. (1963). (1980). *The Civic Culture Revisited.* Boston: Little and Brown.

―――. (1963). *The Civic Culture.* Princeton: Princeton University Press.

Aly, Abd al-Sayid. (1982). "Modern Islamic Reform Movements: The Muslim Brotherhood in Egypt." *Middle East Journal* 36: 326–42.

Amin, Samir. (1978). *The Arab Nation: Nationalism and Class Struggle*. London: Zed Books.

Amnesty International. (1981, 1991). *Amnesty International Report*. London: Amnesty International.

Anderson, Lisa. (1991). "Political Pacts, Liberalism, and Democracy: The Tunisian National Pact of 1988." *Government and Opposition* 26: 244–60.

———. (1986). *The State and Social Transformation in Libya and Tunisia*. Princeton: Princeton University Press.

Ansari, Hamied. (1984a). "Islamic Militants in Egyptian Society." *International Journal of Middle Eastern Studies* 16: 123–44.

———. (1984b). "Sectarian Conflict in Egypt and the Expediency of Religion." *Middle East Journal* 38: 397–420.

Antoun, Richard, and Donald Quataert. (1991). *Syria: Culture, Society and Polity*. Albany: SUNY Press.

Apter, David. (1968). *Some Conceptual Approaches to the Study of Modernization*. Englewood Cliffs, NJ: Prentice Hall.

Arjomand, Said. (1988). *The Turban for the Crown: The Iranian Revolution*. New York: Oxford University Press.

Ashford, Douglas. (1961). *Political Change in Morocco*. Princeton: Princeton University Press.

Ashrafi, Reza. (1994). "An Essay on Islamic Cultural Relativism in the Human Rights Debate." *Human Rights Quarterly* 16: 255–72.

Ayubi, Nazeh. (1995). *Overstating the Arab State: Politics and Society in the Middle East*. London: I. B. Tauris.

Bahireyeh, Hoseyn. (1984). *The State and Revolution in Iran*. New York: St. Martin's Press.

Bakash, Shaul. (1986). *The Reign of the Ayatollahs: Iran and the Islamic Revolution*. New York: Basic Books.

Bani-Sadr, Abol Hassan. (1979). *Unitarian Economic Programs*. Paris: Editions Islamique (French).

———. (1977). *Principles of Islamic Government*. Tehran: Lidiya.

Bannah, Hassan al-. (1981). *The Memoirs of Hassan al-Bannah*. Karachi: International Islamic Publishing.

Barzagan, Mehdi. (1976). "The Causes of the Decline of Islamic Nations." *Islamic Review* 6: 23.

Batatu, Hanna. (1982). "Syria's Muslim Brethren." *MERIP Reports*, November/December: 12–20

———. (1981). "Some Observations on Syria's Ruling Military Group." *Middle East Journal* 35: 331–44.

Belhaj, Ali. (1988). *The Islamic Solution to Algeria's Problems*. Algiers: Unpublished (Arabic).

Bendix, Reinhard. (1967). "Tradition and Modernity Reconsidered." *Comparative Studies in Society and History* 9: 246–92.

Bill, James. (1988). *The Eagle and the Lion: The Tragedy of American-Iranian Relations*. New Haven: Yale University Press.

Binder, Leonard. (1988). *Islamic Liberalism*. Chicago: University of Chicago Press.

————. (1978). *In a Moment of Enthusiasm: Political Power and the Second Stratum.* Chicago: University of Chicago Press.

————. (1976). *The Study of the Middle East: Research and Scholarship.* New York: John Wiley.

Blalock, Hubert. (1978). *Social Statistics.* New York: McGraw-Hill.

Bligh, Alexander. (1984). *From Prince to King: Royal Succession in Saudi Arabia.* New York: New York University Press.

Bollen, Kenneth. (1993). "Liberal Democracy: Validity and Method Factors in Cross-National Measures." *American Journal of Political Science* 37: 1207–30.

Brown, L. Carl. (1984). *International Politics of the Middle East.* Princeton: Princeton University Press.

Bryner, Rex. (1992). "Economics and Post-Rentier Democratization in the Arab World: The Case of Jordan." *Canadian Journal of Political Science* 25: 69–97.

Burgat, Francois. (1993). *The Islamic Movement in North Africa.* Austin: University of Texas Press.

Carrol, Tarrence. (1986). "Islam and Political Community in the Arab World." *International Journal of Middle East Studies* 18: 185–207.

Chelkwoski, Peter. (1988). *Ideology and Power in the Middle East.* Durham, NC: Duke University Press.

Cingranelli, David. (1992). "Democracy and Human Rights in Less Developed Countries." Paper presented at the American Political Science Association annual meeting. Chicago, IL, September.

Claisse, A. (1987). "Mahkzen Traditions." In *The Political Economy of Morocco,* edited by I. William Zartman. New York: Praeger.

Combs-Schilling, E. (1989). *Sacred Performances: Islam, Sexuality, and Sacrifice.* New York: Columbia University Press.

Cordoso, Fernando, and Enzo Faleto. (1979). *Development and Dependency in South America.* Berkeley: University of California Press.

Cottam, Richard. (1964). *Nationalism in Iran.* Pittsburgh: University of Pittsburgh Press.

Crecelius, Daniel. (1970). "The Course of Secularization in Egypt." In *Religion and Political Development,* edited by Donald Smith. Boston: Little and Brown.

Curtis, Michael. (1981). *Religion and Politics in the Middle East.* Boulder: Westview Press.

Dahl, Robert. (1971). *Polyarchy: Participation and Opposition.* New Haven: Yale University Press.

Davis, Joyce. (1997). *Jihad and Salaam: Profiles in Islam.* New York: St. Martin's Press.

Dawisha, Adeed. (1984). "The Motives of Syria's Involvement in Lebanon." *Middle East Journal* 38: 228–36.

Day, Arthur. (1986). *East Bank–West Bank.* New York: Council on Foreign Relations.

Dekmejian, R. H. (1985). *Islam in Revolution.* Syracuse: Syracuse University Press.

————. (1971). *Nasser's Egypt.* Albany: SUNY Press.

Dennis, Anthony. (1996). *The Rise of Islam and the Threat to the West.* Bristol, IN: Wyndham Hall Press.

Deutsch, Karl. (1961). "Social Mobilization, Change and Political Development." *American Political Science Review* 55: 493–514.

Devlin, Art. (1983). *Syria: Modern State in the Ancient Land.* Boulder: Westview Press.

Diamond, Larry, ed. (1993). *Political Culture and Democracy in Developing Countries.* Boulder: Lynne Rienner.

Donnelly, Jack. (1989). *Universal Human Rights in Theory and Practice.* Ithaca: Cornell University Press.

———. (1984). "Cultural Relativism and Human Rights." *Human Rights Quarterly* 6: 411.

———. (1982). "Human Rights and Human Dignity: An Analytical Critique of Non-Western Conceptions of Human Rights." *American Political Science Review* 76: 306–16.

Donohue, John, and J. Esposito. (1982). *Islam in Transition.* Oxford: Oxford University Press.

Downs, Anthony. (1957). *An Economic Theory of Democracy.* New York: Harper and Row.

Drysdale, Alsdair. (1985). "The Succession Question in Syria." *Middle East Journal* 39: 246–57.

———. (1982). "The Assad Regime and its Troubles." *MERIP Reports,* November/December: 3–11.

Duran, Khalid. (1989). "The Second Battle of Algiers." *Orbis* 33: 403–26.

Dwyer, Kevin. (1991). *Arab Voices: The Human Rights Debate in the Middle East.* Berkeley: University of California Press.

Dye, Thomas. (1990). *American Federalism.* Lexington, MA: Lexington Books.

Eckstein, Harry. (1988). "A Culturalist Theory of Political Change." *American Political Science Review* 82: 789–804.

Edgar, Adrienne. (1987). "The Islamic Opposition in Egypt and Syria: A Comparative Study." *Journal of Arab Affairs* 6: 82–110.

Eickelman, Dale. (1987). "Religion in Polity and Society." In *The Political Economy of Morocco,* edited by I. William Zartman. New York: Praeger.

———. (1976). *Moroccan Islam.* Austin: University of Texas Press.

Eisenstadt, S. N. (1973). *Tradition, Change and Modernity.* New York: Random House.

———. (1968). *The Protestant Ethic and Modernization.* New York: Basic Books.

Enayat, Hamid. (1982). *Modern Islamic Political Thought.* Austin: University of Texas Press.

Entelis, John. (1994). "Political Islam in Algeria: Non-Violent Dimensions." *Current History* 94: 13–17.

———. (1992a). *State and Society in Algeria.* Boulder: Westview Press.

———. (1992b). "Crisis of Authoritarianism in Algeria." *Problems of Communism* 4: 71–87.

———. (1989). *Culture and Counter Culture in Moroccan Politics.* Boulder: Westview Press.

———. (1986). *Algeria: The Revolution Institutionalized.* Boulder: Westview Press.

———. (1980). *Comparative Politics of North Africa.* Syracuse: Syracuse University Press.

Esposito, John. (1991). *Islam and Politics.* Syracuse: Syracuse University Press.

————, ed. (1983). *Voices of a Resurgent Islam*. New York: Oxford University Press.

Esposito, John, and J. Piscatori. (1991). "Democratization and Islam." *Middle East Journal* 45: 426–45.

Esposito, John, and J. Voll. (1996). *Islam and Democracy*. New York: Oxford University Press.

Fathi, Schinni. (1994). *Jordan: An Invented Nation?* Hamburg: Deutsch-Orient Institute.

Fleuhr-Lobban, Carolyn. (1994). *Islamic Society in Practice*. Gainesville: University of Florida Press.

Fried, Robert. (1971). "Communism, Urban Budgets and Two Italies." *Journal of Politics* 33: 1008–1051.

Friedman, Thomas. (1990). *From Beirut to Jerusalem*. New York: Doubleday.

Garfinkle, Adam. (1993). "Jordan." In *The Arab World Following the Gulf War*, edited by J. Heller. Boulder: Lynne Rienner.

Gastil, Raymond. (1981, 1991). *Freedom in the World*. New York: Freedom House.

Gellner, Ernest. (1981). *Muslim Society*. Cambridge: Cambridge University Press.

Ghanouchi, Rachid. (1992). *Transcript of a Lecture Given in Houston, Texas*. Houston: Unpublished.

————. (1986). *Positions of Al-Nahda*. Tunis: Unpublished (Arabic).

Glass, Charles. (1990). *Tribes With Flags: A Journey Curtailed*. London: Secker and Warburg.

Gran, Peter. (1979). *Islamic Roots of Capitalism*. Austin: University of Texas Press.

Green, Jerrold. (1982). *Revolution in Iran*. New York: Praeger.

Gubser, Peter. (1983). *Jordan: Crossroads of Middle East Events*. Boulder: Westview Press.

Guillaume, Albert. (1954). *Islam*. London: Penguin Books.

Gurr, Ted. (1994). *Ethnic Conflict in World Politics*. Boulder: Westview Press.

Halliday, Fred. (1979). *Iran: Dictatorship and Development*. New York: Penguin Books.

Halpern, Manfred. (1967). *The Politics of Social Change in the Middle East and North Africa*. Princeton: Princeton University Press.

Harkabi, Yehoshefat. (1971). *Arab Attitudes Towards Israel*. Jerusalem: Keter.

Heikal, Mohammed. (1983). *Autumn of Fury*. New York: Random House.

Helms, Christine. (1981). *The Cohesion of Saudi Arabia: The Evolution of Political Identity*. London: Croon Helm.

Heper, Martin. (1984). *Islam and Politics in the Middle East*. New York: St. Martin's Press.

Hermassi, Elkab. (1991). "The Islamist Program." In *Tunisia: The Political Economy of Reform*, edited by I. William Zartman. Boulder: Lynne Rienner.

Hinnebusch, Raymond. (1990). *Authoritarian Politics and State Formation in Ba'athist Syria*. Boulder: Lynne Rienner.

————. (1988). *Egyptian Politics Under Sadat*. Boulder: Lynne Rienner.

Hiro, Dillip. (1989). *Holy Wars: The Rise of Islamic Fundamentalism*. New York: Routledge.

Hofferbert, Richard, and Ian Budge. (1990). "Mandates and Policy Output: U.S. Party Platforms and Federal Expenditures." *American Political Science Review* 84: 111–31.

Hofferbert, Richard, and Ira Sharkansky. (1973). "Social Structure and Politics in Subnational Systems." In *Legislatures in Comparative Perspective*, edited by L. Kornburg. New York: David McKay.

Hopwood, Derek. (1992). *Bourghiba of Tunisia: The Tragedy of Longevity*. New York: St. Martin's Press.

———. (1985). *Egyptian Politics and Society*. Boston: Allen and Unwin.

Horowitz, Donald. (1985). *Ethnic Groups in Conflict*. Berkeley: University of California Press.

Hourani, Albert. (1991). *A History of the Arab People*. New York: Warner Books.

———. (1962). *Arab Thought in the Liberal Age*. Oxford: Oxford University Press.

———. (1946). *Lebanon and Syria: A Political Essay*. London: Oxford University Press.

Hudson, Michael. (1991). "After the War: Prospects for Democratization in the Arab World." *Middle East Journal* 45: 407–26.

———. (1982). *Arab Politics: The Search for Legitimacy*. New Haven: Yale University Press.

Humphreys, R. Stephen. (1979). "Islam and Political Values in Egypt, Saudi Arabia, and Syria." *Middle East Journal* 33: 7–18.

Hunter, Shireen. (1986). *The Politics of Islamic Revival*. Bloomington: Indiana University Press.

Huntington, Samuel. (1993). "The Clash of Civilizations?" *Foreign Affairs* 72 (Summer): 22–49.

———. (1992). *Democracy and the Third Wave*. New Haven: Yale University Press.

———. (1991). "How Countries Democratize." *Political Science Quarterly* 106: 579–616.

———. (1967). *Political Order in Changing Societies*. New Haven: Yale University Press.

Huyette, S. (1985). *Political Adaptation in Saudi Arabia*. Boulder: Westview Press.

Ibrahim, Saad. (1980). "Anatomy of Egypt's Militant Islamic Groups." *International Journal of Middle East Studies* 12: 423–45.

Inglehart, Ronald. (1990). *Culture Shift in Advanced Industrial Societies*. Princeton: Princeton University.

Inkeles, Alex. (1974). *Becoming Modern*. Cambridge, MA: Harvard University Press.

International Commission of Jurists. (1982). *Human Rights in Islam*. Geneva: International Commission of Jurists.

———. (1964). *Knowledge and Religious Experience*. Lahore: Islamic Publishing.

Iqbal, Mohammed. (1964). "Islam as a Moral and Political Ideal." In *Thoughts and Reflections of Iqbal*, edited by S. Vahid. Lahore: Islamic Editions.

Islamic Research Academy of Cairo. (1979). "Draft of the Islamic Constitution." *Majilat Al-Azhar* 51: 221.

Ismael, Tareeq. (1985). *Government and Politics in Islam*. London: Frances Pinter.

Israeli, Raphael. (1984). "Islam in Egypt Under Nasser." In *Islam and Politics in the Middle East*, edited by M. Heper. New York: St. Martin's Press.

Jackson, Henry. (1977). *The FLN in Algeria: Party Development in a Revolutionary Society*. Westport, CT: Greenwood Press.

Juhayaman, Ibn-Saayif. (1980). *Revolt for Mecca*. Kuwait: Dar Sawt a-Tali'a.

Jullundhri, Rashid. (1980). "Human Rights in Islam." In *Understanding Human Rights: An Interdisciplinary Study*. Dublin: Irish School of Economics.

Jureidini, Paul. (1984). *The Impact of Social Change on Tribes*. New York: Praeger.

Jurgensmeyer, Mark. (1993). *The New Cold War: Religious Nationalism Confronts the Secular State*. Berkeley: University of California Press.

Kaas, Max, and S. Barnes. (1979). *Political Action and Mass Participation in Seven Democracies*. Beverly Hills, CA: Sage Publications.

Kechichian Joseph. (1993). "Islamic Revivalism and Change in Saudi Arabia." *Muslim World* 40: 80–111.

———. (1986). "The Role of the Ulama in the Politics of the Islamic State: The Case of Saudi Arabia." *International Journal of Middle East Studies* 12: 224–43.

Keddie, Nikki. (1983). *Religion and Politics in Iran*. New Haven: Yale University Press.

Kenz, Ali. (1991a). *Algerian Reflections on Arab Crises*. Austin: University of Texas Press.

———. (1991b). *Algeria: The Challenge of Modernity*. London: Codeseria.

Keppel, Gilles. (1994). *The Revenge of God*. University Park: Pennsylvania State University Press.

———. (1985). *Prophet and Pharaoh: Muslim Extremism in Egypt*. London: Zed Books.

Key, V. O. (1984). *Southern Politics*. Knoxville: University of Tennessee Press.

Khaldun, Ibn. (1958). *The Muqadimah: An Introduction to History*. New York: Pantheon.

Khomeini, Rulluah. (1981). *Islam and Revolution: Writings and Declarations of Khomeini*. London: KPI.

King, Anthony. (1973). "Ideas, Institutions, and the Policies of Governments." *British Journal of Political Science* 3: 291–313, 409–23.

Kiskh, Mohammed. (1974). *Words to the Egyptian People*. Beirut: N.p. (Arabic).

———. (1969). *The Defeat and the Ideological Invasion*. Beirut: N.p. (Arabic).

Klingemann, Hans, I. Budge, and R. Hofferbert (1994). *Parties, Policies and Democracy*. Boulder: Westview Press.

Kramer, Martin. (1996). *Arab Awakening and Islamic Revival: Political Ideas of the New Middle East*. New Brunswick, NJ: Transaction Press.

Labat, Christine. (1994). "Islamic Groups in Algeria." In *Islamism and Secularism in North Africa*, edited by J. Reudy. Washington, DC: Georgetown University Press.

Lerner, Daniel. (1958). *The Passing of Traditional Society*. Glencoe, IL: Free Press.

Lewis, Bernard. (1993). *Islam and the West*. New York: Oxford University Press.

———. (1988). *The Political Language of Islam*. Chicago: University of Chicago Press.

———. (1976). "The Return of Islam." *Commentary* 61:39–49.

———. (1961). *The Emergence of Modern Turkey*. London: Oxford University Press.

Lijphart, Arend. (1977). *Democracy in Plural Societies*. New Haven: Yale University Press.

Lipset, Seymour Martin. (1959). "Some Social Requisites of Democracy: Economic

Development and Political Legitimacy." *American Political Science Review* 53:69–105.

Long, David. (1991). "Stability in Saudi Arabia." *Current History* 90:9–14.

Maamiry, Hamoud al-. (1983). *Islam and Economic Prosperity in the Third World.* New Delhi: Lancer's Books.

Mackey, Sandra. (1987). *The Saudis: Inside the Desert Kingdom.* Boston: Houghton Mifflin.

Madani, Abassi-al. (1989). *The Crisis of Modern Thought and the Islamic Alternative.* Algeria: Dar Rihab (Arabic).

Magnuson, Robert. (1991). "Islamic Reform in Contemporary Tunisia: Unity and Diversity." In *Tunisia: The Political Economy of Reform*, edited by I. William Zartman. Boulder: Lynne Rienner.

Mattadeh, Roy. (1985). *The Mantel of the Prophet: Religion and Politics in Iran.* New York: Simon and Schuster.

Mawdudi, Abul A'al. (1980).*Human Rights in Islam.* Leicester, UK: Islamic Foundation.

Mawdudi, Mawlana. (1967). *Islamic Law and Constitution.* Lahore: Islamic Publications.

Mayer, Ann. (1991). *Islam and Human Rights.* Boulder: Westview Press.

Mazali, M. (1985). *An Open Letter to Bourghiba.* Cairo: Ahram Center for Translation and Publishing.

Mazrui, Ali. (1990). *Cultural Forces in World Politics.* London: James Currey.

Mernissi, Fatima. (1992). *Islam and Democracy: Fear of the Modern World.* Reading, MA: Addison Wesley Publishing.

———. (1991). *The Veil and the Male Elite.* Reading, MA: Addison Wesley Publishing.

———. (1988). *Doing Daily Battle: Interviews with Moroccan Women.* London: Women's Press.

———. (1987). *Beyond the Veil: Male-Female Dynamics in Modern Muslim Society.* Bloomington: Indiana University Press.

Milani, Mohsen. (1988). *The Making of Iran's Revolution.* Boulder: Westview Press.

Mitchell, Neil, and J. McCormick. (1988). "Economic and Political Explanations of Human Rights Violations." *World Politics* 40: 476–98.

Moore, Clement Henry. (1990). "Islamic Banks and Competitive Politics in the Arab World and Turkey." *Middle East Journal* 44: 234–55.

———. (1965). *Tunisia Since Independence.* Berkeley: University of California Press.

Morris, Mary. (1993). *New Political Realities and the Gulf War: Egypt, Syria, and Jordan.* Santa Monica, CA: Rand.

Mossadeq, Rika. (1987). "Political Parties and Power Sharing." In *The Political Economy of Morocco*, edited by I. William Zartman. New York: Praeger.

Munson, Henry. (1993). *Religion and Power in Morocco.* New Haven: Yale University Press.

———. (1988). *Islam and Revolution in the Middle East.* New Haven: Yale University Press.

———. (1986). "The Social Base of Islamic Militancy in Morocco." *Middle East Journal* 40: 267–84.

Nahi, Yahya. (1985). *Islamic Government and the Revolution in Iran.* Glasgow: Royston.

an-Naim, Abdulahi. (1995). "Toward an Islamic Hermeneutics for Human Rights." In *Human Rights and Religious Values,* edited by A. an-Naim et al. Amsterdam: Editions Rodopi.

———. (1987). "Religious Minorities Under Islamic Law and the Limits of Cultural Relativism." *Human Rights Quarterly* 9:1–18.

Nevo, Ilan, and J. Papp. (1994). *Jordan in the Middle East.* Essex, UK: Frank Cass.

Norton, A. Richard. (1995). *Civil Society in the Middle East.* New York: Brill.

———. (1987). *Amal and the Shia: Struggle for the Soul of Lebanon.* Austin: University of Texas Press.

O'Donnell, Guillermo. (1986). *Transitions from Authoritarian Rule: Tentative Conclusions About Uncertain Democracies.* Baltimore: Johns Hopkins University Press.

Olson, Robert. (1982). *Syria and the Ba'ath, 1947–1982.* Princeton: Kingston Press.

Owen, Roger, and C. Tripp. (1989). *Egypt Under Mubarak.* London: Routledge.

Park, Han. (1987). "Correlates of Human Rights: Global Tendencies." *Human Rights Quarterly* 9: 405–13.

Peretz, Don. (1994). *The Middle East Today.* Westport, CT: Praeger.

———. (1983). *Islam: Legacies of the Past, Challenges of the Future.* Croton, NY: North River Press.

Perthes, Voelker. (1995). *The Political Economy of Syria Under Assad.* New York: St. Martin's Press.

———. (1980). "Human Rights in Islamic Political Culture." In *The Moral Interpretives of Human Rights: A World Survey,* edited by K. Thompson. Washington, DC: University Press of America.

Piscatori, James. (1986). *Islam in the Political Process.* Oxford: Oxford University Press.

———, ed. (1983). *Islam in a World of Nation States.* Cambridge: Cambridge University Press.

Poe, Steven, and N. Tate. (1994). "Repression of Human Rights to Personal Integrity in the 1980's: A Global Analysis." *American Political Science Review* 88: 853–72.

Price, David. (1979). *The Western Sahara.* Beverly Hills, CA: Sage.

Pye, Lucien. (1988). *The Mandarin and the Cadre: China's Political Culture.* Ann Arbor: University of Michigan Press.

———. (1965). *Political Culture and Political Development.* Princeton: Princeton University Press.

Quandt, William. (1969). *Revolution and Political Leadership in Algeria.* Cambridge, MA: MIT Press.

Qutb, Sayyid. (1981). *Milestones.* Cedar Rapids, IA: Unity.

———. (1975). *Foundations of Islamic Society.* Beirut: Dar al-Shuruq (Arabic).

———. (1974). *Islam and Capitalism.* Beirut: Dar al-Shuruq (Arabic).

Rahman, Hamied. (1983). "The Concept of Jihad in Egypt." In *Islam, Nationalism, and Radicalism in Egypt and the Sudan,* edited by G. Warburg and U. Kupperscmidt. New York: Praeger.

Rath, Katherine. (1994). "The Process of Democratization in Jordan." *Middle East Studies* 30: 530–57.

Reudy, John. (1994). *Islamism and Secularism in North Africa*. Washington, DC: Georgetown University Press.

Robbins, David. (1991). "Jordan's Parliamentary Elections." In *Politics and the Economy in Jordan*, edited by R. Wilson. New York: Routledge.

Roberts, David. (1987). *The Ba'ath and the Creation of Modern Syria*. London: Croon Helm.

Roberts, Hugh. (1992). "The Algerian State and the Challenge of Democracy." *Government and Opposition* 27:433–54.

Roberts, John. (1995). *Vision and Mirage: The Middle East in a New Era*. Edinburgh: Mainstream.

Rodinson, Maxime. (1978). *Islam and Capitalism*. Austin: University of Texas Press.

Rosenthal Erwin. (1962). *Judaism and Islam*. London: World Zionist Organization.

Rostow, W. W. (1960). *The Stages of Economic Growth*. Cambridge: Cambridge University Press.

———. (1958). *The Stages of Economic Growth*. Princeton: Princeton University Press.

Rustow, Dankwart, ed. (1992). *Comparative Political Dynamics*. New York: Harper Collins.

———. (1971). *Middle Eastern Political Dynamics*. Englewood Cliffs, NJ: Prentice Hall.

———. (1970). "Transitions to Democracy: Toward a Dynamic Model." *Comparative Politics* 2:348–67.

Sadawi, Nawal. (1982). *Faces of Eve: Women in the Arab World*. Boston: Beacon Press.

Sadowski, Yahya. (1989). "Egypt's Islamist Movement: A New Political and Economic Force." *Middle East Insight* 5:37–45.

Safran, Nadav. (1961). *Egypt's Search for Political Community*. Cambridge, MA: Harvard University Press.

Said, Abdul Aziz. (1979). "Human Rights in Islamic Perspective." In *Human Rights in Ideological and Cultural Perspective*, edited by A. Pollis. New York: Praeger.

Said, Edward. (1981). *Covering Islam*. New York: Pantheon Books.

———. (1978). *Orientalism*. Berkeley: University of California Press.

Saikal, Amin. (1980). *The Rise and Fall of the Shah*. Princeton: Princeton University Press.

Salehi, M. M. (1988). *Insurgency Through Culture and Religion: Iran's Revolution*. New York: St. Martin's Press.

Salem, Norma. (1989). *Habib Bourghiba, Islam and the Creation of Tunisia*. London: Croon Helm.

Satloff, Robert. (1994). *From Abdallah to Hussein: Jordan in Transition*. New York: Oxford University Press.

———. (1986). *Trouble in the East Bank: Challenges to Domestic Stability in Jordan*. New York: Praeger.

Sayigh, R. (1991). "The Search for a National Identity." In *Politics and the Economy in Jordan*, edited by R. Wilson. New York: Routledge.

Schacht, Joseph. (1964). *An Introduction to Islamic Law*. Oxford: Clarendon Press.

Seale, Patrick. (1990). *Assad of Syria*. New Haven: Yale University Press.

———. (1986). *The Struggle for Syria*. New Haven: Yale University Press.

Shahin, Emad. (1997). *Contemporary Islamic Movements in North Africa*. Boulder: Westview Press.

Shaltut, Sheik Mahmud. (1982). "Socialism and Islam." In *Islam in Transition*, edited by J. Donohue and J. Esposito. Oxford: Oxford University Press.

Shariati, Ali. (1980). *Marxism and other Western Fallacies*. Berkeley: Mizan Press.

———. (1979). *On the Sociology of Islam: Lectures*. Berkeley: Mizan Press.

Shaw, David. (1982). *Saudi Arabia and Modernization: The Impact of Change on Stability*. New York: Praeger.

Shepard, William. (1986). "Islam and Ideology: Towards a Typology." *International Journal of Middle East Studies* 19:307–36.

Sivan, Emmanual. (1990). *Radical Islam: Medieval Problems and Modern Solutions*. New Haven: Yale University Press.

———. (1987). "The Two Faces of Islamic Fundamentalism." *Jerusalem Quarterly* 27:127–49.

Skocpol, Theda. (1994). *Social Revolutions in the Modern World*. Cambridge: Cambridge University Press.

Smith, Donald. (1974). *Religion and Political Modernization*. New Haven: Yale University Press.

———. (1970). *Religion and Political Development*. Boston: Little and Brown.

Spencer, Clare. (1994). "Algeria in Crisis." *Survival* 36:149–63.

Springborg, Robert. (1988). *Mubarak's Egypt: Fragmentation of the Political Order*. Boulder: Westview Press.

Syrian Islamic Action Front. (1981). *Political Program of the Syrian Islamic Action Front*. Beirut: N.p.

Tabandeh, Sultanhussein. (1970). *A Muslim Perspective on the Universal Declaration of Human Rights*. London: F. T. Goulding and Company.

Tabari, Azar. (1983). "The Role of the Clergy in Modern Iranian Politics." In *Religion and Politics in Iran*, edited by N. Keddie. New Haven: Yale University Press.

Tahari, Amir. (1985). *The Spirit of Allah: Khomeini and the Islamic Revolution*. London: Hutchison.

Tahi, Mohammed. (1992). "The Arduous Democratization Process in Algeria." *Journal of Modern African Studies* 30:397–419.

Tal, Lawrence. (1993). "Is Jordan Doomed." *Foreign Affairs* 72:45–81.

Tayyib, Saleh. (1988). *Transition in Algeria: From Reformism to Revolutionary Populism*. Khartoum: Khartoum University Press.

Tessler, Mark. (1987a). "Image and Reality in the Moroccan Political Economy." In *The Political Economy of Morocco*, edited by I. William Zartman. New York: Praeger.

Tessler, Mark, ed. (1987b). *The Evaluation and Application of Survey Research in the Arab World*. Boulder: Westview Press.

Thompson, Michael. (1990). *Cultural Theory*. Boulder: Westview Press.

Tibbi, Bassam. (1983). "The Role of Islam in Political and Social Development in the Middle East." *Middle East Journal* 37: 3–13.

Tlemacani, Rachid. (1986). *State and Revolution in Algeria*. Boulder: Westview Press.

Toqueville, Alexis de. (1956). *Democracy in America*. New York: Mentor.

Tozy, Mohammed. (1989). "Islam et etat au Maghreb." *Maghreb et Machrek* 126: 25–46.

Traer, Robert. (1991). *Faith in Human Rights*. Washington, DC: Georgetown University Press.

Turner, Bryan. (1974). *Weber and Islam: A Critical Study*. London: Routledge.

Universal Islamic Declaration of Human Rights. (1981). London: Islamic Foundation.

U.S. State Department. (1981, 1991). *Country Reports on Human Rights Practices*. Washington, DC: Government Printing Office.

Van Dam, Nikolas. (1981). *The Struggle for Power in Syria*. London: Croon Helm.

Vanderwalle, Dirk. (1988). "From New State to New Era: The Second Republic in Tunisia." *Middle East Journal* 42: 358–89.

Vatikiotis, P. J. (1983). "Religion and State." In *Islam, Nationalism, and Radicalism in Egypt and the Sudan*, edited by G. Warburg and U. Kupperscmidt. New York: Praeger.

———. (1978). *Nasser and His Generation*. London: Croon Helm.

Vatin, Jean. (1983). "Popular Puritanism versus State Reformism: Islam in Algeria." In *Islam in a World of Nation States*, edited by J. Piscatori. Cambridge: Cambridge University Press.

Verbit, Mervin. (1981). "Islam and Judaism." In *Religion and Politics in the Middle East*, edited by M. Curtis. Boulder: Westview Press.

Waltz, Susan. (1994). *Human Rights and Reform*. Berkeley: University of California Press.

———. (1991). "Clientelism and Reform." In *Tunisia: The Political Economy of Reform*, edited by I. William Zartman. Boulder: Lynne Rienner.

———. (1986). "The Islamic Appeal in Tunisia." *Middle East Journal* 40: 651–70.

Walzer, Michael. (1973). *The Revolution of the Saints*. New York: Atheneum.

Warburg, Gabriel, and Uri Kupperscmidt, ed. (1983). *Islam, Nationalism, and Radicalism in Egypt and the Sudan*. New York: Praeger.

Ware, L. B. (1988). "Ben Ali's Constitutional Coup in Tunisia." *Middle East Journal* 42: 332–58.

Waterbury, John. (1970). *The Commander of the Faithful*. New York: Columbia University Press.

Weber, Max. (1958). *The Protestant Ethic and the Spirit of Capitalism*. New York: Charles Scribner's Sons.

Weiner, Myron. (1966). *Modernization: The Dynamics of Growth*. New York: Basic Books.

Wildavsky, Aaron. (1990). "Choosing Preferences By Constructing Institutions: A Cultural Theory of Preference Formations." *American Political Science Review* 84: 3–21.

Wilson, Paul, and D. Graham. (1994). *Saudi Arabia: The Coming Storm*. Armonk, NY: M. E. Sharpe.

Wilson, Rodney. (1991). *Politics and the Economy in Jordan*. New York: Routledge.

World Bank. (1981, 1991). *World Development Report*. New York: World Bank.

Wright, Robin. (1986). *Sacred Rage: The Wrath of Militant Islam*. New York: Simon and Schuster.

Yasin, Abd as-Salaam. (1982). *La Revolution a l'heure de Islam*. Marseille: N.p.

————. (1974). *An Open Letter to the King of Morocco.* N.p. (Arabic).

Yasini, Ayman. (1985). *Religion and State in Saudi Arabia.* Boulder: Westview Press.

Yorke, Valerie. (1988). *Domestic Politics and Regional Security.* Washington, DC: Gowan.

Youseff, Michael. (1986). *Islamic Zealots Against the West.* Amsterdam: E. J. Brill.

Zakaria, Fouad. (1986). "Human Rights in the Arab World: The Islamic Context." *Philosophical Foundations of Human Rights.* Paris: UNESCO.

Zamzani, Mohammed al-. (1979). *The Position of Islam on Wealth and Poverty.* N.p. (Arabic).

Zartman, I. William, ed. (1991). *Tunisia: The Political Economy of Reform.* Boulder: Lynne Rienner.

————. ed. (1987). *The Political Economy of Morocco.* New York: Praeger.

Zghal, Alexander. (1991). "The New Strategy of the Movement of the Islamic Way: Cultural Expression or Manipulation." In *Tunisia: The Political Economy of Reform*, edited by I. William Zartman. Boulder: Lynne Rienner.

Zonis, Marvin. (1991). *Majestic Failure: The Fall of the Shah.* Chicago: University of Chicago Press.

Index

About the Author

DANIEL E. PRICE is Assistant Professor of Criminal Justice Studies at the Trumbull Campus of Kent State University. Professor Price has published in the *Presidential Studies Quarterly*.

ISBN 0-275-96187-7

HARDCOVER BAR CODE